THE ASCENT BEGINS

The World Beyond Empire — Sovereignty in the Age of Collapse

by

Shanaka Anslem Perera

Ash & Seed Press · Melbourne, Australia · 2025

A Bridge & Loom Book

A division of Ash & Seed Press

THE ASCENT BEGINS

The World Beyond Empire — Sovereignty in the Age of Collapse

© 2025 J.A. Shanaka Anslem Perera. All rights reserved.

No part of this book may be reproduced, stored in a retrieval system, or transmitted in any form or by any means — electronic, mechanical, photocopying, recording, or otherwise — without prior written permission of the publisher, except for brief quotations in critical reviews or educational use.

Published by **Ash & Seed Press**, Melbourne, Australia.

First Paperback Edition 2025
Paperback ISBN: 978-1-7643447-0-8
eBook ISBN: 978-1-7643447-1-5
Audiobook ISBN: 978-1-7643447-2-2
Hardcover ISBN: 978-1-7643447-3-9
Publisher: Ash & Seed Press

Printed in Australia & worldwide.

Distributed worldwide by IngramSpark and Amazon KDP.

"Civilizations fall not when they are conquered, but when they forget why they exist."

Library of Congress Cataloguing-in-Publication Data available upon request.

Dedication

For the ones who kept the lamp burning
when the world forgot light.
For every builder who chose repair over revenge.
You are the proof that ascent is possible.

Epigraphs

"In the ashes of the old world lie the blueprints of the new."
— *Fragment from the Ebla Tablets, c. 2300 BCE*

"He who has a why to live can bear almost any how."
— *Viktor E. Frankl*

"The empire ends when meaning returns."
— *Shanaka Anslem Perera*

Table of Contents

Preface 1
Prologue 7

Part I — The Fall 13
Chapter 1: The Frequency Of Collapse 13
Chapter 2: The Anatomy Of Collapse 43
Chapter 3: The Sovereign Stack 73

Part Ii — The Turning 111
Chapter 4: The Psychology Of Dependency 111
Chapter 5: The Mirror Of Power 153
Chapter 6: The Threshold Of Meaning 197

Part Iii - The Builders 229
Chapter 7: The Builders Of The New World 229
Chapter 8: The Economy Of Integrity 261
Chapter 9: The Cultural Rebirth 293

Part Iv · The Future 325
Chapter 10: The Sovereign Future 325
Chapter 11: The Testament Of The Builders 359
Chapter 12: The Children Of Ascent 393

Epilogue 427
The Return — From Dust To Breath To Dawn 427

Acknowledgments 434
Notes 435
Further Reading 436
About The Author 437

Preface

The Frequency of Awakening

There are moments in history when the world seems to exhale — when its systems, stories, and certainties collapse inward, leaving only the silence that follows the fall. For those who live through such hours, it feels as if the air itself has thickened, as if reality has become a sloweddown echo of something once familiar.

I wrote this book from within one of those silences.

In 2022, an island nation ran out of fuel. Buses stopped, hospitals flickered, cities slept without light. I remember the sound most vividly: the hum of generators dying one by one across Colombo's skyline, until the city's heartbeat turned irregular, then faint. It was not the first collapse in history, nor will it be the last — but for millions of us, it was the first time we realized civilization could simply pause.

The experience left a question that refused to leave:

If the world we depend on can vanish overnight, what remains that cannot?

That question grew into this book.

I.

Collapse is never singular. It begins as an economic failure, but behind it lies a moral fatigue — the loss of coherence between what a civilization says, believes, and does. When currency no longer matches value, when words no longer match truth, when power no longer matches responsibility, collapse is already under way. The lights going out are just the symptoms.

But collapse, I have learned, is also a frequency — a shift in vibration between endings and beginnings. When the familiar breaks apart, the inaudible becomes audible again. In that space, one can hear the oldest of sounds: the human will to rebuild.

Every generation inherits its own version of empire — the structure that promises protection in exchange for obedience. For us, empire is not Rome or Britain; it is the network of dependencies that now bind our food, energy, attention, and identity. When these systems strain, the temptation is to panic. Yet beneath the panic lies a choice: will we cling to the collapsing scaffolds, or learn to stand without them?

That is the work of sovereignty. Not nationalism, not isolation, but the quiet capacity to remain coherent amid disintegration. To think, choose, and create from first principles when institutions falter.

II.

The Ascent Begins is a map drawn for that moment of decision. It is not a book of theory, nor of prophecy. It is a field guide for anyone who senses that history's current cycle is closing — and who refuses to end with it.

Its architecture mirrors the rhythm of every civilizational story: **Fall, Turning, Building, Future.** Each part explores how humanity has endured previous descents — from the Late Bronze Age to the Black Death, from Weimar's hyperinflation to digital addiction — and how individuals and communities found coherence again. The patterns repeat because human nature does.

To read these pages is to travel through ruins and workshops, monasteries and marketplaces, myths and laboratories. It is to meet the ancestors who already solved the problems we think are new.

In writing this, I walked the ruins of ancient ports where trade once stitched continents together. I read the diaries of reformers and exiles. I sat with engineers designing solar villages and with farmers coaxing life from exhausted soil. Each conversation traced a single thread: survival becomes renewal when meaning returns.

Meaning is the true currency of civilization.

III ·

This book is written in gratitude to those who kept meaning alive when institutions forgot how. The monks who copied books in plague years. The teachers who opened secret classrooms under occupation. The coders and healers, the artisans and rebels who refused to sell their integrity for comfort.

They are the true lineage of the Builders — the quiet architects of continuity. Every time you choose honesty over ease, every time you restore something broken, every time you teach a skill instead of hoarding it, you join their guild.

What follows is therefore not a manifesto but a manual. Each chapter is a workshop in resilience, structured through five prisms: **history, the present, the mind, the myth, and the method.** The goal is not escape but engagement — to make readers sovereign within their own sphere so that society, rebuilt from sovereign parts, can endure.

You will not find slogans here. You will find stories. History's data, psychology's diagrams, and mythology's symbols converge to remind us that the human pattern of renewal is universal. What changes is only the vocabulary.

IV.

Some readers will approach this book in fear. That is understandable. The age of collapse produces anxiety by design. We are told daily that we are too small to act and too late to matter. But the evidence of history is otherwise: small groups have always been the carriers of civilization's DNA.

When the Roman roads broke, it was villages and abbeys that kept literacy alive. When the Mongols burned Baghdad, knowledge fled not into armies but into poems and manuscripts. When colonialism stripped nations of sovereignty, memory survived in songs and stories.

Every empire is temporary. The impulse to build is eternal.

To awaken to this truth is to shift from despair to design. Once you see the pattern, panic gives way to participation. The world does not end when systems fail; it ends when imagination does.

The Builders' task is therefore simple: keep imagination alive.

V.

Why write this book now? Because we are at an inflection point — a moment when old structures are cracking faster than new ones can form. The energy crisis, the attention crisis, the ecological crisis, the crisis of trust — they are all facets of the same event: the exhaustion of empire.

We need not wait for collapse to end before beginning ascent. The work begins wherever you stand.

This preface is therefore an invitation. You do not need permission from governments or credentials from institutions to reclaim your sovereignty. You need only attention, integrity, and the willingness to build something that will outlast you.

Begin with one act of coherence: cook your own meal, mend your own garment, teach one person what you know, plant one seed. In that act, history restarts.

VI ·

A final note.

This book was written in fragments — some in blackout nights, some in airports between crises, some in quiet mornings when the city slept. Each paragraph was a way of making sense of disarray. As it took form, I realized it was not just a personal record but a collective one. These words belong to everyone who has ever looked at a broken world and refused to surrender.

If you are reading this, you have already crossed a threshold. The rest of the journey is endurance and attention. Read slowly. Reflect often. Share what resonates.

Every age of renewal begins with a few who remember that civilization is not inherited — it is re-created, one choice at a time.

The ascent does not begin in theory.

It begins wherever you stand.

Prologue

The Moment Before the Dawn

There is always a hush before the light returns.

Not silence—something deeper, like the held breath of the earth itself.

In that pause, the world balances between what has been lost and what might still be found.

If you listen closely, you can hear the faint murmuring of civilization in suspension: the last radio frequencies, the sigh of dormant engines, the whisper of wind moving through abandoned glass towers. Nothing moves, yet everything waits. Even decay has rhythm.

From a distance the planet looks unchanged. Continents keep their outlines, clouds trace the same spirals, the moon still drifts across its inherited path. But inside the human field, something irreversible has shifted. The empire of distraction has exhausted itself; the noise has collapsed under its own weight. What remains is attention—raw, unmediated, untraded.

You are standing in that moment now.

I

Night Without Clocks

The cities have dimmed, and for the first time in generations the stars are visible again. Streets once governed by screens now belong to crickets and wind. Time loosens. Without the hum of schedules, people begin to measure hours by smell—bread rising, soil cooling, firewood catching. The night no longer hides; it teaches.

Across one quiet neighborhood, an old man repairs a lantern. In another, a girl writes a word she has never seen before: *begin*. Somewhere, in a small house still connected to the grid, a woman reads by the light of her phone until the battery dies; then she sits in the dark and discovers that her own breathing glows louder than any screen.

This is the threshold state: when technology falters and human senses return.

Every collapse is preceded by arrogance and followed by wonder. The arrogance imagines control; the wonder remembers belonging. Between the two lies this fragile, electric night.

II ·

The Awakening Sense

At first people mistake the quiet for despair. They walk through emptied supermarkets, through fields of unharvested grain, and they grieve. But grief, when felt fully, clears perception. Slowly, new forms of sight emerge.

They begin to hear water again—its weight, its tone. They touch objects they once ignored: the grain of wood, the chill of stone, the pulse inside the wrist. What industrial time erased, sensory time restores.

Children become guides. Unburdened by nostalgia, they adapt fastest. They rediscover play with discarded tools, build windmills from scrap, map constellations on paper instead of phones. Elders, once sidelined, find themselves sought out for memory—how to ferment, weave, mend, read weather. The arc of knowledge bends backward to move forward.

The great reconciliation begins: science shaking hands with myth, data bowing to story, speed yielding to rhythm. Humanity, stripped of noise, starts to listen to its own frequency again.

III ·

The Call of Hands

At dawn's edge, the first communal fires ignite. Not rituals of fear, but of orientation. People gather instinctively in circles—the geometry that has no hierarchy. There are no speeches, only gestures: someone passes bread, someone sharpens a blade, someone sketches a map in dust.

This is how civilizations restart—not through declarations, but through tasks. A wall is patched, a well cleaned, a child taught a new word. Work becomes prayer, competence becomes kindness.

Among the Builders there is a quiet code:

Do not rebuild what failed.

Remember why it failed.

Begin with what you can hold in your hands.

A single repaired hinge, a tuned instrument, a shared meal—each is an act of defiance against entropy. The empire may have fallen, but coordination remains. Cooperation, it turns out, is a biological constant; hierarchy was the experiment.

IV.

The Voice Within the Ruins

As daylight climbs, fragments of language return. Not slogans, but questions.

What is enough?

What is sacred?

What is true?

In the old age, these questions were outsourced to algorithms. Now they resound inside every person like ancestral drums. The act of asking becomes the new literacy.

Some rebuilders turn to philosophy, others to faith, others to soil. The methods differ, but the impulse converges: to weave coherence from chaos. Each community becomes a prototype of the possible world. One plants gardens on rooftops, another revives barter economies, another transforms libraries into seed banks. None of them know if it will work. All of them know it must.

The prophets of despair still whisper through static, predicting endless decline. But even they are outnumbered now by the sound of hammers.

V.

The Rising Light

The moment before the dawn is always the coldest. Fingers stiffen, breaths cloud, doubts creep in. Then, almost imperceptibly, the horizon begins to blush.

First gray, then amber, then the thinnest thread of gold. It touches metal roofs, glances off glass shards, glows in puddles. People look up as if seeing color for the first time. The light reveals not ruin but texture—the honest surface of a world stripped of varnish.

One woman lifts a child to show him the sun. He squints, laughs, reaches toward it with both hands. Around them, birds test their first songs of the day. The air hums with possibility. For a few seconds the entire planet feels weightless.

No one announces the new era. It simply arrives.

VI ·

The Remembering Mind

Memory returns as warmth does—quietly, then all at once. People recall how their grandparents survived previous winters, how their ancestors mapped stars to cross oceans, how every myth of the Flood ends not in death but in planting. The story of humanity rethreads itself through small acts of care.

Archaeologists of the future will find little record of this hour—no grand monument, no date to mark the turning. But they will notice a subtle change in the strata: cleaner soil, fewer toxins, signs of repair. They will call it the *Resilience Horizon*. They will not know that it began in silence.

Inside each person a private resolution forms: never again to trade meaning for convenience. That oath, multiplied millions of times, becomes civilization's true foundation.

VII ·

The First Steps

By mid-morning, the rebuilt world has no anthem, only movement. Farmers till. Poets write. Engineers design water pumps from bicycle parts. Children deliver messages by foot and laughter. Networks reform, not as invisible webs of control but as visible lines of trust.

The Builders have no flag. Their emblem is the open hand—strong enough to shape, empty enough to receive. They do not speak of saving humanity; they speak of serving it. The word *sovereign* no longer means separate. It means whole.

Every act of creation becomes a form of remembrance. They are not escaping history; they are finishing it.

VIII ·

Threshold to the Journey

By the time the sun clears the horizon, you can see the path ahead—a ridge winding toward higher ground. The ruins shimmer in heat behind you. The air smells of iron and rain. In that scent is everything: loss, endurance, beginning.

You step forward.

Each footfall sounds like a promise: that wisdom will not be wasted, that beauty will not be optional, that power will once again mean service. The ascent has no fanfare; it is a rhythm, a breath, a steady climb through ordinary hours.

Far below, the sea glitters, erasing old borders. Above, the sky opens wide enough to hold all contradictions. Between them, humanity walks—unfinished, unafraid.

The dawn expands.

And somewhere in the distance, a new story starts writing itself.

Chapter 1

The Frequency Of Collapse

Part I — The Fall

Key 1 · Historical Mirror · Late Bronze Age Collapse

The first sign of the end was silence.

Not the silence of peace, but the heavy quiet that follows when a network stops singing. In the twelfth century BCE, letters stopped moving across the eastern Mediterranean. The couriers who once ran the roads between palaces carried fewer tablets, and those they brought sounded strange: anxious, clipped, unfinished. One, fired in haste at Ugarit, reads, *"Enemy ships have been sighted."* It was written in the time it took for an empire's heart to miss a beat.

For nearly three hundred years before that moment, the region had been a single web of rhythm. The Hittite kings traded with Egypt; copper from Cyprus flowed north; tin from the far edges of Afghanistan and Cornwall met it in the furnaces of Anatolia; accountants in palaces marked each shipment on wet clay and pressed their seals. Mycenaean craftsmen carved the faces of gods into gold leaf; scribes in Ugarit translated Akkadian into Hurrian and back again; envoys toasted to the same sun gods at different ends of the sea. Civilization was not one place—it was a timing system.

When that timing slipped, everything else followed.

I ·

The Year the Music Faltered

Archaeologists can trace the unraveling like the static of a fading song.

At Hattusa, the Hittite capital, storage rooms filled with unused grain jars—signs of taxation that outpaced distribution. Farther south, the great port of Ugarit shows burn layers atop its final archives. In Mycenae and Tiryns, fortification walls were repaired in panic, thicker but cruder than before. Egyptian reliefs carved for Ramesses III at Medinet Habu depict battles with "Sea Peoples"—coalitions of migrants and raiders whose names still echo like broken chords: Peleset, Shekelesh, Denyen.

No single note caused the discord. Climate data pulled from stalagmites in Anatolia show a thirty-year drought window. Trade networks had already thinned as debts mounted; elites demanded more copper while harvests shrank. The tin routes—the narrow lifelines that allowed bronze to exist—were the most fragile of all. When caravans stalled in the mountains or pirate fleets cut the shipping lanes, smiths waited with cold forges. Bronze was not a metal; it was a contract between lands. Break the contract, and the age ends.

At first, people explained the change as a series of local misfortunes: a poor harvest, a late convoy, a fickle god. Then correspondence dwindled altogether. In the ruins of Ugarit, one unfinished tablet was left unbaked in its kiln. It still carries finger marks from a scribe who never returned. Fire hardened it only when the palace burned.

II ·

What Collapse Sounds Like

Collapse rarely looks like the movies. There is no single day when everyone knows. It sounds instead like delay, excuses, and faint laughter in markets as prices rise faster than comprehension. Merchants promise that the next convoy will arrive. Officials reassure the people that the temples will open again next week. Musicians still tune their lyres for evening feasts; the wine still pours. But each performance shortens, and each promise returns thinner.

In those years, the kingdoms of the eastern Mediterranean behaved like a symphony drifting off key. When a soloist faltered, others overplayed their parts. The Pharaoh of Egypt sent letters begging for wood from Byblos; Byblos asked for grain; grain required peace on the roads, which now hosted refugees. When the balance of imports and offerings broke, even belief staggered. Gods who had guaranteed harvests for centuries suddenly fell silent. Priests doubled the sacrifices. The sky remained dry.

What followed was not annihilation but simplification. Palaces emptied into villages. Literacy fell, not because minds dulled, but because there were no longer enough scribes to justify the cost of clay. Pottery styles became rougher but more personal; new patterns appeared in the margins where people had begun to trade directly again. Collapse was not an explosion. It was a phase change: a civilization moving from the complex to the local, from the imperial to the intimate.

III ·

Physics Beneath the Ruins

Modern science gives this old story a new vocabulary. In condensed-matter physics, a small perturbation can trigger a phase transition when a system has reached critical coupling. Water turns to steam not gradually but suddenly once energy tips a threshold. In superconductors, a tiny rise in temperature ends perfect conductivity. The Bronze Age network behaved the same way: a vast, tightly linked lattice that could move energy—goods, knowledge, ritual—without resistance until one variable drifted too far. When climate stress, debt, and war converged, the network lost coherence. A civilization's phase shifted from ordered to turbulent.

Complexity theorist Joseph Tainter described this long before data models confirmed it: societies expand their problem-solving machinery until the cost of complexity exceeds its return. Then they simplify. The simplification feels like catastrophe to those inside it but is, in physics terms, a return to equilibrium. Energy seeks a lower state. So do empires.

This does not make the suffering less real. It frames it within a pattern older than history. When you understand collapse as a harmonic convergence—stresses resonating until the structure cannot absorb them—you see why small warnings matter. The tremor before the earthquake carries the same frequency as the destruction, only softer. To those who can hear it, it is a rehearsal.

IV.

The Human Frequency

Imagine a scribe in Ugarit, dusk light flickering on his tablet as he presses symbols for "tin shipment delayed." He believes he is writing logistics. He is, without knowing it, chronicling the limits of complexity. His children will not inherit his script; they will trade grain face-to-face instead of writing receipts. And yet, from that narrowing of scale, culture will survive. Languages will blend, smaller communities will relearn forgotten skills, and centuries later, a new alphabet will rise from the ashes of the old.

Collapse strips grandeur but preserves pattern. Every age carries the hum of its own fragility. The Bronze Age kings could not imagine a world without bronze; we struggle to imagine one without electricity or debt. Yet the physics is the same. When synchronization breaks, the song stops.

The courier's run from the palace kiln to the harbor was short—half a mile at most. He carried a clay tablet that still exists, hardened by the very fire that destroyed his city. It outlived every god he served. It outlived the alphabet in which it was written. What remains is a warning and an invitation: listen for the silences. They tell you how close the rhythm is to changing.

Key 2 · Modern Parallel · Sri Lanka 2022

At dawn the queue already curved around the block.

Women wrapped in cotton saris held plastic cans the color of caution; men leaned against motorbikes and trucks, resting on handles slick with diesel mist. Children still half-asleep sat on the curb, guarding their family's place in line. The air at the edge of Colombo smelled of salt, exhaust, and the faint sweetness of tea leaves drying upriver. Overhead, the loudspeakers of a nearby temple carried morning chants that no longer matched the rhythm of the city.

By eight a.m. the power had failed again. Phones lost signal. Shops pulled down their shutters not because of violence but because the generators had no fuel left. Somewhere behind the empty stations, the government's foreign reserves had already slipped below zero. The country's grid was still technically alive; it just no longer had anything left to burn.

I ·

A Modern Island in an Ancient Pattern

For years Sri Lanka had been told it was a model of post-war recovery. Tourism surged after 2009; cranes re-drew the skyline; the southern expressway cut hours off the journey from Galle to the capital. It was the same illusion every rising power sells to itself—the belief that momentum is the same as immunity.

By 2021, the illusion was paid for with borrowed dollars. Pandemic border closures erased tourist income. Debt repayments came due in foreign currency. The government cut taxes in the hope that confidence alone could refill the treasury. Then came a decision as sudden as any divine omen: a total ban on chemical fertilizers and pesticides, announced overnight. It was framed as a leap toward "organic prosperity." Instead, yields of rice and tea—two pillars of national export—collapsed by as much as half within one growing season.

Foreign exchange vanished faster than belief. Importers could not pay for fuel cargoes; ships idled offshore, waiting for letters of credit that would never arrive. Blackouts stretched from two hours to six, then to ten. When pumps went dry, people began sleeping in their vehicles.

II ·

The Queue as a Mirror

By April 2022, the queue had become the true parliament of the nation. It stretched through the night, lit by phone screens and candles. People spoke quietly about rumors—how the port had turned away a tanker; how the currency had been devalued; how ministers' families had left the country. Anger ripened, but slowly, like fruit in a sealed room.

On April 12 the central bank declared the island would suspend external debt payments—its first sovereign default since independence. The next morning a protest encampment appeared at Galle Face Green, the ceremonial lawn facing the colonial-era Secretariat. Tents rose, then a kitchen, then a library made from crates and donated books. Students printed signs that read, **"Gota Go Gama — Village of Refusal."** The city's elite laughed at the name until the camp grew large enough to feed thousands.

The encampment became a living civics lesson: nurses taught first aid, lawyers held workshops on rights, musicians played by generator light. At night, chants rolled across the sea wall: *"Power to the people."* When riot police finally cleared the square months later, the chant outlived the tents. The country had already learned something irreversible—that power can migrate faster than currency.

III ·

The Digital Ration

To calm the chaos, the government launched a National Fuel Pass. Every citizen received a QR code linked to their ID; scanning it at the pump displayed the week's allowance. It was rational, efficient—and deeply revealing. Scarcity had been digitized. The screen at the station became a mirror of personal dependency: how many liters between work and standstill, between modern life and a cart on the roadside.

Economists abroad called the system a success because it reduced fights at the pump. Inside the country, people recognized it as something else: proof that the state had become an app for managing shortage. Where the Bronze Age priest once measured grain to appease the gods, the twenty-first-century bureaucrat measured fuel to appease bondholders.

Every household became an energy accountant. Fans were unplugged. Elevators stood still. The city's heartbeat slowed. The older generation remembered the curfews of civil war, but this silence was stranger—it carried no gunfire, only waiting.

IV ·

Echoes and Equations

When historians compare eras, they often miss the sensory continuity between them. The queues in Colombo smelled not unlike the markets of Ugarit before the fires: sweat, oil, the uncertainty of supply. The same physics governed both crises—too many dependencies, too little slack, feedback loops that reinforce collapse.

If the Bronze Age ended when tin failed to reach the smiths, Sri Lanka's version arrived when dollars failed to reach the fuel importers. Both metals and money served the same role: a medium of synchronization. Both became bottlenecks. The couriers of Ugarit and the truck drivers of Colombo were separated by three millennia but moved along identical fault lines.

Complexity, once efficient, turned predatory. Debt obligations denominated in foreign currency mimicked the old empire's tribute demands. Each payment exported stability to creditors and imported fragility to citizens. The International Monetary Fund's rescue package promised restructuring in exchange for austerity—modern language for enforced simplification.

To outside observers, the crisis looked like mismanagement. To those who stood in line, it felt elemental, as if the island itself were exhaling centuries of borrowed air.

V.

The Sound of Renewal

By mid-2023, power returned to most districts. The IMF deal stabilized the currency; tourist flights trickled back. Yet something deeper had changed. Families who had once relied on the supermarket began planting roof gardens. Neighbors formed car-share circles. A few of the young men who had organized Gota Go Gama registered new cooperatives to distribute rice and medicine without intermediaries. The movement's vocabulary shifted from protest to production.

In the ancient world, after the fires cooled, survivors gathered shards and learned to melt them into simpler tools. The same instinct stirred here. A generation learned that the opposite of scarcity is not abundance but coordination.

One evening, months after the queues had shortened, a retired teacher who had spent nights at the protest camp walked past the fuel station on Galle Road. The lights were bright again; the line had disappeared. On impulse she stopped the car, stepped out, and pressed her hand against the concrete where her jerry can once stood. "Never again," she whispered—not to the government, but to herself.

Transmission

Civilizations do not collapse because people fail to care; they collapse because systems train them to wait for permission to act.

The queues of 2022 were not signs of apathy but of obedience.

The next question is psychological: *what keeps humans from moving until the fuel is gone?*

That is the threshold we cross next.

Key 3 · Psychological Mechanism · Why Denial Precedes Downfall

Collapse begins in the mind before it reaches the streets.

A society does not fall because it runs out of fuel or grain or credit. It falls because it runs out of imagination—because the people inside it cannot picture a different tomorrow quickly enough to respond.

When historians reconstruct the Late Bronze Age or Sri Lanka's queues, they see data: rainfall curves, balance sheets, debt ratios. What they cannot chart is the slow drift of perception. The eyes that looked at withering crops or empty pumps did not see "collapse." They saw temporary inconvenience. Every empire tells its people the same comforting story: *things will return to normal.* That story is the real contagion.

I ·

The Architecture of Denial

Psychologists call it **normalcy bias**—the reflex that causes humans to underestimate both the probability and the impact of disaster.

It is an adaptation, not a flaw. Our ancestors survived by assuming that the rustle in the grass was just the wind most of the time; constant alarm burns more energy than it saves. Normalcy bias keeps daily life bearable. It also guarantees that early warnings are ignored.

In laboratory studies, participants shown footage of an approaching fire often wait for confirmation from others before moving. In simulated emergencies, people cluster near exits yet hesitate to open them until someone of perceived authority acts first. The brain balances two fears:

the fear of the event itself, and the fear of embarrassment for overreacting. The second often wins.

In markets and politics, the same bias becomes policy. Leaders wait for additional data points. Investors call downturns "corrections." Families borrow against next year's harvest because last year's drought was surely an anomaly. Denial is not stupidity; it is a form of faith.

II ·

Cognitive Dissonance: Protecting the Story

When evidence finally pierces the shell of normalcy, the psyche faces an impossible choice: update the story or distort the facts.

Leon Festinger documented this in the 1950s while observing a doomsday cult whose prophecy failed. The members did not abandon their belief; they deepened it. The failure, they decided, meant their faith had saved the world. Dissonance had been resolved not by truth but by invention.

This mechanism scales.

When economies strain, we invent narratives of temporary turbulence. When ecosystems shift, we rename seasons instead of behavior. When digital systems addict entire populations, we call it connection. Each story maintains the illusion of control while quietly surrendering it.

In Sri Lanka, citizens knew the reserves were falling; newspaper graphs made it explicit. Yet public discourse revolved around patriotism and destiny. Ministers promised revival through self-reliance even as ships idled offshore. In the Bronze Age, kings performed extra sacrifices to silent gods rather than admit material limits. Both reactions are identical in structure: to protect the self-image of power, reality must bend.

III ·

Learned Helplessness: When Effort Stops Working

If denial is the opening act, **learned helplessness** is the closing one.

In the 1960s, psychologist Martin Seligman ran an experiment with dogs that were exposed to mild electric shocks. Some animals could escape by pressing a lever; others could not. Later, even when escape became possible, the ones trained in futility simply lay down. They had learned that action was irrelevant.

Societies teach the same lesson through experience. When citizens petition, protest, and vote without visible effect, they begin to conserve effort. Energy collapses inward. This apathy is mistaken for laziness but is in fact self-protection. The reward gradient has vanished.

In collapsing states, you can measure learned helplessness in small gestures: shopkeepers who no longer repaint their signs; civil servants who stop filing reports; families who keep cash under the mattress but make no plans for what comes next. The will to adapt erodes faster than infrastructure. A population that has stopped believing in efficacy becomes easy to manage for a while—then impossible to move at all.

IV ·

The Obedience Loop

Stanley Milgram's obedience experiments at Yale in 1963 revealed another dimension of this paralysis.

When instructed by an authority figure to deliver what they believed were painful electric shocks, 65 percent of participants continued to the maximum voltage. They did so not out of cruelty but because responsibility had been outsourced. The subject's conscience deferred to the lab coat.

Empires exploit this reflex instinctively. Bureaucracy is obedience codified; it teaches citizens to see their role as execution, not interpretation. The larger and more abstract the system, the easier it becomes to follow procedure against reason. During the Bronze Age, scribes tallied shipments long after the mines had ceased production. During the 2008 financial crisis, rating agencies stamped securities "AAA" even as they collapsed. In both cases, the system's operators were sincere. That sincerity is what made the machinery unstoppable.

Obedience is a relief—it converts uncertainty into clarity. Yet it carries the same psychological cost as helplessness: the erosion of agency. When every choice is framed as compliance, the concept of initiative atrophies. People wait for orders even when none are coming.

V.

How Collapse Feels from the Inside

To live through decline is to inhabit contradiction.

You feel both urgency and inertia. You know something fundamental has shifted, yet daily tasks still demand attention. You pay bills, attend meetings, cook dinner. The unreality of the normal becomes its own narcotic.

Frankl, writing from a concentration camp, observed that meaning—not comfort—kept prisoners alive. When the external world becomes unrecognizable, the internal narrative must find a new anchor or dissolve.

That search for meaning is what differentiates a fall from an awakening.

The same human machinery that delays recognition can also produce renewal once denial breaks. Normalcy bias becomes realism. Dissonance becomes curiosity. Helplessness, when reframed through skill and community, becomes discipline. The psyche does not need to be eradicated—it needs to be retuned.

Collapse, viewed from within, feels like exhaustion. Viewed from without, it looks like transformation. The line between them is agency.

VI ·

Listening for the Shift

There is a moment, just before panic, when silence changes flavor. The crowd waiting in line stops chatting; a few faces turn toward the horizon as if something inaudible has spoken. That is the instant when awareness outruns obedience. Most civilizations miss it. A few use it to step sideways into survival.

Psychologically, that moment is a *locus-of-control inversion*: the recognition that external systems are no longer reliable and that responsibility has returned home. It feels terrifying precisely because it is freedom rediscovered. Every sovereignty begins with that discomfort.

The Bronze Age scribe might have felt it when his last shipment failed to arrive. A shopkeeper in Colombo felt it when the pump display read "system offline." You will feel it in your own life when the institution you trusted falters and no replacement appears. The test is whether you interpret that silence as doom or as invitation.

VII ·

Transmission

Myth remembers that silence as a flood—the cleansing of old illusions and the beginning of a new world.

Before we cross into the archetypes that encoded this lesson, pause on a single truth: denial is not the enemy; it is the chrysalis of awareness. When it breaks, sovereignty begins.

Key 4 · Mythic Resonance · The Flood Archetype

Every civilization keeps a memory of water.

It appears under different names—Deucalion, Noah, Manu, Utnapishtim—but the melody is the same: the world becomes too proud, too loud, too heavy with deceit, and the gods decide to wash it clean. The flood myth is not about punishment; it is about recalibration. The sea is the instrument that retunes creation to its proper key.

When Utnapishtim tells Gilgamesh the story of the Deluge in the world's oldest surviving epic, his voice is weary. The gods had quarreled about whether humanity deserved to live. Enlil wanted silence; Ea wanted mercy. The compromise was a storm so vast it erased memory itself. For six days the waters raged, and on the seventh they receded. When the survivors emerged, they offered sacrifice, and the gods—smelling the smoke—remembered that life was sweeter imperfect than erased.

That paradox is the heart of every flood: destruction as remembrance.

I ·

The First Reset

Archaeologists once searched for a single geological event behind the stories—a flood in Mesopotamia, perhaps, or the end of an Ice Age glacial melt. But the persistence of the myth across every continent suggests something deeper: a psychological truth encoded in narrative form. The flood stands for the moment when accumulated complexity exceeds the capacity of the vessel. When the networks of an age choke on their own interconnections, the collective unconscious imagines a cleansing wave.

In Hindu cosmology, Manu, forewarned by a talking fish, builds a boat to preserve seeds of all life. In the Greek myth, Deucalion and Pyrrha survive Zeus's deluge by retreating to a chest on Mount Parnassus; when the waters subside, they repopulate the world by casting stones over their shoulders—each stone becoming a human. The message is consistent: when structure collapses, what endures is pattern. The ark, the chest, the seed vault—all are metaphors for the continuity of form through transformation.

II ·

Myth as Physics

Seen through modern eyes, the flood is a model of entropy and renewal.

In thermodynamics, order requires energy; when a system grows too complex, its internal friction increases until a threshold is breached, and the structure resets to a lower state of organization. That is precisely what the flood enacts: an entropic release disguised as divine will. The deluge is the universe's way of dissipating unsustainable heat.

Physicist Ilya Prigogine, in his work on dissipative structures, showed that systems driven far from equilibrium spontaneously reorganize at higher levels of coherence. Myths anticipated this law millennia earlier. The flood annihilates only to permit reorganization. It is the cosmos exhaling.

When you read of Noah's forty days or Vishnu's cosmic ocean, you are witnessing an intuitive comprehension of non-linear dynamics. The old world was metastable; the flood was its phase change. The survivors are the new attractor points around which order condenses.

III ·

The Moral Geometry of Water

The deluge also encodes ethics.

Water is morally neutral—it destroys palaces and hovels alike—but it carries memory. Each myth makes survival contingent not on power but on attentiveness. Utnapishtim listens to the whisper of a god who speaks through a wall. Noah obeys an impossible instruction. Manu saves the fish rather than eating it. In every case, humility before signals precedes salvation. Those who laughed at omens or mocked preparations vanished with the tide.

This is myth's way of teaching risk perception. The flood punishes arrogance not through wrath but through physics. Those who notice small shifts in the current survive; those who insist that the tide will retreat as usual do not.

In Sri Lanka, the equivalent signal was an empty tanker list. In the Bronze Age, it was a missing convoy of tin. Myths distilled those lessons into story form long before data analysis existed.

IV ·

The Ark as Archetype

Every survivor builds an ark, whether literal or symbolic. The ark is not a luxury yacht of escape—it is a condensed civilization, a portable pattern of meaning. Noah's ark carries pairs; Manu's carries seeds; the ark of the covenant carries laws. Each represents a different strategy of preservation: biological, ecological, ethical.

Carl Jung interpreted the flood as the dissolution of ego boundaries under collective pressure, with the ark symbolizing the resilient Self— the container of consciousness that endures when the outer identity is swept away. Civilization mirrors that psychology. When institutions crumble, individuals must become arks of coherence, holding within themselves the fragments of language, skill, and memory that keep humanity continuous.

The ark is therefore not built once; it is built daily. Each act of learning, storing, writing, or planting is a plank in its hull. The shape of your habits determines whether your mind floats or drowns when systems fail.

V.

The Survivors' Bargain

What happens after the waters recede?

In every version of the myth, the survivors make a covenant. Noah receives a rainbow as promise; Manu establishes the new dharma; Utnapishtim is granted immortality but exiled from the human world. The price of survival is responsibility. Those who live through the reset are bound to remember the conditions that made it necessary.

The rainbow, then, is not decoration—it is accountability written across the sky. Each generation must look at it and recall that equilibrium is temporary. The flood myth persists precisely because humanity keeps breaking that promise. We rebuild faster than we remember.

VI.

Echo in the Modern Mind

Our digital seas follow the same tide. Information floods the planet faster than comprehension. The deluge is no longer of water but of data, washing away meaning in torrents of content. The modern ark is discernment—the ability to carry through noise only what is vital and true. The storm outside the screen mirrors the one that drowned Utnapishtim's world. Both demand the same virtue: restraint.

When energy grids fail, currencies collapse, or algorithms addict, we are not punished by gods; we are corrected by scale. The flood myth's endurance across five millennia is proof that the human psyche recognizes its own cycles. We overconnect, overconsume, overreach, and then rediscover humility through reduction. Every generation re-enacts the flood; the wise prepare the ark before the rain.

VII ·

Return to the Shore

In the Epic of Gilgamesh, after the waters drain away, Utnapishtim releases a dove, then a swallow, then a raven. Only when the raven fails to return does he know that the world has dried. It is a quiet, human moment—the first empirical test in literature. Hope confirmed by observation.

That gesture closes the circle from myth to science. It tells us that renewal requires curiosity, not faith alone. The raven's flight is data gathering; the ark's landing is evidence-based rebirth.

Civilizations collapse when they forget that distinction—when they mistake ritual for measurement, or belief for feedback. The survivors of the next flood will be those who rebuild both heart and method, myth and metric.

VIII ·

Transmission

Myth shows us that the end is a rhythm, not a cliff.

When the waters recede, what matters is what we carried through.

The next task is to translate this understanding into motion—to design practical rituals and systems that make sovereignty tangible.

Every reader of this book is a potential ark.

The next section will show how to build it.

Key 5 · Sovereignty Protocol · The Energy and Fragility Audit

When a civilization trembles, individuals feel the vibration first.

The hum is personal: a fridge that cycles off too often, a price that doubles without warning, an attention span that fragments under constant alerts. These are not random inconveniences. They are micro-faults in the same tectonic plate that cracks nations. Sovereignty begins when you stop waiting for rescue and start treating your life as a small, conscious system—one that can withstand turbulence because it is designed with awareness.

This section is your first blueprint: the *Energy and Fragility Audit*.

It is a 30-day process to map dependence, restore autonomy, and build a self-sustaining rhythm. It does not require wealth or isolation. It requires attention.

I ·

Day 1–5: Awareness — Seeing the Grid You Stand On

Take a notebook and draw five concentric circles. Label them: **Energy, Food, Information, Finance, Community**.

These are the arteries of modern life. Within each, list your single points of failure—the places where one outage could freeze you.

• *Energy*: How many days can you function if the grid fails?

Do you know how to light, cook, or store without electricity?

• *Food*: How many meals in your home right now are dependent on trucks that cross provincial borders?

- *Information*: If your phone and Wi-Fi vanished for three days, who could still reach you, and how?
- *Finance*: What fraction of your savings would evaporate if banking apps froze for a week?
- *Community*: If you fell sick tomorrow, who would feed you? Name them. If you cannot name anyone, that circle is hollow.

Write the answers without shame or pride. The goal is not paranoia but visibility. The first act of sovereignty is measurement.

II ·

Day 6–10: Energy — Reclaiming the Fire

In every collapse story, energy is the first domino. When power dies, everything that depends on it reveals its true nature.

Perform a 48-hour blackout simulation. Turn off breakers except for one light and your fridge.

Observe.

Which habits rely on convenience rather than necessity?

Which spaces of your home remain usable?

The experiment is not punishment; it is reacquaintance.

Now map three tiers of resilience:

1. **Immediate (0–3 days)**: candles, matches, batteries, solar chargers, stovetop coffee, blankets.
2. **Intermediate (1–3 weeks)**: a small generator or shared neighbourhood solar rig; water filters; manual tools.
3. **Long-term (3+ months)**: energy literacy—knowing voltage, wattage, storage, and how to repair rather than replace.

If this feels mundane, remember that knowledge was once sacred. In Egypt, the priesthood's power derived from its control of irrigation schedules—the original energy code. When you learn how your home's current flows, you inherit that priesthood.

III ·

Day 11–15: Consumption — The Fragility Ratio

Every resource you use has two hidden costs: distance and dependence.

Distance measures how far it travels to reach you. Dependence measures how many intermediaries stand between you and the source.

Take one week and log ten ordinary items: bread, coffee, phone charger, medicine, clothing, water, data plan, news feed, transportation, security.

For each, write:

- Origin distance (km or source country).
- Number of hands between you and origin.
- Whether you could replace it locally if imports stopped.

The higher the product of distance × dependence, the more fragile that item is.

This is your **Fragility Index**.

Example: imported coffee—distance 8,000 km × dependence 6 intermediaries = 48,000 fragility units. Local bread—distance 10 × dependence 2 = 20 units.

Visualize this as a bar graph. You will immediately see where sovereignty leaks. The goal is not to abandon global trade but to anchor essentials close enough that a broken ship or sanction cannot starve you.

In the Bronze Age, the failure of a single tin route ended an era. The same logic governs your morning routine.

IV.

Day 16–20: Attention — Reclaiming Cognitive Energy

Modern collapse is as much psychological as material.

Our nervous systems are power grids; constant input is a form of brownout.

For five days, perform an **information fast**:

—No social media before noon.
—No doom-scrolling after sunset.
—News limited to two 15-minute windows.

Replace the remainder with physical tasks: cooking, repairing, walking, writing by hand.

Within 72 hours, your mental bandwidth expands. Studies on digital detox programs (University of Pennsylvania, 2018) show anxiety reduction of 25% and concentration improvement of 35% after one week. The data confirms what monks already knew: silence is infrastructure.

This regained attention is capital. Use it to notice small inefficiencies, delayed maintenance, forgotten skills. Sovereignty grows in the space between reaction and creation.

V.

Day 21–25: Finance — The Reserves of Trust

Money is a promise wrapped in code. When faith in the issuer wavers, the code unravels.

Calculate your personal liquidity horizon: how many days could you function if ATMs, cards, and apps were offline?

Convert one week's expenses into hard currency or alternative mediums—cash, commodities, or community credit. Store them discreetly but accessibly.

Then audit your income sources. Classify each as **Dependent** (requires complex external systems) or **Independent** (based on direct human exchange or skill).

Your goal over the next year is to raise the independent share by at least 10%. It could be tutoring, repair work, design, food production—anything that generates value without digital intermediaries.

Every hour spent cultivating such a skill is an investment that appreciates regardless of market swings. In the long cycles of history, skills outlast coins.

VI.

Day 26–28: Community — The Network of Trust

Collapse isolates before it unites. The antidote is pre-emptive alliance.

List ten people within a one-kilometre radius whose abilities you respect. Reach out to three this week with a genuine offer: trade a skill, share a tool, cook a meal. Do not speak of collapse; speak of collaboration.

Sociological data from post-disaster zones (Aldrich, *Building Resilience*, 2012) proves that social capital—not income or infrastructure—correlates most strongly with recovery speed.

A community that shares before crisis thrives after it.

Begin a **Commons Ledger**: a simple notebook tracking shared assets—a drill, a ladder, a solar charger, a seed library. Ownership is less useful than access. The Bronze Age palaces hoarded; the surviving villages shared. The pattern endures.

VII ·

Day 29: Reflection — The Audit of Time

Collapse distorts time. Hours stretch during scarcity, then vanish in crisis.

Spend one day tracking how you use time across the five circles—energy, food, information, finance, community.

Where does attention accumulate? Where does it leak?

The audit's purpose is not to shame distraction but to re-synchronize your internal clock with the real world's rhythms. When you cook, walk, read, or build at natural pace, you exit the empire of speed and enter the domain of presence. Sovereignty is not rebellion; it is rhythm regained.

VIII ·

Day 30 and Beyond: Integration — From Audit to Practice

After 30 days, you will have a map: weak points, reserves, potential alliances.

Translate it into three permanent practices:

1. **The One-Month Buffer:** store one month's essentials—food, cash, water, and knowledge of where to get more.
2. **The Weekly Skill:** every week, learn or refresh one low-tech ability—repair, first aid, planting, barter arithmetic.
3. **The Monthly Council:** gather friends or neighbours to discuss mutual preparedness, not as paranoia but as culture. Rotate hosts. Share data. Eat together.

The repetition is the secret. Systems fail when maintenance lapses. Civilizations collapse when citizens forget maintenance is sacred work.

IX ·

The Physics of Sovereignty

At its core, this protocol mirrors natural law. In physics, a structure's resilience depends on three variables: redundancy, modularity, and feedback.

Redundancy: multiple paths to the same outcome.

Modularity: parts can fail without collapsing the whole.

Feedback: the system can sense its state and adjust.

Apply this to your life. Redundancy means multiple energy and income sources. Modularity means diversified communities and skills. Feedback means honest tracking of consumption and emotion.

The mathematics of survival and the ethics of integrity are the same equation viewed from different sides.

X.

Closing Reflection — The Sovereign Pulse

At night, turn off every artificial light in your home. Sit in the dark for one minute and listen.

You will hear the faint pulse of appliances, perhaps the hum of a distant road, or only your heartbeat. That sound is the base frequency of existence—the one civilizations forget when they chase perpetual brightness.

The goal of this audit is not austerity but attunement.

When you can hear that pulse without fear, you have exited dependency and entered authorship.

From this stillness, all building begins.

Transmission

Collapse, viewed clearly, is not annihilation but invitation.

The systems that fail around you are messages in a forgotten tongue, asking you to remember how to stand without them.

The next chapter—*The Anatomy of Collapse*—takes this awareness from the personal to the structural. It dissects how entire societies overshoot, how signals multiply and cancel, and how the same physics that fractures also teaches us to rebuild.

Chapter 2

The Anatomy of Collapse

Part I — The Fall

Key 6 · Historical Mirror · The Maya Civilization's Overreach and Ecological Fall

The jungle still hides their bones.

In the Yucatán heat, you can hear the breath of the past between ceiba trees and vines, where stone steps rise from undergrowth like vertebrae. The temples of Tikal, Calakmul, and Copán pierce the canopy as if the forest is slowly swallowing a dream it once allowed. For six centuries the Maya ruled these highlands and lowlands—a lattice of city-states more like living organisms than kingdoms. Each pulsed with its own heartbeat of maize, calendar, and divine mathematics. They built time into architecture, aligning doorways to solstices and counting Venus's revolutions as the priests recited in meter. Then, slowly, the rhythm began to misfire.

Collapse came not with conquest but with exhaustion.

I ·

The Empire of Cycles

Between 250 and 900 CE, the Classic Maya transformed the limestone basins of Mesoamerica into a self-referential machine of abundance. Water from cenotes fed raised fields; limestone became both building material and lime for plaster; maize and cacao sustained populations larger than any previous civilization in the region. Their glyphs, carved on stelae, traced lineages and victories with obsessive precision. Kings called themselves *k'uhul ajaw*—holy lords—and their legitimacy rested on balancing cosmic and ecological time.

But the balance grew fragile as success multiplied. Cities competed not for survival but for spectacle: taller pyramids, more ornate ball courts, richer offerings. The gods demanded proof of devotion in the currency of stone and sacrifice. To quarry, carve, and transport each new monument, forests were felled. The sacred ceiba—axis of the Maya world—became scaffolding and fuel.

By the eighth century, pollen cores from Petén lakes show a sharp decline in tree species and a rise in weeds and maize pollen. The green lung that had sheltered them was thinning.

II ·

Drought and Denial

Nature, indifferent to grandeur, shifted rhythm.

Speleothem data—mineral layers in caves that record rainfall—reveal a sequence of megadroughts between 820 and 950 CE. The rainy season shortened; reservoirs cracked. In response, Maya engineers built more reservoirs, deeper cisterns, and elaborate canal networks. For a time, it worked. The priests declared that new rituals had appeased Chaac, the rain god. Yet each adaptation raised complexity—and thus vulnerability.

The cities began to cannibalize one another. Armies marched for captives and tribute; kings performed bloodletting rituals to feed the sky. The inscriptions grow frantic near the end, filled with dates and names but less meaning, as if language itself was burning. Then, silence. The stelae stopped.

Population models suggest the central lowlands lost up to 80% of inhabitants within a century. Some migrated to the coasts; others simply vanished into oral legend. Jungle reclaimed limestone, vines smoothed history's sharp edges. The Maya did not disappear—they decentralized—but the integrated system that had bound them collapsed.

III ·

The Equation of Overreach

What happened was not mystery but mathematics.

Each pyramid, festival, and war required energy—labour, food, wood, water. As the network expanded, its cost of maintenance rose exponentially. Joseph Tainter's principle of diminishing returns on complexity applies with uncanny precision: when each additional unit of organization yields less benefit than it costs to sustain, the system slides toward collapse.

In Maya terms, every new temple demanded more lime; each lime kiln devoured five tons of wood for every ton of plaster. Multiply that across hundreds of cities and centuries, and the equation becomes untenable.

As forests vanished, rainfall declined further. Fewer trees meant less transpiration, less local rain, more drought—feedback loops the priests could not see because their cosmology interpreted weather as divine mood rather than systemic feedback. The gods, in truth, were simply obeying physics.

Collapse, in this view, is the moment a civilization's story can no longer metabolize its own consequences.

IV ·

The Human Texture of the End

Archaeology reconstructs economics; imagination restores emotion.

Picture a scribe in Copán around 820 CE. The plaza still fills with dancers for the solstice, but fewer torches are lit. The ruler's headdress grows heavier even as his people grow thinner. In the marketplace, cacao beans—once currency—buy less maize each week. Traders whisper that the northern cities have gone silent. The scribe dutifully carves another date into stone, perhaps suspecting that no one will read it.

Elsewhere, mothers grind maize into thinner gruel. Farmers dig new canals that dry within months. The youngest generation inherits rituals without confidence. The ceremonies continue, but the link between offering and rain has dissolved. Belief persists out of inertia—the same inertia that will one day make modern nations defend currencies long after value has evaporated.

Every sign of collapse hides inside ordinary days until hindsight illuminates them.

V.

Echoes Beyond the Jungle

For centuries after, European chroniclers misread the ruins as evidence of a "lost" people. Only later did archaeologists realize that the Maya world had not vanished but retreated into distributed fragments. Small towns continued to farm maize and speak the language; descendants still calculated the sacred calendar in secret under colonial rule. The collapse was not extinction but simplification—a reversion from empire to ecosystem.

That pattern repeats endlessly. Rome fell, yet its roads carried pilgrims. The Khmer temples of Angkor drowned in their own hydraulic overreach, yet Cambodia endures. The Soviet Union disintegrated, yet its satellites still orbit above. Collapse is not the death of a culture but the moment it stops pretending it can defy ecology.

The Maya's great lesson is not about catastrophe but calibration: prosperity without humility becomes entropy.

They carved that truth in stone long before we rediscovered it in data.

VI ·

Transmission

The Maya reveal the skeleton of all collapses:

1. **Overreach** — expansion beyond ecological carrying capacity.
2. **Feedback delay** — interpreting signals through ideology instead of systems.
3. **Fragmentation** — the center can no longer synchronize its periphery.
4. **Simplification** — survival through contraction and localism.

In the next section we cross from the jungle to the printing press and banknote—to another empire that burned value faster than it could print it.

If the Maya's temples were made of limestone, Weimar's temples were made of paper.

Key 7 · Modern Parallel · Weimar Germany and the Logic of Hyperinflation

Berlin, August 1923.

A man stands in line for bread with a wheelbarrow full of money.

He isn't poor in theory; he's poor in time. By the time he reaches the counter, the price has doubled. Behind him, a woman counts notes so fast that her fingers blur, stacking bundles in shapes that no longer look like currency but like kindling.

Outside, the air smells of coal dust and decay. Newspapers run twice a day, not to inform but to update exchange rates. One morning coffee costs 5,000 marks; by evening, it costs 12,000. Children play with bricks of cash because toys are unaffordable, but paper is suddenly cheaper than wood. Germany's money, once the envy of Europe, has lost its story.

I .

A Crisis Born from Paper

To understand how an advanced industrial nation reached this absurdity, we must trace the same anatomy that doomed the Maya: complexity outrunning control, feedback delayed until useless.

After the First World War, the Treaty of Versailles demanded reparations equal to roughly 132 billion gold marks—an astronomical sum indexed to gold, not paper. Germany's industrial base was crippled, its debt denominated in a currency it could no longer mint. Politicians faced a trilemma: raise taxes and risk revolt, default and invite invasion, or print marks and pray. They chose the printing press.

At first, it seemed elegant. Inflation lubricated the economy, reduced the real value of debt, and allowed short-term growth. But each new note issued required more notes to sustain prices. By 1922, the mark had already lost 90% of its pre-war value. Foreign investors fled. The government responded not with contraction but acceleration. Money creation became the new ritual sacrifice to the gods of stability.

II ·

The Physics of Inflation

Economists describe inflation as "too much money chasing too few goods," but that phrase hides the psychological element. What collapses is not supply or demand but *belief*. Money functions only as long as collective imagination holds its shape. Once that consensus wavers, feedback loops behave like fire.

Each citizen, trying to protect savings, accelerates the burn: they spend faster, convert cash into goods, or flee into foreign currency. The velocity of money—the rate at which it changes hands—skyrockets. The act of preservation becomes indistinguishable from destruction.

By July 1923, prices were doubling every three days. Bank clerks received pay twice daily so their families could shop before value evaporated. Workers negotiated not wages but *frequency of payment*. The Reichsbank ran twenty-four-hour shifts printing new notes; the ink supply became a strategic resource. The paper itself—cellulose and cotton blend—ran out, forcing the government to recycle school notebooks, bonds, even train tickets into blank currency stock.

III.

Collapse as Theater

Weimar's inflation was not merely economic—it was cultural implosion performed in real time.

Artists turned panic into innovation: Dadaists pasted banknotes into collages mocking the absurdity of value; cabarets filled with songs about hunger and lust. The city's nightlife exploded precisely because tomorrow's money was worthless. Hedonism became hedging.

Meanwhile, the rural hinterlands starved. Farmers hoarded grain, refusing to sell for paper that devalued hourly. Urban dwellers, their savings annihilated, bartered jewelry for potatoes. Food riots broke out from Hamburg to Munich. The state's authority—once rooted in fiscal order—eroded into improvisation. Bureaucrats paid taxes in goods, judges accepted livestock as collateral, and prostitutes priced services in cigarettes.

When society loses a universal measure of value, every transaction becomes negotiation. That is not commerce; it is entropy.

IV.

The Psychology of Acceleration

Hyperinflation reveals the same mental architecture as the drought-stricken Maya or the fuel queues of Sri Lanka: the inability to act before the curve steepens.

Early warnings appeared years before the peak—charts, editorials, protests—but the public response was familiar: *things will normalize.* Normalcy bias, cognitive dissonance, and learned helplessness combined with institutional arrogance to sustain denial.

Even as prices multiplied, many citizens continued to deposit wages in banks out of habit, believing bureaucracy itself carried magic. That obedience prolonged the illusion. Each small adaptation—printing more money, raising nominal wages, pegging new indices—temporarily restored calm while increasing fragility. The Weimar economy became a self-cannibalizing machine, feeding on future confidence to survive present panic.

Hyperinflation is not chaos; it is an order that has lost feedback control. Like a microphone howling when its signal loops into itself, the economy amplifies its own noise until systems overload. By the time leaders recognize the screech, the speakers have melted.

V.

The Reckoning

On November 15, 1923, the government introduced the **Rentenmark**, a new currency backed not by gold but by land and industrial assets. The exchange rate was fixed: one Rentenmark equaled one trillion old marks. Overnight, the illusion was reset. Prices stabilized, not because wealth returned but because narrative coherence did. People could once again tell themselves a believable story about value.

The Weimar experiment left scars deeper than any spreadsheet could show. Middle-class savings evaporated; social trust collapsed. Those who had thrived on credit were ruined, while those with tangible assets—factories, farms, foreign currency—emerged dominant. The stage was set for radical politics. Within a decade, economic trauma became the psychological fuel of authoritarianism. When money lies, people crave certainty in flesh.

The ruin of the mark was not just a fiscal event; it was the moral disintegration of exchange itself.

VI ·

Echoes in the Digital Century

We like to believe our currencies—fiat, crypto, or otherwise—are safer because they move faster, because algorithms watch for imbalance. But speed amplifies feedback as much as it stabilizes it. A globalized financial system can inflate or crash across continents in seconds. The same pattern that consumed Weimar now hides in derivative markets, sovereign debt spirals, and the invisible money of quantitative easing. The paper is gone, but the story remains.

Modern monetary crises—Argentina's peso, Zimbabwe's dollar, Venezuela's bolívar—repeat Weimar's script with updated technology. Each begins with a noble justification (growth, justice, independence) and ends with citizens bartering essentials while leaders print promises.

The medium evolves; the myth persists.

VII ·

Transmission

The Maya exhausted soil; Weimar exhausted trust.

Both prove that collapse begins when symbols lose correlation with reality—when harvest quotas or currency digits expand faster than the system that anchors them.

The next section dissects the psychology beneath that overreach: how comfort breeds blindness, how helplessness becomes culture, and how the mind can be rewired to detect the tremor before the fall.

Key 8 · Psychological Mechanism · The Biology of Surrender

Civilizations do not collapse from lack of resources alone.

They collapse when their people forget how to respond to pain.

At the core of every downfall lies a neurological malfunction: the gradual rewiring of a society's collective nervous system from action to waiting. The Maya watched the rains vanish and doubled their rituals. Weimar's citizens watched prices triple and queued politely for bread. Sri Lankans watched tankers drift offshore and refreshed government apps for news. Each culture, though separated by centuries, exhibited the same response: compliance as anaesthesia.

I ·

The Laboratory of Despair

In 1967, psychologist Martin Seligman conducted an experiment that became a grim mirror of history. Dogs were placed in harnesses and exposed to mild electric shocks. Some could end the pain by pressing a lever; others could not. After repeated exposure, when given a chance to escape, the animals who had learned helplessness stayed still. They had internalized futility.

When the same principle is applied to humans, the pattern expands.

Citizens subjected to chronic uncertainty—economic crises, shifting rules, political betrayal—begin to interpret failure as personal inevitability. Motivation decays not from laziness but from conditioned despair. The cost of trying exceeds the reward of success.

In modern cities, this manifests subtly: people stop applying for jobs after too many rejections; voters stop believing reforms matter; families stop saving when inflation mocks discipline. Each small surrender becomes neurological—an efficiency adaptation of the brain's reward circuitry. The collective result is paralysis.

II ·

The Mechanism of Normalization

The human brain is built to normalize anything that repeats.

Neuroscientists call it **habituation**—the dampening of response to persistent stimuli. It kept early humans from panicking at every thunderclap, but in a collapsing society, it becomes fatal. When power outages occur weekly, they become "routine." When corruption headlines appear daily, outrage fades into irony. When debt becomes infinite, it becomes invisible.

This process turns instability into the new normal. The Maya endured decades of irregular rains before admitting drought. Weimar citizens recalibrated value every morning as if insanity were accounting. The mind, desperate for predictability, redefines chaos as order.

That redefinition feels like resilience but functions as anesthesia. It keeps the organism alive while stripping its capacity for adaptation. The final stage is resignation disguised as patience.

III·

The Dopamine Trap

Modern collapse introduces a new layer: algorithmic control.

Our nervous systems, once trained by weather and work, are now tuned by digital reward loops. Social media platforms exploit the same dopamine circuits that Seligman's levers once targeted. Each notification delivers micro-pleasure, regardless of substance. The more uncertain the world becomes, the more compulsively we seek these tiny confirmations of existence.

This is the new opiate: intermittent reinforcement.

Like lab animals pressing levers, citizens press screens. The illusion of agency replaces agency itself. Political and corporate power thrive in this trance because outrage can be quantified, predicted, and redirected. A population fed on stimulus becomes incapable of sustained focus—the cognitive resource collapse that precedes physical collapse.

Neuroscientist Anna Lembke describes it bluntly: "In dopamine nation, pleasure and pain share a single balance." The more we consume to escape discomfort, the deeper the deficit becomes. A civilization addicted to its own distractions cannot sense the storm until it arrives.

IV·

The Comfort Paradox

As living standards rise, resilience falls.

In evolutionary terms, comfort is recent. For most of human history, hardship was the default state; survival demanded constant learning and cooperation. The twentieth century inverted that ratio. We outsourced difficulty to machines, discomfort to policy, uncertainty to experts. The result was convenience—our most seductive form of captivity.

Comfort shortens time horizons. It trains the brain to expect frictionless feedback: a click, a delivery, a solution. When systems that provide this comfort falter, the withdrawal is psychic. Panic replaces patience. Instead of adapting, people rage or freeze. The energy that once drove exploration becomes grievance.

In this sense, decline is the body remembering that ease was never guaranteed. Collapse is not the apocalypse; it is physical reality reclaiming attention from abstraction.

V.

The Ritual of Waiting

Anthropologists studying late-stage societies—from Byzantium to the Soviet Union—observe a phenomenon they call *anticipatory obedience*. Citizens begin adjusting behavior in advance of new decrees, not because they are forced but because they assume inevitability. The bureaucrat fills out forms no one reads; the shopkeeper restocks goods no one buys. Everyone continues the ritual of maintenance long after purpose dissolves.

This ritual has deep psychological roots. Humans equate motion with meaning. Continuing the familiar, even when futile, feels safer than confronting the void. In Weimar, people counted zeros instead of calories. In the final years of the Maya, temples rose even as crops failed. Rituals expanded as results vanished.

That is why collapse looks orderly until the final hour. Everyone is still at their post.

VI ·

The Biology of Awakening

The same brain that learns helplessness can unlearn it—but only through shock or purpose.

In experiments where the barrier between the shocked dogs and safety was removed, most still did not cross it—until a researcher physically lifted them over once. Thereafter, they learned to escape on their own. The implication is profound: consciousness requires demonstration of possibility, not mere instruction.

Historically, moments of renewal follow exposure to undeniable failure. The Black Death birthed humanism; Weimar's trauma spawned both totalitarianism and modern psychology. In each case, a portion of the population recognized futility and pivoted from obedience to authorship.

At the neurochemical level, agency reactivates dopamine balance. Each successful act of problem-solving—planting food, repairing, organizing—rebuilds the circuitry of hope. The feedback loop reverses: effort becomes rewarding again. Sovereignty is not an ideology; it is a neurobiological condition.

VII ·

Training for the Unthinkable

To reverse societal paralysis, individuals must perform controlled discomfort.

Cold showers, fasting, silence, manual labor—each small hardship is rehearsal for autonomy.

These are not spiritual affectations but neurological retraining. They re-teach the body that effort leads to outcome, that discomfort signals growth rather than doom. Monks, athletes, and soldiers have long known this instinctively. The collapse-aware citizen must relearn it.

Psychologists term this **stress inoculation**—voluntary exposure to manageable stress to build tolerance for larger shocks. Civilizations that neglect it grow brittle. Citizens who practice it become the backbone of recovery.

VIII ·

Transmission

Collapse begins as neurological feedback failure and ends as myth.

The next section turns to the oldest story of all—the tale of hubris and consequence.

Just as the Maya raised monuments higher to prove control and the Weimar bankers printed faster to buy time, the mythic figure of Prometheus captures this eternal temptation: to steal fire without foresight.

From here we descend into the archetype of overreach—the myth that explains why knowledge and pride so often share the same flame.

Key 9 · Mythic Resonance · Prometheus and the Fire of Hubris

Every civilization believes it has mastered fire.

It begins with warmth and ends with worship. The first flames tamed beasts, forged tools, and baked clay into the shapes of gods. Then fire became symbol—of innovation, rebellion, and divine theft. No myth captures that transformation more completely than the story of Prometheus, the Titan who defied the heavens to bring light to humankind.

His name means "forethought." His crime was compassion. His punishment was eternity.

I ·

The Theft of Light

In Hesiod's *Theogony*, Prometheus tricks Zeus by offering him two piles at a feast: one of fat covering bones, the other of meat hidden inside a foul stomach. Zeus chooses the deceptive offering, establishing sacrifice forever—humans would burn the best portion for the gods and keep the rest. Enraged, Zeus withholds fire from mankind. Prometheus, pitying the shivering mortals, steals it back in a hollow reed.

Fire becomes the first technology, the first rebellion, and the first debt.

Zeus retaliates by chaining Prometheus to a mountain, where an eagle devours his liver each day and it regenerates each night. The punishment is cyclical, like the human condition itself: knowledge and suffering renewing each other indefinitely.

II ·

The Archetype of Overreach

Prometheus is the father of civilization's ambition and its anxiety.

He represents the moment when humanity decides that divine order is too slow. The Titan's fire ignites metallurgy, craft, and reason—but also pride. In Aeschylus' version, Prometheus boasts that he gave humans mathematics, navigation, medicine, architecture. In short, he gave them the power to imitate gods. His rebellion was altruism fused with arrogance.

Every empire inherits that same impulse. The Maya believed their astronomical precision guaranteed cosmic harmony; Weimar believed its printing presses could rewrite scarcity. In both, forethought mutated into hubris. Prometheus's flame never extinguishes—it just changes fuel.

In psychological terms, the myth encodes the reward circuitry of mastery. Each success reinforces risk-taking until feedback vanishes. When the returns of innovation are immediate and the costs are delayed, cultures climb mountains they cannot descend. Zeus's eagle is not vengeance; it is consequence.

III ·

The Fire and the Algorithm

The modern descendant of Prometheus no longer carries reeds but circuits.

Our species has stolen new fires: nuclear energy, genetic engineering, artificial intelligence. Each promises liberation, each demands discipline we have not yet proven. When Oppenheimer watched the first atomic flash, he whispered from the *Bhagavad Gita*: *"Now I am become Death, the destroyer of worlds."* It was the same mountain, the same flame, and perhaps the same eagle.

Technology, like mythic fire, amplifies human intention without improving its ethics. The internet democratized knowledge and created new empires of distraction. Genetic editing can heal or weaponize. Artificial intelligence, if left to markets alone, will mirror our appetites rather than our ideals. We have again taken light from the gods and forgotten to ask if we are ready to see everything it reveals.

Prometheus's wound—his regenerating liver—symbolizes perpetual consequence. Every advancement heals the surface while leaving the scar beneath. Progress without reflection is immortality without peace.

IV.

The Counterbalance: Pandora

Zeus's revenge did not end with Prometheus. From the ashes of stolen fire, he crafted Pandora—the first woman—molded from clay and given gifts from every god: beauty, charm, curiosity. Her jar (later mistranslated as a box) contained all evils: disease, greed, envy, deceit. When she opened it, these escaped into the world, leaving only *hope* trapped inside.

The mythic balance is exact. Fire expands possibility; Pandora releases consequence. Together they form the dual heartbeat of civilization: creation and correction.

Without Pandora, fire would consume everything. Without fire, Pandora's evils would have no theater.

Hope's imprisonment at the bottom of the jar is the final paradox. It reminds us that survival depends not on extinguishing risk but on managing it. Hope remains precisely because it is the one force that can coexist with awareness of danger. Every age opens Pandora's jar anew; every generation redefines what hope means after overreach.

V.

The Psychological Code

In depth psychology, Prometheus represents the ego's rebellion against limitation. Jung saw him as the archetype of individuation—the spark that drives humans to differentiate from the collective. Yet unintegrated, this impulse becomes narcissism: creation without conscience. The modern world, obsessed with disruption, worships the Promethean hero but forgets his chains.

Healthy forethought requires humility before consequence. The mature psyche does not extinguish ambition but surrounds it with awareness—Zeus within Prometheus. This is the equilibrium of sovereignty: innovation guided by restraint.

The Maya lost it in limestone; Weimar lost it in paper; we risk losing it in code.

Every builder must therefore become their own eagle, inspecting the cost of their creations daily. Without that self-devouring vigilance, civilization mistakes momentum for morality.

VI.

Fire as Covenant

There is another reading—quieter, redemptive.

In later myths, Prometheus is eventually freed by Heracles, who slays the eagle. Zeus permits it, having recognized that humanity cannot return to ignorance. The punishment ends not through rebellion but through acceptance of responsibility. Fire becomes sacred again, tended in temples rather than stolen.

This is the forgotten half of the myth: the reconciliation between creation and discipline.

Ancient Greece instituted the **Prometheia**—a torch relay where runners carried flame from altar to altar without letting it die. The ritual taught that knowledge must be passed, not hoarded, and that its continuity depends on stewardship. The torch of the Olympic Games descends from that practice—a secular echo of a sacred vow.

The lesson is simple: innovation without ritual is theft; innovation with ritual is culture.

VII ·

Transmission

Prometheus warns us that overreach is inevitable but not irreversible.

His chains are self-forged, his fire self-sustaining. Each civilization must learn how to hold light without burning.

The next and final section of this chapter translates that wisdom into practice: a *Household Early-Warning Dashboard*—a modern divination table for detecting imbalance before the fire spreads.

Key 10 · Sovereignty Protocol · The Household Early-Warning Dashboard

No empire believes it is collapsing until the data goes quiet.

Before statues topple or currencies die, the signals shrink into daily noise: a shipment delayed, a headline rewritten, a rumor of rationing. The difference between survival and surprise is not genius but vigilance. The *Household Early-Warning Dashboard* is the tool that restores that vigilance. It turns observation into discipline, turning every home into a miniature civilization with sensors tuned to reality.

You cannot control the system, but you can read its pulse.

I ·

The Logic of Foresight

All collapses share one pathology: *signal blindness*.

In stable times, citizens outsource observation to specialists—priests, economists, algorithms. When the specialists fail, feedback dies. The dashboard reverses that dependency by teaching pattern recognition at the scale of the kitchen table.

Think of it as your personal seismograph. It doesn't predict earthquakes; it detects strain.

Its purpose is not panic but adaptation: to give you a three-month advantage on the future.

The structure follows five modules—Energy, Price, Supply, Governance, and Sentiment—each with measurable indicators. The numbers themselves are less important than their *trend velocity*. What matters is how fast they change relative to your lived experience.

II.

Module 1 — Energy Pressure

Energy is civilization's heartbeat. When it stutters, everything else trembles.

Track these three metrics weekly:

1. **Fuel-to-Income Ratio:** the cost of your primary energy source (electricity, gas, or transport fuel) as a percentage of household income. Historically, when this exceeds 15 %, unrest follows within six months.
2. **Outage Frequency:** count blackouts or supply cuts longer than one hour. The shift from rare to regular marks the transition from strain to breakdown.
3. **Maintenance Delay Index:** days between a fault and its repair. Infrastructure decay begins not with explosions but with longer waits.

Keep this record on paper, not cloud. When the lights go, paper remembers.

III.

Module 2 — Price Anomalies

Hyperinflation, scarcity, and corruption all begin as small distortions in price symmetry.

Build a *basket of essentials*: bread, rice, oil, eggs, soap, and one staple unique to your region. Record prices every Sunday at the same store.

Plot them monthly on a simple graph.

- **Early Alarm:** two consecutive months above 10 % increase across the basket.
- **Critical Alarm:** when prices diverge—one good stable, another doubling—indicating hidden subsidies or hoarding.
- **Cultural Alarm:** when luxury items (alcohol, cigarettes, entertainment) drop in price while basics rise; that gap measures despair.

In Weimar, prices of pianos collapsed while potatoes soared. Watch what the culture stops valuing.

IV ·

Module 3 — Supply Integrity

The Maya lost tin; modern societies lose microchips or fertilizer. The medium changes, the pattern doesn't.

Your task: create a **Lead-Time Map** of essentials—how many days between purchase and replacement.

For each category—food, medicine, water, tools—mark three thresholds:

- **Green:** easily replaced within 24 hours.
- **Yellow:** takes 3–7 days or depends on one supplier.
- **Red:** unavailable locally or import-dependent.

Revisit quarterly. The goal is not hoarding but diversification. A household with ten supply chains has options; one with two has beliefs.

Note the *feel* of scarcity: longer queues, smaller packaging, subtle quality decay. These are your early signals—the whisper before the crash.

V.

Module 4 — Governance Lag

Collapse accelerates when institutions speak slower than events.

Track the **Gap Between Announcement and Action.** When public officials announce a measure—fuel subsidy, wage adjustment, import restriction—note the date and when it materializes.

- **Stable phase:** action within two weeks.
- **Strain phase:** one month lag.
- **Break phase:** policies contradicted or reversed within days.

Record also the tone of language. Bureaucratic optimism ("temporary challenge") often precedes confession ("unexpected difficulty") by exactly one quarter. When metaphors replace numbers, truth has fled the room.

Governance decay is audible before it is visible.

VI.

Module 5 — Sentiment Field

Numbers warn; emotions confirm.

Every society generates an ambient frequency—how people talk in markets, transport, social feeds. Learn to sample it consciously.

Create a **Weekly Mood Index.**

Each Friday, note in a single line the dominant tone you perceive: hope, fatigue, anger, absurdity, silence. Over months, patterns emerge.

When humor turns self-destructive and silence replaces complaint, you have entered the zone of moral exhaustion. At that stage, systems no longer reform; they reset.

Sentiment analysis may sound unscientific, but it kept entire villages alive in past collapses. When gossip changes rhythm, logistics soon follow.

VII ·

Turning Data into Action

Observation without motion is voyeurism. The dashboard's second phase converts awareness into micro-responses:

- **Diversify Dependencies:** If any module flashes red twice consecutively, redesign one habit—change supplier, skill, or routine.
- **Quarterly Council:** gather trusted peers to share findings. Compare notes; local data averages out fear.
- **Practice the 3-Day Rule:** keep autonomy for seventy-two hours—food, water, cash, and communication. Three days separates inconvenience from emergency.

Each act rewires helplessness into authorship. The dashboard is less about metrics than muscle memory.

VIII ·

Calibration with History

Test your dashboard against precedent:

- *Maya (820 CE):* forest pollen decline preceded abandonment by 30 years.

- *Weimar (1923):* paper shortages predated currency collapse by 6 months.
- *Sri Lanka (2022):* fertilizer import drop forecast food riots a year ahead.

In every case, data existed; interpretation failed. The household that reads patterns before experts becomes the new oracle. Sovereignty in the modern age is not prophecy but attentiveness.

IX.

The Ethics of Foresight

Knowledge carries burden. Once you see the signs, cynicism is tempting—*why warn others if they won't listen?* Resist that instinct. The dashboard's highest purpose is communal, not individual.

Share calmly, model preparedness without preaching. Panic is contagious; so is composure.

In moral terms, foresight is stewardship: the ability to hold awareness without arrogance. The Promethean error was giving fire without guidance. Your task is to keep the flame steady enough that others can gather around it.

X.

The Daily Practice of Sovereignty

Each morning, glance at your dashboard before the newsfeed.

Ask five questions:

1. Did my environment change faster than my habits?
2. Do I rely on one story to explain all signals?

3. Have I spoken with my neighbors this week?
4. What one action restores balance today?
5. If systems froze tonight, what still works?

Write answers in shorthand. Over time, they become intuition.

Collapse stops being apocalypse and becomes feedback—loud, painful, but comprehensible.

XI ·

The Long View

Civilizations recover not by avoiding stress but by transforming it into information.

Your dashboard is the first draft of a new social contract—citizens as sensors, communities as processors, leaders as listeners. When the state forgets to measure honestly, the people must.

Three thousand years after the Bronze Age, we have satellites and sensors, yet the oldest instrument remains the human pattern-spotter. The goal is not to out-predict the future but to re-enter dialogue with it.

Collapse will visit again; it always does. The sovereign learns its language early.

XII ·

Closing Reflection

In the dark, after the day's counts and graphs, turn off the lights and look at the faint glow from your devices. That is your fire—the modern reed of Prometheus. It can illuminate or consume.

The discipline of foresight is how you decide which.

The anatomy of collapse ends where vigilance begins. From this threshold onward, the task is no longer detection but design—the reconstruction of systems worthy of endurance.

Transmission

Chapter 1 taught awareness.

Chapter 2 taught anatomy.

Now the ascent turns inward.

In **Chapter 3 — The Sovereign Stack**, we begin building: the layered architecture of financial, cognitive, social, and cultural independence that turns foresight into foundation.

Chapter 3

The Sovereign Stack

Part I — The Fall

Key 11 · Historical Mirror · The Jewish Diaspora and the Architecture of Portable Identity

When an empire collapses, stones crack first, then stories.

In 70 CE the Second Temple burned above Jerusalem's valley. Roman legions under Titus dismantled not only a sanctuary but a civilization's spatial anchor. For the Jews who survived, sovereignty did not vanish—it migrated. Over the next two millennia they built something that no conqueror could occupy: a nation inside the mind.

I ·

From Kingdom to Code

The Temple's destruction forced a radical innovation: religion without geography.

With no altar, no priesthood, and no homeland, Jewish thinkers encoded nationhood into *Torah as text* rather than *temple as place*. The Mishnah and Talmud—compiled in dispersed academies from Yavneh to Babylon—became the first portable constitution. Law, language, and learning turned into the triad of survival.

Every scroll was a server; every scholar a node.

It was the birth of distributed sovereignty—a network civilization centuries before blockchain metaphors existed. The exile taught that identity could be replicated by memory and maintained by ritual.

The lesson was brutal but elegant: when land is lost, structure the sacred as information.

II ·

Commerce as Citizenship

By the 10th century, Jewish merchant families known as the Radhanites traversed the Old World from Lyon to Chang'an.

They wrote in Hebrew but spoke Arabic, Persian, Greek, and Slavonic; they carried letters of credit recognized across hostile borders. Their trust network—rooted in shared law and lineage—functioned as a proto-financial internet.

A trader in Cordoba could ship spices to Baghdad through cousins he had never met, confident that debts would clear because moral obligation was enforceable through communal reputation. The community was both regulator and insurer.

When medieval kings expelled Jewish populations—from England in 1290 to Spain in 1492—their capital fled with them. Each expulsion hollowed a state's treasury and enriched another's. Portability became leverage: a quiet power exercised not by armies but by the ability to reconstitute life anywhere within one lunar cycle.

III ·

Memory Infrastructure

Synagogues in exile were not merely houses of prayer; they were time machines.

Every architectural element pointed back to a lost center—the Aron ha-Kodesh toward Jerusalem, the eternal lamp symbolizing the Temple's fire. Festivals became annual rehearsals of collective trauma and renewal: *Passover* for liberation, *Tisha B'Av* for destruction, *Sukkot* for impermanence.

Psychologically, these rituals accomplished what fortresses could not: coherence.

They stabilized identity through repetition, a principle modern neuroscience now confirms. Repetition under emotional charge rewires neural pathways; shared ritual makes memory communal, resilient against erasure.

A people scattered across seventy kingdoms could still synchronize sunsets by the same calendar. In information-theory terms, they achieved *signal coherence across noise*.

IV.

Education as Defense

While medieval Europe reserved literacy for clerics, Jewish communities mandated it for every child—girls included in many regions centuries before modern schooling.

Study was worship. The Hebrew verb *limmud* conflates learning and devotion; knowledge itself became sacred infrastructure.

This educational sovereignty produced disproportionate survival outcomes.

During the persecutions of the 14th and 15th centuries, families that could read laws, count debts, and interpret contracts could migrate, bargain, and adapt. Where others depended on feudal lords, Jews depended on portable intellect.

Later, this same discipline birthed disproportionate modern achievements—Einstein, Freud, Marx, Kafka—not accidents of genetics but of culture engineered for cognitive endurance.

Learning, in this lineage, was not self-improvement; it was self-defense.

V.

The Covenant as Operating System

What held the network together was not empire but ethic.

The *brit*—the covenant between God and people—functioned as a social contract more binding than constitutions. It specified duties before rights: care for widow, orphan, and stranger; honor the Sabbath; redeem captives; balance mercy with justice.

Each commandment was both legal code and behavioral protocol. Violating it threatened the system's integrity; obeying it reinforced feedback loops of trust.

This covenantal design turned morality into infrastructure—the true secret of civilizational uptime.

Where imperial decrees required armies, the covenant required conscience.

That is why Jewish civilization survived without borders: its walls were internalized.

VI.

Resilience Through Recursion

Every exile repeated the same pattern—displacement, adaptation, renewal.

From Babylon to Alexandria, Toledo to Vilnius, Baghdad to New York—the network rebuilt itself recursively. Each community began with three constants: a place of learning, a place of worship, a fund for the poor. Within months a micro-nation reappeared.

Sociologists later called this *social capital*.

Historians called it miracle.

In truth it was protocol: the Sovereign Stack before the phrase existed.

Financial layer — trust and credit.

Cognitive layer — education and law.

Social layer — mutual aid and ritual.

Cultural layer — story and moral memory.

Add technology, and you have the template for every resilient society to come.

VII ·

The Psychological Core: Internal Locus of Control

The diaspora trained individuals to believe that agency survives environment.

Even when stripped of citizenship, they retained authorship. This internal locus of control—later measured by psychologist Julian Rotter (1966)—correlates with higher problem-solving, health, and income. Entire communities embodied it centuries before science named it.

While empires externalized blame—on enemies, gods, or markets—diasporic culture internalized responsibility: if covenant is broken, repair it; if exile persists, adapt faster.

That self-regulating mindset transformed powerlessness into momentum.

Sovereignty, they proved, is a state of consciousness before it is a state of law.

VIII ·

The Modern Echo

Every refugee camp, digital nomad community, and remote-work collective inherits this lineage, knowingly or not.

When identity becomes portable, geography loses monopoly over belonging. The future will resemble the diaspora more than the nation-state. Bitcoin wallets, encrypted communication, and online learning are secular Torahs—scripts of continuity independent of borders.

But the warning endures: without ethic, portability becomes rootlessness. The covenant must evolve, not vanish. Networks without moral gravity drift into chaos.

What held the Jewish world through forty generations was not innovation but integration—knowledge bound to conscience.

IX ·

Transmission

The diaspora's genius lay in transforming displacement into design.

That is the foundation of *The Sovereign Stack*: a system of layered independence built to outlast empires.

Next, in the modern mirror, we descend into another crucible of deprivation and ingenuity—**Cuba's Special Period (1991–2000)**—to see how an island under embargo rebuilt its economy from bicycles, gardens, and grit.

Key 12 · Modern Parallel · Cuba's Special Period and the Art of Decentralized Survival

When the Soviet Union dissolved in 1991, Cuba awoke to silence.

Tankers stopped arriving from Murmansk, the sugar-for-oil exchanges collapsed overnight, and ninety percent of imports vanished. Buses halted mid-route. Factories went dark. Even oxygen for hospitals ran low because it came in tanks made in Ukraine.

Fidel Castro called it the *Período Especial en Tiempo de Paz*—the "Special Period in Time of Peace."

Peace was not the right word. It was famine without bombs, siege without invaders.

Yet from that deprivation, a new kind of civilization emerged—one that rediscovered the mechanics of autonomy.

I ·

The Collapse

At the dawn of the 1990s, Cuba was more industrially entangled with Moscow than any nation on Earth. It exported sugar and nickel; it imported oil, food, and fertilizer. When the Soviet bloc imploded, GDP shrank 35 percent in three years. Public transport collapsed by 80 percent. Power blackouts averaged sixteen hours per day. Caloric intake fell from 3,000 to barely 1,800 per person.

Doctors recorded weight loss across the population—an accidental nationwide fasting experiment.

The government rationed everything: soap, matches, meat, milk. Bicycles replaced buses, oxen replaced tractors.

For any other modern state, this would have been terminal. Cuba, however, improvised a new operating system.

II ·

The Return of the Garden

Deprived of imported fertilizer and fuel, cities turned green.

Abandoned lots became *organopónicos*—organic urban gardens. By 1995, Havana alone had over 10,000 micro-farms producing more than half its vegetables locally. Compost replaced chemicals; earthworms replaced diesel. Farmers re-learned hand tools from grandparents.

These were not romantic gestures but necessity-driven design.

The *organopónico* movement fused three principles of sovereignty:

1. **Localization:** produce what you consume within walking distance.
2. **Circularity:** every waste is an input for another process.
3. **Community Stewardship:** ownership is distributed through cooperatives, not ministries.

The government legalized private food markets for the first time since the revolution, turning black-market survival into sanctioned adaptation.

It was agrarian regression on paper, but ecological acceleration in reality—Cuba became the only country in the world to reach both the UN's minimum food security threshold and sustainability metrics during that decade.

III.

The Bicycle Economy

Transportation mirrored the same pivot.

With fuel imports cut by half, Cuba imported one million Chinese bicycles and produced half a million more domestically. Citizens commuted by pedal, forming spontaneous convoys through cities. Workshops sprouted to recycle ball bearings and weld spare parts from scrap.

Energy descent turned into community rhythm.

Doctors visited patients by bicycle; teachers pedaled to rural schools; entire offices cycled together. The average Cuban burned 5,000 calories daily just moving between errands, but the air cleared, accidents dropped, and streets filled with conversations again.

It was not utopia—people fainted in queues and sold heirlooms for protein—but the social fabric held. Cuba demonstrated that a nation could decouple well-being from petroleum without civil war.

IV.

The Energy Monks

Inside that hardship arose an unexpected hero: the engineer-philosopher.

Scientists from the University of Havana began documenting small-scale energy systems—solar cookers made from mirrors, wind turbines built from car alternators, methane digesters made from abandoned fuel tanks.

They called themselves *energéticos comunitarios*—community energy monks.

Their laboratories were rooftops and alleyways.

They kept notebooks of experiments like medieval alchemists, except their gold was resilience.

This network—informal, decentralized, and open-source—produced the world's first large-scale proof that industrial-scale production is not the only path to modernity. They hacked scarcity into stability.

The idea later inspired sustainability movements from Detroit to Dhaka: if you can power a house with refuse and design a life around bicycles, you can outlast empires.

V.

The Cultural Immune System

What saved Cuba was not just improvisation but meaning.

While material conditions collapsed, ideological coherence—however imperfect—gave suffering a frame. The narrative of resistance turned hunger into sacrifice, blackout into discipline. Songs, humor, and community kitchens preserved morale.

Psychologists observed that suicide rates remained far lower than expected for such deprivation. The key was *colectivo*—the felt sense of belonging. Isolation kills faster than hunger; shared ordeal can extend life.

Street murals declared *Resistir es Vencer*—to endure is to win. In neighborhoods, grandmothers cooked one communal meal from pooled rations. In schools, children wrote diaries to document "how we lived through the Special Period," ensuring memory became testimony, not trauma.

Cultural immune systems are built exactly this way: story as metabolism.

VI ·

The Shadow Economy and Adaptive Ethics

Necessity also birthed a shadow network—barter, remittances, unlicensed taxis, underground markets.

The moral line blurred between survival and corruption. A mechanic fixing a generator with stolen parts was both criminal and savior. Women traded soap for rice; teachers moonlighted as vendors.

Yet these informal circuits functioned as parallel governance. They distributed resources when official channels froze.

Anthropologists later coined the term *resolver*—"to resolve, to make do"—as a philosophy of Cuban pragmatism.

Every household became its own ministry of economics. The lesson for modern readers is clear: morality during collapse is situational but coherence must remain. Sovereignty means navigating grey zones without losing a core ethic.

VII ·

Health and Science Resilience

Despite shortages, Cuba's public health system adapted remarkably.

Doctors reverted to herbal remedies, acupuncture, and locally synthesized pharmaceuticals. Medical schools emphasized preventive care and epidemiology. Infant mortality remained among the lowest in Latin America.

The island's biotech sector—ironically born from scarcity—eventually produced vaccines and exportable medicines. By the 2000s, Cuba had turned health itself into an export economy, sending doctors abroad in exchange for fuel or currency.

This transformation revealed a deeper form of sovereignty: knowledge as currency. When material inputs vanish, intellectual capital sustains trade.

The diaspora built memory; Cuba built muscle.

VIII ·

Energy as Ethics

By the late 1990s, solar panels began dotting rural schools.

Students learned to wire circuits, monitor voltage, and measure sunlight hours. Energy education became moral education: every watt was sacred. Waste equaled disrespect.

In contrast to industrial nations where consumption signified success, Cubans learned a reversed equation—discipline as dignity.

The paradox: the same socialist ideology that created dependence on the USSR also generated unity strong enough to survive its collapse. Ideology, like fire, destroys or purifies depending on how it's tended.

The Promethean theme returns here: fire reclaimed from gods, handled by mortals with care.

IX.

Psychological Mechanism: The Rebirth of Agency

Martin Seligman's theory of learned helplessness describes how repeated failure erodes will. Cuba's Special Period demonstrated the inverse: repeated *problem-solving* restores it.

Each garden, each jury-rigged bicycle, each communal meal was a micro-dose of agency. Small wins recalibrated dopamine loops; collective success released oxytocin; scarcity turned neurochemical. The population rewired itself for self-efficacy.

In behavioral economics, this mirrors *nudge dynamics*—structural constraints forcing creative adaptation. A population conditioned for scarcity can outperform one spoiled by abundance, because it reads feedback more accurately.

Sovereignty begins in neurons before it reaches nations.

X.

The Aftermath

By 2000, Cuba had stabilized. The gardens remained. The bicycle culture persisted. Even as oil imports returned, citizens resisted total re-industrialization.

When Venezuela's collapse decades later caused new shortages, the island responded calmly—the muscle memory of sovereignty intact.

No one romanticizes the hunger. But every nation facing future shocks—climate, energy, digital—can learn from Cuba's experiment: resilience scales downward, not upward.

If the Jewish diaspora proved that identity can be carried in memory, Cuba proved that civilization can be rebuilt from compost.

Both show that sovereignty is fractal: it begins in the smallest self-correcting system and grows outward.

XI ·

Transmission

The past two chapters traced the anatomy of collapse; here we have witnessed adaptation made art.

Next comes the mind beneath it—the *psychological architecture of sovereignty.*

In the **Next Key — Psychological Mechanism: The Internal Locus of Control and the Cognitive Geometry of Freedom**, we map the mental shift that turns survival into creation and dependence into authorship.

Key 13 · *Psychological Mechanism · The Internal Locus of Control*

Empires collapse when their citizens forget that control begins in the mind.

The greatest revolutions—spiritual, political, or scientific—have always begun as private cognitive uprisings: the invisible moment when a person stops waiting for permission.

Sovereignty is not inherited; it is remembered.

I ·

The Invisible Axis

Psychologists define the *locus of control* as the degree to which people believe their actions influence outcomes.

An *external locus* blames luck, fate, or systems.

An *internal locus* accepts responsibility for cause and effect.

Julian Rotter's 1966 studies showed that individuals with internal orientation outperform their peers in health, income, and happiness across every demographic. The same principle scales to civilizations. When cultures externalize agency, they stagnate; when they internalize it, they ascend.

Collapse, therefore, is not merely political or economic—it is cognitive dislocation.

The sovereign mind reclaims that axis.

II ·

The Psychology of Helplessness

Martin Seligman's 1967 experiments remain one of the most haunting parables in modern psychology.

Dogs subjected to unavoidable shocks eventually stopped trying to escape—even when doors were left open. Repeated failure rewired them for paralysis.

This is the blueprint of decline.

When citizens believe systems are unchangeable, they stop innovating, voting, even imagining alternatives. Learned helplessness metastasizes into national fatalism. Empires fall not when they are conquered, but when they no longer believe escape is possible.

Sri Lanka's queues, Weimar's inflation lines, Rome's bread doles—each was the same nervous system response: collective resignation.

III ·

Agency as Neurochemistry

Control is not a metaphor; it is measurable.

Every act of self-determination releases dopamine and activates the ventral striatum, the brain's reward center. Small wins are neurological proof of sovereignty. Conversely, chronic dependency depresses serotonin and shrinks the hippocampus, impairing learning and memory.

When individuals outsource agency to algorithms, employers, or ideologies, their biology mirrors captivity.

The modern empire is not Rome—it is the smartphone. Infinite scroll replaces infinite frontier. Notifications simulate control while draining willpower.

To reclaim sovereignty, one must redesign neurochemistry through deliberate effort: direct feedback, real skill acquisition, tangible consequence. Gardens, bicycles, crafts, fasting—all ancient rituals of internal locus—are, in biological terms, rewiring protocols.

IV.

The Geometry of Freedom

Imagine the psyche as a compass with two coordinates: *autonomy* and *connection.*

When autonomy dominates without connection, you get narcissism.

When connection dominates without autonomy, you get servitude.

Sovereignty balances both: self-rule harmonized with responsibility to others.

This geometry explains why the Jewish diaspora survived—strong vertical autonomy (inner law) nested within horizontal solidarity (community). The same pattern reappears in Cuba's Special Period—localized independence balanced by collective ethic.

Freedom is not isolation; it is integration without dependency.

That distinction defines whether power liberates or corrupts.

V.

The Myth of the Savior

Every fallen empire shares a reflex: the longing for rescue.

Citizens wait for a leader, a god, or a policy. The savior narrative soothes helplessness by externalizing hope. But saviors often become new tyrants because they centralize what must remain distributed.

The internal locus dismantles that illusion. It reframes the citizen as micro-sovereign, each responsible for one node of civilization.

This psychological decentralization is the cognitive twin of the blockchain: trust built horizontally, not vertically.

Once a population internalizes that truth, the age of empires ends automatically. Power no longer concentrates because belief no longer demands it.

VI.

Attention as Territory

Modern dependency is cognitive colonization.

In the attention economy, sovereignty begins with focus. Social media platforms harvest it; algorithms weaponize it; governments measure it. Each notification is a tax on consciousness.

Regaining control requires treating attention as land—finite, sacred, defensible.

Practices like digital fasting, journaling, and controlled information intake are not lifestyle trends; they are acts of decolonization.

When Gandhi led salt marches, he reclaimed physical resources. When a modern reader deletes addictive apps, they reclaim psychic territory. Both are forms of nonviolent revolution.

Attention is the currency of the mind-state. Spend it like gold.

VII ·

The Discipline of Reality

A mature internal locus demands radical honesty.

The sovereign mind does not confuse optimism with denial. It measures energy use, tracks expenses, faces decay without narrative anesthesia. This realism is not cynicism—it is faith grounded in evidence.

In behavioral economics, this maps to *feedback loops with short intervals.* Systems that see results quickly self-correct faster.

At a psychological level, that means designing life so consequence follows action immediately: cook instead of order, repair instead of replace, walk instead of drive.

Reality is the only teacher that never flatters.

The closer your feedback loop, the truer your sovereignty.

VIII ·

Moral Autonomy

Immanuel Kant called autonomy "the property of the will by which it is a law to itself."

True freedom, therefore, is self-legislation—acting from principles one could rationally wish universal.

The diaspora's covenant, Cuba's communal ethic, Stoic philosophy—all express this same logic.

Moral autonomy is the firewall against collective madness. When propaganda floods the system, internally legislated ethics prevent contagion.

Each person becomes a constitutional unit of civilization.

This is why tyranny fears conscience—it decentralizes law.

IX ·

Resilience as Ritual

Agency must be rehearsed or it decays.

Ritual—daily, repeated, sensory—keeps the neural pathways of control alive. Morning routines, breath practices, cold showers, skill drills, even journaling are micro-acts of self-government.

They form what neuroscientists call *predictive stability*: the brain's sense that it can anticipate and influence reality. Societies that ritualize self-efficacy through rites, education, or craft inoculate themselves against despair.

Collapse, by contrast, erases ritual. Days lose structure; time dissolves into crisis. Rebuilding begins the moment someone lights a candle or plants a seed on schedule. Consistency resurrects meaning.

Ritual is the muscle memory of sovereignty.

X ·

The Physics of Responsibility

In thermodynamics, systems that dissipate energy without feedback collapse into entropy.

Human systems follow the same law. Responsibility is feedback. It recycles energy—turning waste into wisdom.

Without responsibility, power leaks until structures rot.

To possess an internal locus is to recognize yourself as both cause and effect.

You are the entropy or the order. No middle ground.

That awareness is terrifying at first; then liberating. It ends excuses and begins authorship.

XI ·

Practical Reconstruction

To move from theory to practice:

1. **Audit Control Beliefs:** For seven days, note every complaint. After each, ask, "What part of this can I influence in 24 hours?" Act on that part only.
2. **Design Feedback Loops:** Choose activities with visible outcomes—gardening, cooking, repairing, writing. They rebuild cause-effect intuition.
3. **Build Peer Circles:** Form small groups that share metrics of progress—skills learned, hours reclaimed from distraction.
4. **Refuse Victim Narratives:** Replace "they should" with "we can." Language precedes reality.

5. **Sabbath of Attention:** One day a week without screens or transactions—reset perception.

These are not wellness practices; they are political technologies of consciousness.

XII ·

Transmission

The mind of sovereignty is now forged.

Next, we descend into its mythic mirror—the ancient story that encodes humanity's first attempt to centralize control and the divine correction that followed: **the Tower of Babel.**

In the next **Key**, we will decode Babel not as punishment, but as the birth of plural sovereignty—the moment unity shattered into languages so that freedom could diversify.

Key 14 · Mythic Resonance · The Tower of Babel and the Birth of Many Sovereigns

In the beginning, the world spoke one tongue.

Brick by brick, humanity built upward—an axis of ambition reaching toward heaven.

They called it Babel.

The builders were united by language, purpose, and pride. They sought to make a name that could never be erased.

And then, according to Genesis, "the Lord came down to see the city and the tower."

He scattered their speech, confused their understanding, and dispersed them across the earth.

What most read as punishment was, in truth, protection.

The Tower of Babel is not the story of divine wrath. It is the story of decentralization.

I ·

The Myth as Mirror

Every civilization dreams of total order.

The Babylonians built ziggurats that touched the clouds; modern nations build data centers that touch the sky of information. The desire is the same: to connect all minds under one architecture, one code.

Babel was the first empire of unbroken bandwidth—unity so absolute that no dissent could exist.

When language is singular, thought narrows. When understanding is perfect, imagination dies.

God's "confusion" was creative sabotage, a reboot of diversity.

In scattering words, the myth suggests, the divine preserved difference. Multiplicity became humanity's firewall against totalitarian perfection.

II ·

Architecture as Psychology

A tower is not a building; it is a cognitive structure—hierarchical, vertical, control-oriented.

At Babel, each layer depended on the one above. The higher it rose, the more fragile it became.

This is how most societies operate: centralized command, uniform ideology, single narrative.

The collapse of such towers is not a glitch; it is entropy correcting imbalance.

The diaspora, by contrast, built horizontally—networks instead of towers, scrolls instead of spires.

Cuba built laterally, too—gardens instead of grids, bicycles instead of buses.

Babel fell because it violated the geometry of resilience.

Diversity is the load-bearing structure of survival.

III ·

Language as Sovereignty

Language is the first currency of power.

Whoever names reality controls its meaning. The builders of Babel sought to monopolize naming—to encode the world in one syntax under one command.

The scattering of tongues decentralized that authority. Each language became a micro-nation of perception, carrying unique metaphors, cosmologies, and cognitive patterns.

Modern linguistics confirms what myth foresaw: language shapes thought.

A culture that speaks in future tenses saves less money (per Keith Chen's research on linguistic relativity).

A culture that lacks gendered pronouns displays lower gender bias.

Speech is governance.

When the tongues multiplied, so did the possible worlds.

The birth of plural language was the birth of plural sovereignty.

IV ·

The Psychological Reading

The Tower symbolizes the ego's attempt to ascend without integration.

In Jungian terms, it is the inflation of consciousness—reason severed from instinct, intellect detached from humility.

The "confusion of tongues" is the psyche's self-correction, forcing awareness to reconcile with shadow.

Every individual repeats Babel internally. We build towers of belief, productivity, identity—then wonder why communication collapses between our own parts.

Healing requires the same medicine: multiplicity.

We must let the many voices within us speak—the rational, the intuitive, the wounded, the visionary. When we allow inner languages to coexist, the psyche decentralizes. The self becomes a network, not a fortress.

The gods didn't destroy humanity's ambition; they diversified it.

Confusion was consciousness expanding.

V.

The Modern Parallels

Babel lives again—in server farms and supercomputers.

The drive toward a single global algorithm, a unified database, or an omniscient artificial intelligence is the modern echo of that tower.

The promise is order; the risk is obedience.

When every human transaction is recorded in one digital language, dissent dies by optimization.

Diversity becomes inefficiency; inefficiency becomes heresy.

Yet even here, scattering persists: new dialects of code, open-source forks, decentralized ledgers. Each is a rebellion of tongues—a reassertion that creativity depends on plurality.

The future of sovereignty depends on keeping Babel fragmented enough to stay human.

VI ·

Mythic Economics

In economic terms, Babel represents monoculture.

A single global currency, a single supply chain, a single financial model—efficient but brittle.

The scattering represents diversification—the principle that resilience emerges from redundancy.

When systems distribute control across nodes, they mimic ecosystems, not empires.

The Jewish diaspora practiced this intuitively; Cuba rediscovered it accidentally; nature has always done it perfectly.

Forests, not towers, endure storms.

The sovereign society of the future will look less like Wall Street and more like mycelium: unseen, connected, antifragile.

VII ·

The Moral Geometry

The moral lesson of Babel is not "do not build." It is "build with boundaries."

Ambition without humility breeds collapse. Diversity without purpose breeds chaos. Sovereignty requires the balance of both.

The moment the builders declared "let us make a name for ourselves," the tower ceased to serve creation and began to serve ego.

The divine descent—"the Lord came down to see"—is an image of feedback, of reality inspecting fantasy. The scattering is the consequence of feedback ignored.

Modern institutions repeat the sin when they dismiss warning signals, suppress whistleblowers, or homogenize discourse.

Collapse is the inevitable descent of truth upon arrogance.

VIII ·

Babel Reimagined

Imagine if the builders had paused mid-tower and invited difference—each floor a different culture, each dialect respected, each design unique.

The tower might still stand, not as monument to pride but as mosaic of voices.

This is the true Sovereign Stack: not one hierarchy reaching heaven but many communities reflecting it.

Pluralism is not weakness; it is civilization's shock absorber.

Babel's ruins remind us that unity enforced is tyranny, but unity chosen is harmony.

IX.

Personal Application

On the individual level, Babel teaches a simple sovereignty practice:

Translate your own life into multiple languages.

Speak in numbers when managing finance, in feeling when loving, in silence when praying, in action when leading. Each mode preserves a facet of truth.

When one language dominates—money, ideology, or intellect—your internal tower tilts.

To stay balanced, scatter your words and listen for the sacred confusion that follows.

Multiplicity is not noise; it is music unfinished.

X.

Transmission

The myth of Babel closes the first arc of *The Sovereign Stack*.

We have seen the architecture of resilience in exile, the ingenuity of survival in blockade, and now the cosmology that forbids uniform tyranny.

Next, in **Key 15— Sovereignty Protocol: The 30-Day Stack Plan**, we build the framework—the practical architecture of financial, cognitive, social, and cultural sovereignty that readers can begin implementing immediately.

The tower will not be rebuilt. Instead, we will lay foundations that can never fall.

Key 15 · Sovereignty Protocol · The 30-Day Stack Plan

Civilizations collapse in decades, but sovereignty can be rebuilt in days.

Not by waiting for governments to reform, but by restoring coherence within one's own system — mind, money, community, and culture.

The *Sovereign Stack* is the operating system for that restoration.

It is a four-layer framework that converts awareness into action, collapse into design.

Over thirty days, the reader becomes a micro-civilization: self-reliant, interdependent, and ungoverned by illusion.

I.

The Architecture of the Stack

Think of sovereignty as a living pyramid inverted — its base not resting on earth but rooted in consciousness.

Each layer reinforces the next:

1. **Financial Sovereignty** — control of resources and the time they purchase.
2. **Cognitive Sovereignty** — mastery of attention and narrative.
3. **Social Sovereignty** — networks of trust and mutual aid.
4. **Cultural Sovereignty** — meaning, ritual, and story that bind identity.

Technology serves all four but rules none. When these layers align, collapse cannot erase you; it can only test your coherence.

II·

Days 1–7: Financial Sovereignty — The Base Layer

The first week rewires your relationship to value.

1. **Audit the Stream:** Record every expense for seven days. Not amounts, but *energy flows* — what nourished, what numbed.
2. **Extract from Empire:** Open one account outside your primary banking system (credit union, local co-op, or Bitcoin wallet). The goal is not speculation but optionality.
3. **Three-Tier Reserve:**
   - *Tier 1:* Cash for 3 days (local currency).
   - *Tier 2:* Assets for 3 months (savings, precious metals, stable digital store).
   - *Tier 3:* Skills for life (tradeable knowledge).
4. **Map Dependencies:** List five essentials you cannot produce or source locally. For each, research one backup channel.

Financial sovereignty begins not with wealth but awareness of exposure.

By Day 7 you will have seen how your labor translates into control — and where it leaks into obedience.

III·

Days 8–14: Cognitive Sovereignty — The Mind Layer

The second week reclaims your attention from algorithms and fear.

1. **Information Fast (Days 8–10):** No news, no feeds, no screens before noon. Replace with reading one historical page and one physical page — book or journal.
2. **Perception Journal (Days 11–12):** Each evening, note three moments you misjudged reality that day — wrong assumption,

rumor believed, emotion exaggerated. This trains *epistemic humility*.
3. **Reconstruction (Days 13–14):** Choose three reliable signal sources (data, field experts, first-hand observation). Ignore all else for a week.

By Day 14, you will feel withdrawal — proof of liberation.

The sovereign mind treats attention as sacred territory: guarded, disciplined, intentionally spent.

IV.

Days 15–21: Social Sovereignty — The Network Layer

The third week restores interdependence. No one endures alone.

1. **Trust Map:** Write down the 10 people you would call in crisis. Then, beside each, what skill or resource they embody.
2. **Reciprocity Ledger:** Offer one favor per day without expectation of return. This transforms charity into alliance.
3. **Micro-Circle:** Convene a 3–5-person weekly gathering — dinner, craft, study, or garden. No ideology, only exchange.
4. **Communication Protocol:** Practice "slow correspondence." Replace instant messaging with one long, intentional weekly letter or voice note.

By Day 21, you will sense the rebirth of local gravity. Networks of trust outlive networks of convenience.

Social sovereignty is not networking; it is remembering who stands beside you when systems fail.

V.

Days 22–28: Cultural Sovereignty — The Story Layer

A culture dies when it forgets its songs. The fourth week restores meaning.

1. **Personal Creed:** Write ten sentences that define what you will not betray under pressure. This is your inner constitution.
2. **Ancestral Study:** Research one story from your lineage that embodies endurance — a grandparent's struggle, a local myth, a forgotten ritual. Rewrite it in modern language.
3. **Ritual Design:** Choose one act to repeat weekly that links work, body, and gratitude — lighting a candle before tasks, tending a plant, preparing food from scratch.
4. **Transmission:** Teach one skill to someone younger. The act of instruction transforms memory into continuity.

By Day 28, you will no longer chase meaning — you will generate it.

VI.

Days 29–30: Integration — The Reassembly

In the final two days, the four layers align.

You are now a living node — financially prepared, mentally sovereign, socially embedded, culturally rooted.

Use this closing protocol:

- **Day 29:** Silence for three hours. No music, phone, or talk. Let your thoughts surface. Observe which layer feels weakest. Plan reinforcement for the coming month.
- **Day 30:** Write the *Sovereign Covenant* — one page summarizing your commitments across all layers. Sign and date it. Store a copy physically.

This document is your personal constitution — proof that you have reentered authorship.

VII ·

The Metrics of Mastery

Measure sovereignty not in possessions but in latency:

- How long can you function if systems pause?
- How quickly can you recover from shock?
- How often do you act from intention rather than reaction?

The shorter the latency between awareness and response, the stronger the stack.

VIII ·

The Ethics of Power

Sovereignty without conscience becomes tyranny.

Every gain in autonomy must expand empathy, not shrink it. The sovereign serves as stabilizer within chaos — the calm node others orbit when signals fail.

You do not prepare to escape society; you prepare to preserve its memory.

To be sovereign is to be of service to the unprepared without surrendering to their panic.

IX.

Long-Term Calibration

After thirty days, repeat quarterly.

Each season, upgrade one layer:

- Financial: learn a new exchange system or skill.
- Cognitive: master one domain deeply, abandon one distraction permanently.
- Social: form a new mutual-aid cell.
- Cultural: create one artifact—a song, essay, or ritual—that will outlive you.

After one year, the four layers converge into sovereignty as rhythm. You will have built not a bunker, but a beacon.

X.

Closing Reflection

The empires of the future will not rise by conquest but by coherence.

When enough individuals build internal stacks, external systems reorganize around them.

Collapse becomes compost.

From the ruins of Babel, new languages of freedom grow.

The sovereign does not wait for permission, praise, or policy.

They begin.

Transmission

The first act of the book ends here — *The Fall*.

We have traced the descent from collapse to consciousness, and now we stand at the threshold of renewal.

In **Part II — The Turning**, we cross from survival into transformation.

Next: **Chapter 4 — The Psychology of Dependency**, where we confront the invisible empire within — the mind's addiction to obedience — and learn how to break it.

Chapter 4

The Psychology of Dependency

Part II — The Turning

Key 16 · Historical Mirror · The British Raj and the Rebellion of Satyagraha

Every empire begins by promising order and ends by producing obedience.

The British Raj perfected this alchemy: a system so vast it conquered not only territory but the Indian mind. It did not merely tax; it trained. It conditioned millions to see dependence as civilization and submission as stability.

Yet within that obedience, a man emerged who saw freedom not as revolt but as *truth-force*.

His name was Mohandas Karamchand Gandhi, and his weapon was refusal.

I ·

The Machinery of Control

At its height in the late 19th century, the British Raj governed over 300 million people with fewer than 100,000 administrators.

Its genius was psychological: the colonized internalized their own inferiority. English education replaced local languages, clerks aped Victorian manners, and merit flowed only through imperial validation.

Factories in Manchester consumed Indian cotton, while Indian weavers starved under tariffs. Salt—pulled from their own shores—was taxed by law. Even time was colonized: the railways ran on London's clock, not the monsoon's.

The empire's violence was efficient because it became invisible. Once dependency is emotional, physical chains are redundant.

II ·

The Birth of Satyagraha

In 1893, a young lawyer was thrown off a train in Pietermaritzburg, South Africa, for refusing to leave the first-class compartment. That night on the platform, Gandhi conceived the seed of resistance—not rage, but moral geometry.

He called it *Satyagraha*: from Sanskrit *satya* (truth) and *agraha* (firmness).

Truth-force. Soul-force. The refusal to cooperate with untruth.

Unlike revolutions that mirror their oppressors' violence, Satyagraha sought purification through suffering. It treated freedom as a psychological condition before a political one. "The moment the slave resolves that he will no longer be a slave," Gandhi wrote, "his fetters fall."

Dependency, therefore, was not material—it was habitual.

III ·

Salt and Sovereignty

In March 1930, Gandhi set out from Sabarmati Ashram to the Arabian Sea—a 240-mile walk through India's villages.

He carried no weapon, only a staff. His target: salt.

By picking up a handful of salt from the shore, he defied the law that reserved it for the empire.

The act was symbolic and systemic at once. Salt was life's mineral, shared by all, yet monopolized by the crown. In reclaiming it, Gandhi reframed rebellion as reclamation.

Tens of thousands followed him, boiling seawater in clay pots. The British arrested sixty thousand. The prisons overflowed, but the psychological order cracked. An empire cannot survive when its moral logic dissolves in its own salt.

IV.

Dependency as Design

The Raj had survived by rewarding compliance and punishing initiative.

Its bureaucracy transformed citizens into clerks, merchants into middlemen, warriors into servants. The system depended on the illusion that only imperial systems could manage complexity.

This dependency model persists today in modern forms—technological, financial, bureaucratic.

Apps tell us what to eat; systems manage our savings; institutions interpret our morals. The colonial architecture never vanished—it digitized.

Dependency is addictive because it feels efficient. It saves us from the anxiety of choice.

Satyagraha shattered that comfort. It demanded decision, endurance, and the courage to suffer for truth.

It was not merely political disobedience—it was cognitive decolonization.

V.

The Inner Empire

Gandhi understood that the true colonizer lived inside the mind.

He fasted to discipline appetite, spun cotton to discipline consumption, and walked barefoot to discipline comfort.

Each gesture rewired the Indian nervous system from compliance to conscience.

When questioned why he spun his own thread, he replied, "Because the world is not destroyed by wickedness but by dependence on the wicked."

The spinning wheel became a meditative machine: each rotation a reminder that liberation is manual labor.

He turned production into prayer and autonomy into rhythm.

Dependency thrives in abstraction; sovereignty is always tactile.

VI.

The Psychology of Obedience

Stanley Milgram's 1963 experiment at Yale—where ordinary people delivered what they thought were lethal shocks to strangers under authority's command—revealed obedience as one of humanity's most dangerous instincts.

The subjects were not sadists; they were normal citizens. They complied because an expert told them to.

The Raj exploited that same circuitry centuries earlier: uniforms, rituals, paperwork—all triggering the obedience reflex.

Milgram's finding that 65 percent of participants obeyed until the supposed death threshold confirms Gandhi's insight: violence begins in compliance long before action.

Freedom begins when the mind disobeys first.

VII ·

The Quiet Revolution

By 1947, Britain left not because it was overthrown but because it could no longer rule minds that had withdrawn consent.

The independence movement was a slow implosion—millions of individuals silently disconnecting from the empire's narrative.

Each village that spun its own thread, each teacher that taught in vernacular, each protester who refused to strike back—they hollowed out the empire's legitimacy.

When rulers lose belief in their own right to rule, collapse becomes ritual.

The British left with ceremonies and parades, not sieges and smoke.

The revolution had already happened in consciousness.

VIII ·

The Paradox of Liberation

After independence came new hierarchies, new dependencies. Bureaucrats replaced viceroys; ideology replaced faith.

This is the recurring pattern: emancipation that imitates the logic of its oppressor.

Satyagraha's unfinished work was not political—it was psychological.

The lesson for the modern reader is clear: external revolutions fail if internal obedience remains.

To exit empire is not to move borders but to reprogram desire.

IX ·

From Satyagraha to Sovereign Practice

Gandhi's tools can be translated into modern rituals of autonomy:

1. **Truth Audit:** Identify one lie you cooperate with daily—professional, emotional, or financial. Refuse it once this week.
2. **Salt Act:** Reclaim one resource monopolized by convenience. Bake bread instead of buying; fix instead of discarding.
3. **Silence March:** Walk one hour without phone or noise. Let discomfort surface; name each dependency revealed.
4. **Constructive Program:** Dedicate one weekly hour to communal creation—garden, repair, teach, or clean.

Each act shrinks the empire inside you. Sovereignty expands inversely to dependency.

X ·

Transmission

Satyagraha marked the turning of India's soul—the moment obedience cracked and agency returned.

But the empire never truly dies; it mutates.

In the **Next Key — Modern Parallel: Big Tech and the Architecture of Algorithmic Dependency**, we will explore how the new colonizer is not a nation but a network—how attention itself became the salt of the 21st century, and how the next Satyagraha must begin in the human nervous system.

Key 17 · Modern Parallel · Big Tech and the Architecture of Algorithmic Dependency

Empires no longer tax salt.

They tax attention.

The 21st century's most powerful colonial system fits not on a map but in a pocket — a glowing rectangle that speaks every language and listens back.

It is the empire of Big Tech: an invisible Raj built from algorithms, behavioral data, and dopamine. Its missionaries are interfaces; its weapons are notifications.

Its colonies are human nervous systems.

I .

The Digital Raj

In the early 2000s, Silicon Valley promised liberation.

The internet would democratize knowledge, dissolve hierarchies, empower individuals.

What emerged instead was feudalism with better branding.

A handful of corporations — Google, Meta, Amazon, Apple, Tencent — now mediate nearly every human transaction.

They own the platforms, the data, and increasingly, the desires.

Where the British Raj controlled trade routes and telegraphs, the Digital Raj controls information routes and attention graphs.

And like its predecessor, it survives through dependency disguised as convenience.

You don't pay for the product because you are the product.

II ·

The Architecture of Addiction

Social networks are behavioral laboratories disguised as playgrounds.

Every color, vibration, and timing interval is engineered using neuroscience.

Variable rewards — the same mechanism that drives slot machines — govern notification schedules.

B.F. Skinner's pigeons pecked levers for random pellets.

Modern humans scroll for variable social validation.

The neurotransmitter dopamine, once evolution's incentive for exploration, is now hijacked for retention metrics.

In biological terms, Big Tech has weaponized curiosity.

In political terms, it has privatized free will.

Dependency has evolved from salt monopolies to stimulus monopolies.

III ·

Algorithmic Authority

The British Empire had governors; the digital one has recommendation engines.

These algorithms dictate what we read, who we love, what we buy, and even what we believe.

They learn faster than any bureaucracy ever could because they optimize not for truth, but for engagement.

Their command structure is invisible but absolute.

The user feels free because they choose — yet every choice is statistically preloaded.

The Milgram experiment has been automated: authority no longer wears a lab coat, it wears personalization.

We obey because the machine flatters us.

IV ·

The Economics of Extraction

Colonialism extracted raw materials; data colonialism extracts behavioral exhaust.

Every click, pause, or hesitation becomes a resource mined for predictive power.

Zuboff's *The Age of Surveillance Capitalism* calls it the unilateral claim to human experience as free raw material for translation into behavioral data.

The revenue model is simple: sell certainty to advertisers and addiction to users.

The longer you scroll, the less you remember choosing to.

The cost is not just privacy; it is agency itself.

The new dependency is informational: reality outsourced to feeds curated by unseen algorithms.

V.

The Psychological Loop

Each time we refresh a timeline, we reenact a ritual of helplessness.

The gesture mimics slot machines, tapping into intermittent reinforcement — the most powerful conditioning mechanism known in psychology.

We have become *learned dependents*: anxious in silence, restless without stimulus, lost without signal.

Attention spans shorten, dopamine baselines crash, and cognitive endurance declines.

By 2023, average screen time exceeded 7 hours daily. Studies from the University of Pennsylvania linked heavy social media use to a 30% rise in anxiety and depression among youth.

Our nervous systems are colonies under occupation.

Dependency is no longer cultural — it is biochemical.

VI.

The Empire of Convenience

The colonial tactic of comfort persists.

Why rebel when the empire feeds you entertainment, delivery, and illusion?

Every convenience purchased from Big Tech removes one small muscle of self-reliance.

Navigation apps erode spatial memory.

Streaming erodes cultural transmission.

Instant gratification erodes patience — the nervous system's most sacred virtue.

Dependency feels like progress until the power goes out.

Then we realize the invisible cords that bound us were not fiber optics but habits.

VII ·

The Illusion of Freedom

The Digital Raj learned from its ancestors: true control is invisible.

Unlike totalitarian states, it allows dissent because dissent generates data.

Unlike dictators, it does not command obedience — it induces participation.

The system doesn't need to silence you; it just needs to drown you in noise.

Every post, argument, and outrage becomes fuel for the algorithm's next iteration.

Anger has become monetized attention.

In psychological terms, the empire externalizes the internal locus of control.

We no longer ask, "What do I think?" but, "What did the feed show me?"

The colonized mind has returned — wearing wireless earbuds.

VIII ·

The New Satyagraha

If Gandhi's rebellion was to refuse salt tax, ours must be to refuse algorithmic tax.

The next *Satyagraha* begins with attention fasting.

It requires the same principles: discipline, patience, moral clarity.

1. **Truth-Force (Satyagraha):** Verify before sharing. Speak less, mean more.
2. **Refusal:** Log off deliberately one hour per day. Withdraw cooperation from exploitative systems.
3. **Constructive Program:** Replace passive consumption with creation — write, build, record, repair.
4. **Collective Action:** Support open-source, privacy-first tools. Each switch weakens the empire's monopoly.

Resistance today is digital asceticism: freedom regained by voluntary friction.

IX ·

Reclaiming Cognitive Sovereignty

The antidote to algorithmic dependency is not abstinence but authorship.

To reclaim authorship, one must restore the feedback loop between curiosity and consequence.

- Keep one analog habit: journaling, drawing, woodworking — something with texture.
- Consume content deliberately: one hour of study, one hour of silence.
- Replace "infinite scroll" with finite study — topics you choose, not those chosen for you.

Each act re-teaches the nervous system that attention is choice, not compulsion.

That is cognitive sovereignty.

X.

The Ethical Reckoning

Big Tech's architects are not villains; they are mirror-builders.

They reflect our desires for convenience, connection, and control. The empire survives because it feeds appetites we refuse to discipline.

Dependency thrives when citizens outsource moral agency to code.

Sovereignty begins when they demand ethics embedded in design — transparency, consent, decentralization.

The next civilization will be written not in constitutions but in protocols.

Freedom will belong to whoever controls the update.

XI ·

The Next Frontier

Artificial intelligence now writes, paints, recommends, and predicts.

Soon it will persuade.

We stand at the edge of algorithmic intimacy — machines that know us better than we know ourselves.

The question is not whether they will control us, but whether we will remain conscious of the exchange.

Satyagraha for the 21st century demands spiritual technology: awareness strong enough to hold the tool without worshipping it.

Dependency is worship without awareness.

Sovereignty is awareness without worship.

XII ·

Transmission

The first two mirrors—Gandhi's salt and Silicon Valley's code—reveal the same geometry of control: systems that feed obedience by erasing consequence.

Now we descend inward to the mechanism beneath both—**the psychology of obedience itself.**

In the **Next Key — Psychological Mechanism: The Obedience Reflex and the Anatomy of Submission**, we will trace the neural, cultural, and emotional circuits that make humans compliant—and how to break them without breaking society.

Key 18 · Psychological Mechanism · The Obedience Reflex and the Anatomy of Submission

Every system that endures learns one secret: control the reflex, not the reason.

Armies, corporations, religions, and algorithms all rely on the same invisible mechanism—a deep neural shortcut that confuses compliance with safety.

This is the *obedience reflex*: humanity's oldest survival instinct, weaponized for governance.

I ·

The Reflex Beneath Thought

In 1961, Stanley Milgram, a Yale psychologist, recruited ordinary citizens to deliver electric shocks to a stranger in another room whenever that person answered a question incorrectly.

The shocks were fake, but the participants believed them real.

Sixty-five percent continued to the "lethal" level because a man in a lab coat told them to.

No threats, no guns—only symbols of authority.

The experiment revealed a brutal truth: moral reasoning often yields to hierarchy.

Obedience is not taught; it is triggered.

Our brains evolved to defer under threat; the modern world simulates threat through structure. Uniforms, logos, official tone—each activates that primitive circuitry.

Civilizations run on it. Collapse begins when individuals learn to override it.

II ·

The Neurobiology of Submission

Neuroscientist Naomi Eisenberger's research on social pain shows that exclusion activates the same brain regions as physical injury.

Disobedience, in social species like ours, once meant exile—and exile once meant death.

The obedience reflex, then, is a vestige of our evolutionary dependency on the tribe.

When someone defies authority, cortisol spikes; the amygdala interprets conflict as mortal danger.

To preserve status and belonging, the body defaults to compliance before the mind can intervene.

Modern systems exploit this: corporations call employees "family"; governments call citizens "patriots"; digital platforms count "followers." Each reactivates the primal need to belong, making defiance feel like betrayal.

Freedom begins at the somatic level: calming the body enough to contradict the tribe.

III ·

Cultural Conditioning

Across centuries, cultures perfected obedience through ritual.

The Roman army drilled daily; monasteries rang bells hourly; modern schools replaced bells with schedules. Each trains the nervous system to equate predictability with virtue.

In industrial society, obedience was moralized as efficiency.

The good worker followed orders, the good citizen trusted experts, the good believer surrendered will.

By adulthood, compliance becomes identity.

Gandhi recognized this conditioning. His fasts and marches retrained the nervous system toward voluntary discomfort—a spiritual counter-conditioning. To break dependency, he made rebellion feel holy.

Obedience dissolves when courage feels safer than compliance.

IV ·

The Banality of Evil

Hannah Arendt, reporting on Adolf Eichmann's trial in 1961, described him as terrifyingly ordinary—not a monster, but a bureaucrat who "never realized what he was doing."

He obeyed rules, filed reports, followed procedure.

His evil was administrative.

Arendt called it the *banality of evil*: atrocity committed by people who simply refused to think.

Dependency creates Eichmanns in every age—managers who optimize exploitation, engineers who code surveillance, citizens who scroll past suffering.

When obedience detaches from conscience, civilization becomes a machine without brakes.

Freedom, then, is not rebellion but reattachment—restoring conscience to cognition.

V.

The Modern Reflex

In the age of automation, obedience has been redesigned as convenience.

We no longer take orders; we accept defaults.

Phones auto-suggest responses; GPS dictates routes; algorithms curate outrage.

We rarely choose—we confirm.

Behavioral economist Richard Thaler proved that default options guide most decisions. Auto-enrollment in pension plans raised participation by 80%.

The same mechanism, applied ethically, helps citizens save; applied unethically, it manufactures consent.

Modern dependency is obedience rebranded as usability.

To resist, one must reintroduce *friction*: pause before clicking, question every default, reclaim the time to decide.

Sovereignty is measured in seconds between impulse and response.

VI ·

The Obedience Economy

Entire industries profit from predictability.

Marketing algorithms forecast behavior not to understand you, but to reduce uncertainty.

The obedient consumer is the most valuable asset in capitalism's balance sheet.

Even protest can be monetized: movements are tracked, hashtags predicted, outrage harvested for engagement.

Resistance becomes another data point in the obedience economy.

This is why the new dissident must master paradox—rebelling within systems without feeding them.

True defiance today is subtle: silence, abstention, non-participation. The sovereign weapon is refusal.

VII ·

Breaking the Reflex

The obedience reflex cannot be destroyed, only redirected.

It must serve principles, not power.

Three techniques retrain it:

1. **Somatic Neutralization:** Before reacting to authority, slow breathing to eight cycles per minute. This restores prefrontal control over the amygdala.
2. **Moral Interrogation:** Ask, "Would I obey this if I were alone?" If no, pause. Group pressure distorts ethics.

3. **Discomfort Training:** Daily minor discomforts—cold water, fasting, manual labor—build tolerance for defiance. Autonomy requires a nervous system unafraid of unease.

Civilization programs obedience through comfort; sovereignty restores freedom through discipline.

VIII ·

The Anatomy of Courage

Courage is not absence of fear; it is the refusal to let fear issue commands.

Neuroimaging studies show that in courageous individuals, the anterior cingulate cortex—responsible for conflict monitoring—remains active under stress. They feel fear but interpret it as signal, not sentence.

This is the biology of sovereignty: awareness larger than reaction.

Empires collapse when enough citizens learn to sustain awareness under pressure.

Gandhi's marchers, Rosa Parks' stillness, Tiananmen's lone man—each moment of composed defiance rewrote collective wiring. One nervous system calm in truth can neutralize thousands vibrating in fear.

IX ·

The Ethics of Disobedience

Not all defiance is liberation.

Rebellion driven by ego becomes tyranny's twin.

Mature sovereignty pairs courage with conscience: refuse only what violates the sacred, obey only what preserves life.

Aristotle called this *phronesis*—practical wisdom.

It distinguishes anarchic impulse from moral resistance.

In a world addicted to performative rebellion, discernment is the new revolution.

The sovereign obeys law when it is just, resists it when it is not, and always remains awake while doing either.

X ·

The Inner Republic

Within each human exists a parliament of selves: desire, fear, reason, memory, conscience.

Dependency begins when one voice rules unchecked.

Sovereignty begins when all voices deliberate.

This is inner democracy—the mind as republic.

Meditation, journaling, and dialogue are its sessions; silence is its constitution.

When this inner parliament functions, external tyrants lose leverage. You cannot be ruled from without when you are governed from within.

XI ·

The Practice of Lucid Obedience

The goal is not disobedience for its own sake but *lucid obedience*: obeying consciously, rejecting reflexively.

Before acting on any command—legal, digital, or social—pause long enough to choose.

Choice transforms reaction into ritual.

That pause, even half a second long, is the birth of freedom.

A sovereign obeys gravity, not coercion.

XII ·

Transmission

We have now exposed the neural, cultural, and moral mechanics of dependency.

Next we ascend to myth—the symbolic mirror where obedience and freedom first battled in the human imagination.

In the **Next Key — Mythic Resonance: Plato's Cave and the Shadow of Dependency**, we will enter the oldest allegory of liberation: prisoners mistaking shadows for truth, and the one who dares to turn his head toward the light.

Key 19 · Mythic Resonance · Plato's Cave and the Shadow of Dependency

I ·

The Prison of Shadows

Plato begins his *Republic* with a story so precise that twenty-four centuries later, it still defines the architecture of control.

He imagines prisoners chained in a cave since birth, forced to look only at the wall before them.

Behind them burns a fire; between the fire and the prisoners walks a parade of puppeteers, their shadows cast on the wall.

The captives watch these shadows and call them reality.

One day, a prisoner breaks his chains.

He turns around, blinded by the fire's light, staggered by the realization that the shapes were illusions.

When he climbs out into the sun, he sees the world as it is — not symbols but substance.

He returns to the cave to free the others, but they reject him.

They prefer the comfort of the shadows to the pain of illumination.

The myth is simple and absolute: dependency begins when perception replaces truth, and ends when truth is chosen over comfort.

II ·

The Cave Today

The cave now glows blue.

It fits in your palm.

Each feed, each algorithmic timeline, each curated narrative — these are the shadows on the wall.

We live chained not by iron but by attention loops.

We mistake information for understanding, opinion for knowledge, and stimulation for meaning.

In the Digital Raj, the puppeteers are invisible: machine-learning models predicting what will keep our eyes fixed on the flicker.

Behind them burns not fire but data centers, consuming megawatts to project illusions across the world.

Plato's cave is no longer metaphor. It is infrastructure.

III ·

The Fear of Light

The liberated prisoner's first reaction was pain.

Light burns the eyes accustomed to darkness.

So too does truth burn the mind accustomed to comfort.

Modern dependency is maintained not by chains but by preference: the voluntary avoidance of discomfort.

To unlearn illusions requires cognitive pain — the death of old certainties.

Each generation invents anesthetics to avoid that pain: propaganda, entertainment, and now algorithmic distraction.

The greater the pain of awakening, the greater the fear of the sun.

This is why the world defends its illusions with violence — because every dependency hides a comfort it refuses to lose.

IV.

The Fire and the Sun

Plato's fire and sun are two types of light.

The fire is artificial illumination — flickering, partial, deceptive. It represents human-made stories that imitate truth but lack substance.

The sun, in contrast, is pure being — reality itself, visible only through discipline.

Every empire uses the fire: control through narrative.

The British Raj used it through bureaucracy and scripture; Big Tech through engagement and code; consumer capitalism through advertising.

To see the sun, one must leave the cave's geometry entirely — not fight the shadows, but abandon the wall.

Sovereignty is not control within illusion; it is the refusal to live by borrowed light.

V.

The Role of the Rebel

The freed prisoner who returns to the cave is the archetype of the heretic, prophet, or reformer — every truth-teller who brings daylight to those still chained.

Socrates, whom Plato modeled in the story, was executed for "corrupting the youth."

The truth is rarely punished for being false; it is punished for breaking dependency.

Gandhi, too, walked back into the cave — into an empire hypnotized by its own civilizing myth.

He did not attack the shadows; he simply refused to obey them.

In doing so, he revealed their unreality.

Every sovereign must eventually return to the cave — not to save others by force, but to remind them they can stand.

VI.

The Inner Cave

Dependency does not begin in politics or algorithms; it begins within the psyche.

Each human being carries an inner cave: the mind's comfort zone, built from habits and unexamined stories.

Our shadows are our fears, projected onto the world.

When you defend an ideology with anger, you are defending your own chains.

When you react automatically to challenge, you are the prisoner mistaking motion for freedom.

The act of turning toward the light is internal first: to look behind your own fear and ask, *Who is holding the torch?*

VII ·

The Myth's Hidden Geometry

The cave allegory is not a simple ascent — it is cyclical.

The prisoner escapes, sees truth, returns, and is rejected.

Civilizations follow the same rhythm: enlightenment, decadence, collapse, renewal.

Each cycle resets when enough individuals turn their heads simultaneously.

This pattern mirrors the Hero's Journey that Joseph Campbell later formalized: departure, initiation, return.

But where the hero seeks adventure, the sovereign seeks clarity.

The journey is not outward but upward — from projection to perception, from illusion to awareness.

The cave, then, is the blueprint of human evolution: consciousness learning to see itself seeing.

VIII ·

Other Myths of Awakening

Nearly every civilization has its version of the cave.

- In Hindu cosmology, *Maya* veils ultimate reality, and enlightenment (*moksha*) is awakening from illusion.
- In Buddhist teaching, ignorance (*avidyā*) binds beings to the wheel of suffering until mindfulness dissolves the shadows.
- In the Egyptian *Book of the Dead*, the soul passes through twelve gates, shedding illusions before meeting the sun god Ra.
- In the Navajo philosophy of *Hózhó*, harmony is restored when one perceives the world as it truly is — whole, interconnected, luminous.

Across epochs, the message is identical: freedom is not escape but sight.

IX ·

Dependency as Voluntary Blindness

Every cave survives because its prisoners police themselves.

They mock the liberated, punish dissent, and praise conformity as sanity.

Modern institutions reward this: consensus metrics, social proof, algorithmic popularity.

This is the paradox of dependency — we mistake our chains for community.

We trade awareness for belonging.

In every timeline, empire succeeds not because rulers are strong, but because subjects fear light.

Dependency is collective cowardice sanctified as stability.

X.

The Light as Responsibility

To see truth is not triumph but burden.

The freed prisoner cannot return to ignorance; he must live with the full weight of clarity.

Sovereignty, therefore, is responsibility for perception.

It demands vigilance against self-deception.

The sovereign studies not only power structures but their reflection within — pride, fear, and the desire to dominate.

For even awareness can become an idol if not tempered by humility.

The final test of the myth is compassion: to walk back into the cave, hold the torch gently, and remember that once, you too were chained.

XI.

The Sacred Turn

Every civilization renews itself when enough people turn their heads at once.

The turn is the universal gesture of awakening: a rotation of perception that realigns being with truth.

- The Renaissance was Europe's collective turn toward inquiry.
- Decolonization was humanity's turn toward self-determination.
- The digital exodus now beginning is our turn toward conscious technology.

Each turn begins with one person daring to face the light — and refusing to forget the way.

XII ·

Transmission

We have explored the inner and outer caves — from Plato's allegory to the algorithmic labyrinths of the present.

But myth, however profound, remains incomplete without practice.

In the final movement of this chapter, we descend from symbol to system.

In the **Next Key — Sovereignty Protocol: The 14-Day Attention Fast and Information Diet**, we will transform awakening into method — a precise, practical discipline for reclaiming focus, purging dependency, and restoring the mind's autonomy.

Key 20 · Sovereignty Protocol · The 14-Day Attention Fast and Information Diet

---

I ·

The Return from the Cave

After every awakening, there is a descent.

The philosopher who has seen the sun must walk back into the shadows with steady eyes.

It is not enough to perceive the mechanics of control; one must rewire them.

Awareness without discipline collapses into exhaustion.

Dependency is not only political or economic—it is rhythmic. It colonizes time itself.

The empire enters not through force but through frequency, through the tempo of distraction.

Therefore the first act of sovereignty is not rebellion but rhythm repair.

You cannot rebuild civilization until you rebuild your day.

II ·

Principle One: The Physics of Attention

Energy follows attention.

Every watt of consciousness fuels a circuit somewhere—your body, a thought, an app, an empire.

Neuroscientists describe attention as a limited-capacity resource. Each moment of focus consumes glucose and oxygen; every notification forces a "task switch," costing an estimated 23 minutes to restore deep concentration (University of California, Irvine, 2014).

On a planetary scale, humanity burns billions of hours daily in micro-interruptions—each one a siphon from creative energy to consumption.

Dependency thrives on this entropy.

If energy is life, then distraction is slow death.

Sovereignty begins with the redirection of energy from extraction back into creation.

This is the physics behind the 14-Day Attention Fast.

III ·

Principle Two: The Metabolism of Information

The brain metabolizes information the way the body metabolizes food.

Too little leads to ignorance; too much leads to toxicity.

A single human nervous system evolved to process a village's worth of input, yet modern feeds deliver empires' worth before breakfast.

Information overload triggers chronic stress: cortisol elevation, sleep disruption, and dopamine burnout.

In evolutionary terms, the organism interprets constant input as constant threat.

Thus, dependency masquerades as curiosity while eroding the very clarity it promises.

Sovereignty requires fasting not from knowledge but from noise.

We fast to remember the taste of truth.

IV.

The 14-Day Attention Fast

The fast is not abstinence but recalibration—a return to deliberate consumption.

It unfolds in three phases:

Phase 1: Deconstruction (Days 1–4)

You begin by mapping your dependencies.

- Record every digital touchpoint for 48 hours—emails, feeds, notifications, advertisements.
- Note not the time spent, but the *state induced* (calm, agitated, hollow, inspired).
- Patterns emerge quickly: most inputs drain more than they deliver.
- Disable all non-essential notifications.
- Uninstall one app that exists solely for dopamine—usually social media.
- Replace morning screen time with physical movement or silence.

Within 72 hours, your dopamine receptors begin to normalize. Sleep deepens.

The mind feels withdrawal—proof that the empire existed inside.

Phase 2: Reconstruction (Days 5–10)

Now rebuild your day as if designing a sovereign state.

- Establish two sacred hours daily: one for creation (writing, building, study), one for contemplation (silence, walking, meditation).
- Reclaim mealtime from screens. Eat slowly. Taste becomes awareness.
- Limit information intake to three intentional windows—morning briefing, afternoon learning, evening reflection.

This is cognitive intermittent fasting: compression of input to restore digestive clarity.

Within a week, focus sharpens. Boredom returns—but boredom is fertile. It is the soil of originality.

Phase 3: Expansion (Days 11–14)

In the final days, reintroduce digital contact with sovereignty intact.

- Reopen feeds only after setting a 20-minute timer.
- Speak online as if addressing your future self.
- Seek one conversation daily that is unrecorded, unposted, unoptimized.

By Day 14, you will recognize dependency not as necessity but as noise.

Freedom has a sound: quiet.

V.

The Information Diet

Just as nutrition separates the living from the lethargic, informational diet separates the sovereign from the sedated.

Three rules govern the diet: purity, balance, and synthesis.

1. **Purity** – Consume from primary sources whenever possible.

- Read historians, not headlines.
- Read scientists, not summaries.
- Read books, not feeds.
- Secondary information decays like reheated food—each reheating loses nutrients of truth.
2. **Balance** – Alternate between ingestion and digestion.
    - For every hour of reading, take ten minutes of stillness.
    - For every complex idea, write one paragraph of your own reflection.
    - The brain integrates knowledge only when idle.
3. **Synthesis** – Cross domains.
    - Pair physics with poetry, economics with ethics, technology with myth.
    - Knowledge without synthesis breeds specialists; synthesis breeds civilizations.

The goal is not less information, but meaning-dense information.

VI ·

The Architecture of a Sovereign Day

Time is the smallest unit of sovereignty.

Design it as an engineer would design a city:

Time Block	Domain	Purpose
Dawn	Silence / Ritual	Orient attention before exposure.
Morning	Creation	Output before input.

Time Block	Domain	Purpose
Midday	Exchange	Work, communication, service.
Dusk	Reflection	Integrate lessons, gratitude, slowing.
Night	Restoration	No screens, no consumption—dream as data compression.

This daily architecture acts as firewall and temple simultaneously.

It protects the psyche from colonization while creating conditions for flow.

The sovereign day becomes the unit cell of a sovereign civilization.

VII ·

Rituals of Attention

Rituals rewire behavior faster than willpower.

Four micro-rituals fortify the mind against dependency:

1. **The One-Minute Reset:** Before opening any device, breathe and state intention: *"I choose what I see."*
2. **Analog Morning:** No digital contact for the first hour after waking. Light, movement, and hydration only.
3. **Focused Deep Work:** One 90-minute session of single-task immersion per day; neuroscience shows this yields up to 4x productivity gains (Csikszentmihalyi, 1990).
4. **Digital Sabbath:** One full day weekly without screens. Discomfort is purification.

Over time, the rituals become identity. Sovereignty ceases to be effort and becomes nature.

VIII ·

Metrics of Liberation

The empire measures you through metrics—clicks, views, retention.

Measure yourself differently: through stillness, presence, and creative yield.

Create your own dashboard of autonomy:

Metric	Indicator	Tracking Method
Focus Duration	Minutes of uninterrupted creation	Use a manual timer, not an app
Noise Exposure	Number of notifications per day	Keep below 10
Silence Hours	Total daily time without digital input	Aim for 2–3
Output Quality	Completed meaningful actions	Journal or track by reflection

When these metrics stabilize, dependency has been reversed.

Freedom is quantifiable when measured in awareness, not approval.

IX.

The Economics of Attention

Attention is the new currency; its interest compounds in creativity.

Each reclaimed hour, when directed toward skill, relationship, or invention, produces exponential returns.

Studies in deliberate practice show that 10,000 focused hours—uninterrupted by distraction—can transform an amateur into a master (Ericsson, 1993).

Therefore, every hour stolen by distraction is not lost—it is converted into someone else's mastery.

When you withdraw attention from the empire, you stop funding it.

When millions do so, GDP shifts from consumption to creation.

That is the macroeconomics of sovereignty.

X.

From Fast to Feast

After the 14 days, you will not return to the old consumption pattern because the palate changes.

Just as sugar dulls the tongue, stimulation dulls discernment.

Once detoxed, even mild distraction feels abrasive.

At this stage, introduce the **Feast of Creation**: dedicate one day to total immersion in building, studying, or making without external input.

The mind, now purified, becomes generative again.

Dependency collapses not by denial but by rediscovery of joy.

Freedom is pleasurable when consciousness tastes its own power.

XI ·

Transmission

The final task of sovereignty is not isolation but transmission.

Share your practices not as doctrine but as invitation.

Teach the fast to one friend, one colleague, one child.

Dependency spreads virally; so must liberation.

Every person who regains attention strengthens the collective immune system of civilization.

A society that can focus can heal.

A culture that can be silent can think.

An individual who can choose can lead.

XII ·

The Closing Benediction

For fourteen days, you withdraw.

On the fifteenth, you return — the same world, new perception.

Screens glow the same, yet no longer command.

The feed still scrolls, yet no longer hypnotizes.

The empire still stands, but its magic has dissolved.

You are no longer the prisoner watching shadows, nor the rebel breaking chains.

You are the architect of your own rhythm — the quiet frequency from which the new world will rise.

Remember:

Silence is not absence.

It is sovereignty manifest.

XIII ·

Transmission

The psychology of dependency ends with discipline; the psychology of power begins with reflection.

In the next chapter, **The Mirror of Power**, we will climb into the citadel of authority itself—its illusions, its isolations, and its inevitable collapse from within.

Where dependency obeys, power isolates.

To master one, you must understand the other.

Chapter 5

The Mirror of Power

Part II — The Turning

Key 21 · Historical Mirror · The Late Ottoman Empire and the Anatomy of Control

When power loses its reflection, it loses itself.

In the late nineteenth century the Ottoman Empire stood at the mirror's edge—trying to modernize fast enough to survive while unable to see the truth of its own decay. The story begins in 1839, when the *Tanzimat Fermanı* promised equality, law, and reform; it ends in 1909, when Sultan Abdülhamid II was led away under guard. Between those dates stretches a single parable: how control, once mistaken for order, becomes blindness.

I ·

The Proclamation of Light

On a cold November morning in Constantinople, clerks unrolled a parchment that glittered with hope. Mustafa Reşid Pasha read aloud the decree of renewal: every subject equal before the law, property protected, tyranny banned. Cannon fire echoed across the Bosphorus; cafés toasted progress in French and Ottoman tongues.

For a brief season, it worked. Schools opened, railways broke the old geography, and telegraph lines stitched the provinces to the capital. But the more the empire extended its nervous system, the less it could feel. Information pooled at the center and stopped there. Reforms became edicts, edicts became paper, and paper became illusion.

II ·

Debt and Dependency

Modernity was expensive. By 1875, half the treasury went to interest on foreign loans. London and Paris financed Ottoman railways, then seized the revenues when repayment failed. The creation of the *Public Debt Administration*—foreign bureaucrats collecting imperial taxes—was the quietest colonization in history.

In the bazaars of Galata, French bankers and Armenian merchants tallied ledgers in five languages while officials in silk robes argued about tariffs. The empire was globalized before globalization had a name. Each borrowed franc bought another layer of submission.

III ·

The Young Sultan

Abdülhamid II ascended the throne in 1876—a cautious intellect shaped by exile, poetry, and paranoia. He inherited an empire in flames and a parliament newborn. Within two years he dissolved it, convinced that talk of liberty invited collapse.

He withdrew to the hilltop palace of Yıldız, where roses bloomed under wire screens and every whisper was recorded. There he created a masterpiece of surveillance: private telegraph lines, police informants, translators sifting foreign journals for hints of dissent. Ministers became messengers; provinces became dossiers.

At first the system worked. Famine reports arrived within hours; governors deferred to the central eye. But sight without hearing distorts. The Sultan soon trusted only written reports, then only the ones that agreed. His empire turned from a body into an archive.

IV.

The Architecture of Fear

Censorship spread like plaster over a cracked wall. Novels were banned for single words—"revolution," "dream," "freedom." Cartographers erased borders that showed lost lands. Even geography was treason.

Poets adapted by inventing metaphor: roses meant blood, nightingales meant prisoners, gardens meant forbidden thought. The result was a culture of exquisite ambiguity—language perfected to evade authority.

The bureaucracy mirrored its master. Officials passed memoranda upward, each layer softening the truth. By the time famine petitions reached Yıldız, statistics had replaced starvation. The empire learned to survive by lying politely.

V.

The Mirror Shatters

Outside the palace, the world changed faster than censorship could conceal. Telegraph poles sprouted nationalism. Bulgarian rebels printed manifestos on smuggled presses; in Salonica, young officers studied French treatises on liberty.

In 1908 the mutiny began. When troops marched on Constantinople demanding restoration of the constitution, Abdülhamid hesitated. The generals no longer answered; the people no longer feared. Crowds filled the streets shouting *"Hürriyet!"*—Freedom.

The Sultan restored the parliament, but the mirror had already cracked. The following year he was deposed, escorted through the same gates that once guarded his secrets. He looked out from the carriage window toward the city's domes, now glittering with flags of revolution. The empire he tried to preserve by control had dissolved in transparency.

VI ·

The Psychological Core

Abdülhamid's tragedy was not malice but isolation. Each reform meant tighter grip; each warning confirmed suspicion. Psychologists would later call it *the isolation effect of authority*: power severs feedback until it can no longer tell reflection from reality.

The Sultan believed his empire survived through vigilance. In truth, it suffocated under it. When every voice becomes potential treason, silence reigns—and silence is the slowest form of collapse.

VII ·

Legacy of the Mirror

After his fall, the archives of Yıldız revealed a mind both meticulous and afraid: notes on foreign conspiracies beside sketches of schools and hospitals. The same pen built railways to Mecca and prisons for poets. History remembers him as the "Red Sultan," yet his color was not blood but dusk—the hour when light fades slowly, and every shape in the mirror looks true.

Empires since have followed the pattern. Bureaucracy hardens; surveillance expands; leaders drown in information and starve for insight. The Ottoman mirror did not break—it multiplied.

VIII ·

Transmission

Power's blindness began in marble halls and ended in ledgers and telegrams.

Next we turn to the modern echo—to boardrooms and server rooms where numbers replace edicts and illusions are measured in market capitalizations.

Key 22 · Modern Parallel · Enron, 2008, and the FTX Mirror of Opacity

When the modern world looks into its own glass, it sees spreadsheets instead of sultans. Yet the reflection is the same: abstraction masquerading as vision, numbers replacing truth.

At the start of the twenty-first century, three collapses—Enron, the 2008 financial crisis, and FTX—exposed how empires built on data can decay from the inside exactly as the Ottomans once did. Each believed transparency was its strength. Each was destroyed by its mirrors.

I ·

The Cult of Complexity

Houston, 1999. A glass tower bearing Enron's blue logo caught the Texas sun like a blade. Inside, executives in Hermès ties spoke a new dialect of profit—mark-to-market accounting, derivatives, structured entities. The company no longer sold gas; it sold predictions of gas.

Every morning a floor of traders re-valued contracts whose value no one could independently test. Profits were booked the day deals were signed, losses postponed to subsidiaries hidden offshore. Analysts called it innovation; in truth it was architecture without load-bearing walls.

The rot was invisible because complexity itself became the currency of credibility. The more abstruse the model, the more brilliant its author appeared. When a junior accountant questioned a balance sheet, a superior smiled: *"If you can't understand it, you're not meant to."*

Empires of paperwork once hid behind seals and silk; empires of finance hide behind jargon. Both rely on awe to prevent inquiry.

II.

The Moment of Unveiling

In October 2001 a single memo breached the illusion. Vice-president Sherron Watkins warned that the company's structures were "an elaborate accounting hoax." Weeks later, Enron imploded, erasing $60 billion in market value and the pensions of thousands. The shock was not merely financial—it was epistemic.

Shareholders realized they had trusted a mirage of numbers. Regulators realized they had been auditing shadows. The system discovered that transparency without comprehension is just light on fog.

What followed was ritual purification: hearings, scapegoats, reforms. Yet the deeper pattern persisted. The empire of abstraction rebuilt itself under new symbols and software.

III.

2008 — The Machine Breaks Its Maker

Seven years later the illusion metastasized into global scale. Mortgage-backed securities, collateralized debt obligations, credit default swaps—each a linguistic labyrinth designed to transmute risk into revenue. Rating agencies, meant to test the system, became its choir.

When subprime defaults began, executives still declared confidence. Spreadsheets said everything was fine. Like Abdülhamid reading reports of prosperity as famine spread, modern financiers trusted models more than streets.

Then the models failed. Lehman Brothers fell; markets convulsed. The world glimpsed how thin its reality had become—an economy built on leveraged belief.

Governments poured trillions into rescue, nationalizing private folly. In that moment capitalism revealed its own version of the Ottoman paradox: centralized intervention masquerading as free market, control disguised as liberty. Every bailout was a firman in digital ink.

IV.

Data as Deity

The century turned again and worship migrated from banks to blockchains. The new prophets preached decentralization: code instead of kings, transparency instead of trust. For a moment it seemed the mirror might finally reflect honestly.

But by 2022 another tower rose—FTX, headquartered in the Bahamas, radiant with logos of virtue. Its founder was hailed as a philosopher-king, tweeting about effective altruism and rational ethics while moving billions through shell accounts.

When liquidity vanished, the curtain dropped: customer deposits missing, governance nonexistent, risk models built on friendship and faith. Auditors found spreadsheets labeled "DO NOT SHOW." The illusion had evolved, not vanished.

Like the Ottoman clerks who rewrote famine into plenty, digital courtiers rewrote debt into yield. The language changed; the blindness remained.

V.

The Psychology of Abstraction

Why do intelligent people build systems they cannot understand?

Because complexity flatters ego and hides guilt. The modern executive, like the sultan in his archive, mistakes data accumulation for wisdom.

Neuroscientists studying cognitive overload note that information surfeit reduces empathy and foresight. When decisions are mediated entirely through screens, consequences become theoretical. In finance, this manifests as *moral distance*: the trader sees numbers, not lives. In empire, the ruler sees reports, not people.

Both forms of detachment create moral anesthesia. The crash or the coup is simply the nervous system remembering pain.

VI ·

The Echo of Secrecy

After each collapse, the response is identical: more oversight, more data, more surveillance. Yet oversight becomes its own blindness. Sarbanes-Oxley begat compliance bureaucracy; post-crisis regulations birthed risk committees whose memos read like poetry of self-exoneration.

The empire of paper transformed into empire of code—algorithms policing algorithms. Transparency now means volume, not clarity. The result is a world monitored yet unseen, quantified yet misunderstood.

We have built a digital Yıldız Palace: vast dashboards, constant metrics, no conversation. CEOs watch real-time profit charts as Abdülhamid once studied telegrams, convinced omniscience ensures control. Both stare into mirrors that only confirm belief.

VII ·

The Moment of Recognition

When FTX collapsed, investors scoured chat logs and balance sheets like archaeologists decoding hieroglyphs. They discovered the same artifact across centuries: hubris carved into policy.

The auditors' report read like a modern epic of ruin—passwords stored in plaintext, billions moved on the whim of a message, a company run on first-person pronouns. It was the late Ottoman court translated into crypto slang: one man, infinite trust, zero transparency of substance.

And yet amid the wreckage, something honest glimmered—the realization that systems fail not from evil but from distance. The further power drifts from consequence, the faster it loses gravity.

VIII ·

The Mirror Restored

After Enron came ethics courses; after 2008, stress tests; after FTX, blockchain audits. Each is necessary, none sufficient. No reform endures unless perception itself changes.

Sovereignty begins when leaders re-enter the world they quantify—when the banker visits the neighborhood behind the spreadsheet, the policymaker the household behind the statistic, the engineer the worker behind the code. Without embodiment, information decays into illusion.

In physics, mirrors do not create light; they only return it. In governance, data does the same. The problem was never lack of transparency but lack of eyes willing to see.

IX.

Transmission

From the Ottoman archive to the crypto exchange, power repeats the same equation: information × distance = delusion.

To understand why individuals inside these systems cannot see the collapse forming beneath them, we turn next to psychology—to the neural mechanics of authority, isolation, and empathy's slow erosion.

Key 23 · Psychological Mechanism · The Isolation Effect of Authority

Power alters perception long before it corrupts intention.

It begins invisibly, with distance—the few extra steps between the leader and the door, the assistant who answers first, the silence that follows a casual command. The higher one climbs, the fewer honest echoes return. Over time that silence hardens into blindness. This is the isolation effect of authority: the neurological and social drift that severs feedback from power until the powerful live inside mirrors of their own design.

I ·

The Height and the Hollow

Every human brain is built to navigate reciprocity. Eye contact, tone, touch—these micro-signals regulate behavior through immediate feedback. In hunter-gatherer bands, reputation was survival; empathy calibrated dominance.

But hierarchy rewires that circuitry. The moment status creates asymmetry, ordinary feedback collapses. Subordinates modulate truth to protect position, and leaders receive a filtered world.

Neuroscientist Sukhvinder Obhi's work at McMaster University proved the physiology behind it. When subjects were primed to feel powerful, their mirror neurons—the cells that simulate others' experiences—fired less. Empathy literally dimmed. Power does not just change perspective; it edits the brain's code for recognition.

II·

The Feedback Desert

A CEO, a president, a sultan—each begins by listening. Over time, listening becomes optional, then ornamental. Executives surround themselves with courtiers fluent in optimism. Ministers learn which facts please the throne. A culture of self-censorship blooms without orders.

This is the paradox of command: the more one needs truth, the harder it is to hear.

Psychologists call it *pluralistic ignorance*—each subordinate privately doubts a decision but believes everyone else supports it. Dissent evaporates, conformity calcifies, and catastrophe matures unseen. When disasters finally arrive, they appear sudden but have been gestating in silence for years.

Empires and corporations both die of the same disease: feedback starvation.

III·

The Euphoria of Control

Dacher Keltner calls it the power paradox: empathy and restraint earn authority, yet authority erodes empathy and restraint. MRI scans reveal reduced error detection activity in powerful subjects' anterior cingulate cortex—the region that signals "I may be wrong."

With diminished self-correction, confidence swells into conviction.

History's archives are filled with men and women who mistook this chemical surge for destiny. The Ottoman Sultan reading only reports that confirmed loyalty; the CEO convinced every market is his dominion; the autocrat who equates applause with approval. Each suffers the same hallucination: that their vision is shared because no one dares contradict it.

Power becomes a drug disguised as duty.

IV.

Loneliness at the Summit

If the powerless suffer exposure, the powerful suffer enclosure.

In 2012 Harvard researchers found half of CEOs feel isolated, and 61 percent believe it harms performance. The throne and the corner office share the same acoustic problem: they absorb sound but do not return it.

Authority transforms friendship into hierarchy. Every relationship acquires a shadow of motive. To confide becomes risky; to relax, dangerous. The leader's public smile conceals private disorientation.

Abdülhamid walked alone in his gardens; Lincoln wrote, "I walk alone." Between palaces and boardrooms stretches the same corridor of solitude.

V.

The Sycophant's Algorithm

Flattery is not a vice; it is a survival instinct. In any system where dissent costs more than deceit, praise becomes currency.

Ottoman poets composed odes to the Sultan's wisdom; modern staff compose emails of alignment. Social media amplifies it through digital applause—the new court of likes and retweets.

Each click rewards conformity. Each metric penalizes nuance.

Power today is surrounded not by courtiers in silk but by dashboards optimizing for affirmation. The result is identical: self-reinforcing illusion.

When the leader finally fails, everyone feigns surprise. Yet the algorithm performed perfectly—it protected the hierarchy, not the truth.

VI ·

The Neurochemistry of Detachment

Power floods the bloodstream with dopamine and lowers cortisol, producing calm under stress but also dulling sensitivity to consequence. Leaders under this influence take greater risks, interrupt more often, and show decreased capacity for perspective-taking.

Neuroscience thus explains what philosophers observed for millennia: unchecked command separates ruler from reality.

The Roman Stoics warned of it; so did Confucian scholars. Modern science simply found the receptors.

To inhabit command without compensation—without deliberate humility or ritualized contradiction—is to drift into cognitive myopia. Eventually, every empire mistakes its reports for the world itself.

VII ·

The Mirror's Trap

In the palace, the sultan's courtiers described the empire's health in glowing terms because the sultan demanded reassurance. In the corporation, analysts present rising graphs because executives expect them. Both forget that mirrors reverse the image. What looks like ascent may in fact be decline.

Leaders often say, "Show me the data." But data, like mirrors, reflects what stands before it. Without independent angles, all analysis becomes self-portrait.

This is the terminal stage of isolation: when metrics replace meaning and correction becomes unpatriotic.

VIII ·

The Ethics of Hearing

Ancient systems designed antidotes. The Chinese emperor's censors could submit petitions of protest; the Caliph of Baghdad employed poets licensed to mock; Roman generals had slaves whisper during triumphs, *"Remember you are mortal."*

Modern equivalents are rare. Performance reviews flatter upward; news networks segment by ideology; social media tailors reality to preference. Without friction, no truth emerges.

Humility must therefore be engineered. Quarterly meetings should allocate time for contradiction; leaders should appoint designated dissenters; institutions should rotate perspective as deliberately as positions.

Listening is not virtue signaling; it is infrastructure maintenance.

IX ·

Isolation as Decay

Empires do not fall because rulers are cruel; they fall because rulers are deaf.

Abdülhamid's palace, Lehman's trading floor, FTX's group chat—each became a closed ecosystem circulating stale air. The first symptom is silence, the second surprise. When the shock arrives, the leader calls it betrayal. In truth, it is the return of the real.

Collapse is hearing restored too late.

X ·

Humility as Technology

The cure is not abdication but calibration.

Mandela rotated advisors to avoid echo chambers; Pope Francis refused the papal palace for proximity; Elizabeth I walked among her subjects in disguise. Each ritualized humility as feedback device.

Modern organizations can replicate this with simple mechanics:

shadow sessions where juniors challenge seniors; *reverse briefings* where leaders explain policies to frontline workers; *empathy immersions* where executives perform low-level tasks.

Humility is not softness—it is sensory reattachment.

XI ·

The Inner Dimension

Isolation also occurs within the psyche. The ego constructs an inner court of advisers: ambition, fear, pride, doubt.

When pride becomes the sole counselor, perception distorts internally. Meditation, journaling, and confession traditions across cultures serve the same biological purpose: to reintroduce feedback into consciousness.

A sovereign individual, like a sovereign state, requires internal opposition.

Without it, even private thought becomes propaganda.

XII ·

The Threshold of Stewardship

Power becomes sustainable only when reframed as stewardship.

Stewardship replaces ownership with guardianship, hierarchy with horizon. The steward asks not "What can I command?" but "What can I sustain?"

This psychological shift restores empathy because it converts consequence into purpose.

The steward's identity expands outward; isolation collapses inward. Every civilization that survives long enough—Ashoka's India, Tokugawa's Japan, postwar Europe—rediscovers this frame.

XIII ·

Transmission

Authority's blindness begins as biology, matures as bureaucracy, and ends as mythology.

To understand how civilizations translate this cycle into story, we turn next to the archetype that has defined hubris for three thousand years: the boy who mistook the sun for destiny.

Key 24 · Mythic Resonance · The Fall of Icarus and the Delusion of Height

I ·

Wax and Wings

Before there were skyscrapers or trading floors, there was Daedalus—the engineer imprisoned by his own genius. The labyrinth he built for King Minos was so cunning that even its creator could not find the exit. In that cell of corridors he fashioned wings from wax and feather, fastening them to his son's shoulders with trembling hands. He warned, "Fly not too high, or the sun will melt your bindings."

The myth begins as craft and ends as consequence. It is the oldest caution against the seduction of elevation. Icarus is not punished for flight; he is undone by disregard. The ascent itself is sacred—humans are meant to rise—but to forget the physics of proximity is to mistake radiance for immunity.

Every empire eventually rehearses this fable. Power, like the sun, does not burn intentionally; it burns inevitably.

II ·

The Archetype of Overreach

Greek myth encoded psychological truth in narrative form. Icarus symbolizes the intoxication of autonomy—the moment when creative capacity outpaces self-awareness. He rises from confinement into freedom and confuses expansion with invulnerability.

Across civilizations the pattern repeats. In Mesopotamia, Gilgamesh seeks immortality and loses his friend instead. In the Hindu

Mahabharata, Duryodhana's pride blinds him to destiny's law. In the Mayan *Popol Vuh*, the Hero Twins ascend to the heavens only after dying to self. These stories are not warnings against ambition; they are cartographies of equilibrium.

Each teaches the same structural law: power without proportion collapses into tragedy.

III ·

The Physiology of Ascent

Modern psychology reinterprets the myth through the neurochemistry of success. Dopamine and serotonin spike with achievement, creating sensations of elevation indistinguishable from literal height. The body misreads reward as altitude; the mind, surrounded by flattery and control, loses friction.

This is why leaders describe triumph as "heady." The language is literal: blood flow increases to the brain's pleasure centers, narrowing focus and suppressing caution. Icarus's wings melt not from external heat but from internal chemistry—his euphoria becomes entropy.

When the Ottoman sultans adorned their domes with gold leaf or CEOs order towers piercing clouds, it is ritualized ascent: architecture as hormone. The higher the spire, the greater the need for humility at its base.

IV ·

The Symbol of the Sun

In ancient iconography the sun represented divine order, truth, and illumination. To draw near was to approach revelation. But sunlight also exposed hubris. Egyptian pharaohs called themselves children of Ra;

their monuments aligned with solstices. Yet even they built burial chambers underground, acknowledging that ascent requires descent.

The modern sun is artificial—screens, spotlights, algorithms of attention. Leaders today do not melt under literal heat but under visibility. Scandals, leaks, exposure—each beam of public scrutiny liquefies pretense. The same myth replays on new thermodynamics: the digital sun burns through illusion faster than the real one.

In both cases, the law holds. The closer one flies to unchecked admiration, the thinner the atmosphere of truth.

V.

Daedalus's Lament

The myth's tragedy is not Icarus's fall but Daedalus's witnessing. The father, symbol of wisdom and craft, engineers liberation yet cannot transmit restraint. His genius solves the problem of confinement but not the problem of pride.

In civilizational terms, Daedalus represents the technocrat—the planner whose inventions liberate society materially while destabilizing it morally. The scientist who splits the atom, the engineer who designs the algorithm, the financier who creates leverage: each crafts wings for others to fly. Yet once the mechanism is airborne, intention loses control.

Daedalus's grief is modern management's inheritance. We are a civilization of inventors watching our creations ignore altitude warnings.

VI ·

The Fall as Revelation

When Bruegel painted *The Fall of Icarus* in the sixteenth century, he placed the boy's plunge in the corner of the canvas. Farmers plough, ships sail, shepherds whistle—life continues. The tragedy of overreach is not only that the hero falls, but that the world barely notices.

Empires dissolve quietly. The Ottoman treasury empties, yet markets hum; the corporation implodes, yet timelines scroll on. The collective attention moves elsewhere. Icarus sinks not into punishment but into indifference.

That is the final cruelty of hubris: insignificance.

VII ·

The Pattern in History

Every empire's climax carries its seed of descent. Rome at Trajan's height stretched beyond administrative coherence; the Ming bureaucracy ossified under its own paper; the British Empire mistook moral mandate for divine endorsement.

The Ottoman sultans, encased in ceremony, could no longer sense the empire's texture. Reports were embellished, maps idealized, reforms announced and forgotten. The empire did not fall to invasion but to insulation.

The myth, when mapped onto history, becomes diagnostic:

1. **Innovation** creates expansion.
2. **Expansion** breeds complexity.
3. **Complexity** demands control.
4. **Control** breeds isolation.
5. **Isolation** collapses coherence.

This sequence is the flight path of Icarus written in bureaucratic ink.

VIII ·

The Shadow in Modernity

In corporate towers, data replaces the sun. Leaders chase illumination through metrics, quarterly earnings, and stock prices. Each new summit demands a higher one. The cult of growth is the myth industrialized.

When markets overheat, it is not greed alone but gravitational law. Systems that forget entropy believe infinite ascent is sustainable. The myth survives as economic physics: the melt of 1929, 2008, 2022—each a wax moment.

Technological culture inherits the same blindness. Artificial intelligence, social media, and biotech all carry Daedalus's signature: brilliance untempered by foresight. Each promises liberation yet risks confinement within its own labyrinth of dependency.

The moral is neither regression nor rejection but calibration. Wings must adapt to heat.

IX ·

The Psychological Reversal

Icarus is remembered for ascent, but the myth's wisdom lies in the fall. The descent is not failure but feedback. It restores proportion, reconnecting the individual to gravity. Psychologically, collapse is a recalibration of scale—the body re-learning boundaries the mind forgot.

Therapists observe this in burnout and recovery. Ambitious personalities often misread exhaustion as weakness until the fall forces rest. The crash, humiliating as it seems, is nature's intervention—a correction, not a curse.

So too with civilizations. Collapse is collective therapy, forcing humility where counsel was ignored.

X ·

The Ethics of Flight

The myth does not forbid flight; it instructs preparation.

Daedalus's craft was meticulous: measured wax, aligned feathers, calculated lift. What doomed Icarus was neglect of maintenance.

In leadership, ethical flight requires three disciplines:

1. **Friction** — deliberate exposure to contradiction.
2. **Cooling** — rituals of humility to dissipate heat.
3. **Tether** — values that remind one of ground.

Without these, every ascent becomes pathology. With them, flight becomes art.

XI ·

The Father and the Son

Every generation repeats the tension between Daedalus and Icarus: elders warn, youth test limits. The dialogue sustains progress. Too much caution yields stagnation; too much defiance, disaster. Civilization evolves by oscillating between both impulses.

In personal development, this dynamic manifests as mentorship and autonomy. The wise teacher must allow ascent but equip the student to survive sunlight. In this sense, Daedalus's true failure was not engineering but education: he built wings but not wisdom.

Every leader, parent, and nation faces the same mandate—to pass on capacity without inflating ego.

XII ·

The Mirror of Power

The myth's central metaphor—height as isolation—returns to our chapter's theme. Power is altitude, and altitude distorts perception. Clouds of privilege obscure terrain; oxygen of empathy thins. The higher one rises, the more one must rely on instruments of feedback—moral compasses, independent counsel, transparent metrics.

Without them, vision blurs into mirage. The palace mirror becomes sky.

Icarus's fall is thus not an accident but an inevitability once feedback fails. The wax is data untested by dissent; the feathers are reputation; the heat is unchecked praise. When these combine, flight ceases to be freedom—it becomes delusion.

XIII ·

Renewal in Descent

Yet every fall seeds renaissance. The splash of Icarus feeds the sea; Daedalus continues to Sicily, where he dedicates his wings to Apollo. The myth concludes not in despair but in devotion—knowledge returned to source.

For civilizations, this is the moment of reformation: humility leading to reconstruction. After the Ottoman collapse came new republics; after financial crashes, new regulations; after personal failures, new conscience. Descent fertilizes ascent.

The story's geometry is cyclical, not linear. The wings are remade each generation, lighter and wiser.

XIV ·

Bridge

Imagine Icarus not falling but gliding lower, wings intact, learning to navigate between heat and sea. This is the unpainted ending—the possibility of sustainable flight.

The myth asks not that we stop rising but that we rise awake.

XV ·

Transmission

To master height, one must re-engineer grounding.

Next we translate this mythic insight into structure—the *Sovereignty Protocol* of Chapter 5: practical systems that transform hierarchy into feedback, leadership into stewardship, and power into service.

Key 25 · Sovereignty Protocol · The Leadership Feedback Engine and the Architecture of Transparent Power

I ·

Power as a System to Be Engineered

Leadership fails when it is treated as charisma instead of circuitry.

Empires, companies, and communities alike collapse not because people grow evil but because systems grow opaque. Transparency is not moral theater; it is the oxygen of feedback. A sovereign order must therefore design power the way engineers design engines—built for stress, cooled by contradiction, and maintained through regular calibration.

The Leadership Feedback Engine begins with one principle: **information must flow in both directions faster than ego can filter it.**

When that law is obeyed, authority becomes stewardship. When ignored, it becomes entropy.

II ·

The Architecture of Transparent Power

Every enduring civilization embeds mechanisms of hearing. The Athenians had ostracism, a crude but effective citizen veto. The Ottomans, before sclerosis set in, maintained the *divan*, an open audience with the Sultan where commoners could present petitions directly. Modern democracies replicate fragments of this through free press, whistleblower laws, and audits, though each decays when captured by fear or faction.

To rebuild trust, we must reconstruct these architectures at every scale—from family to firm to federation—using four feedback pillars:

1. **Visibility** — decisions must be observable.
2. **Accountability** — power must be traceable.
3. **Reversibility** — errors must be correctable.
4. **Proximity** — decision-makers must feel consequences.

Each pillar converts hierarchy into circulation, preventing the stagnation that precedes collapse.

III ·

Visibility — Seeing the Machine

Visibility begins with design. In aviation, every critical system is instrumented; pilots trust dials more than intuition. Governance needs the same instrumentation.

A leader should be surrounded by metrics that reveal reality, not reinforce delusion—cash flow, morale, environmental footprint, public sentiment—each updated by independent sensors.

For households, visibility means open budgets and shared planning. For organizations, it means transparent decision logs and error reporting. For governments, it means public data and sunset clauses.

Opacity is not security; it is suffocation. The empire that hides rot breeds rumor; the company that hides loss breeds scandal. Transparency does not weaken authority—it purifies it.

IV.

Accountability — The Chain of Return

In electrical circuits, current flows because every node completes the loop. Authority requires the same closure.

Accountability is the return path of power: the assurance that influence meets consequence. Without it, command becomes abstraction.

Practical forms:

- **Peer auditing:** rotating committees that evaluate leadership performance.
- **Public ledgers:** financial transparency accessible to contributors or citizens.
- **Reverse mentorship:** juniors brief seniors monthly on ground truth.

Each mechanism reminds leaders that leadership is leased, not owned. The lease renews only when performance matches trust.

V.

Reversibility — Designing for Error

No system remains perfect under stress. The wise build for recovery, not illusion of infallibility.

Reversibility ensures that bad decisions can be undone before they metastasize.

The ancient Romans allowed dictatorships for six months only; early software engineers introduced "rollback" functions; pilots rehearse abort sequences before takeoff.

Reversibility in governance could mean trial policies, pilot zones, or automatic reviews after defined intervals.

In personal sovereignty it means regular life audits—reviewing habits, finances, relationships, and beliefs for error accumulation.

To be sovereign is not to avoid mistakes but to make them safely reversible.

VI ·

Proximity — Restoring Sensation

When rulers stop feeling the cost of their commands, morality detaches from reality.

In ancient Japan, shoguns inspected rice fields; in Bhutan, ministers trek to remote villages. Exposure preserves empathy.

Modern leaders need sensory reconnection: field immersion, shadowing workers, reading unfiltered messages. The same applies to households and teams. When decision-makers experience outcomes directly, authority regains conscience.

Power must be embodied or it turns spectral. Proximity is the antidote to abstraction.

VII ·

The Human Sensor Network

Technology can amplify transparency but cannot replace trust.

Build concentric circles of honest voices—the inner ring of challengers, the middle ring of implementers, the outer ring of citizens or customers. Rotate members regularly to prevent echo chambers.

In personal life, this becomes an advisory triad:

- One who tells you truth regardless of consequence.
- One who executes your vision faithfully.
- One who represents those affected by your choices.

This triad transforms solitude into structure. It prevents Icarus moments before they begin.

VIII ·

Rituals of Humility

Power must cool itself through ritual the way engines use coolant.

Every tradition discovered humility technologies: confession in Christianity, *zikr* in Sufism, *seiza* in Japanese discipline, daily accounting in Stoicism. Each reintroduces vulnerability into authority.

Modern equivalents can be secular: weekly reflection logs shared with teams, failure postmortems conducted publicly, gratitude briefings before decision cycles.

Such practices normalize fallibility and transform shame into learning.

A leader who cannot say "I was wrong" invites history to say it louder.

IX ·

The Sovereign Feedback Cycle

1. **Signal Capture** – Gather raw truth from multiple sources without filtration.
2. **Signal Processing** – Distinguish pattern from noise using diverse perspectives.
3. **Signal Response** – Implement adjustments rapidly, publicly.

4. **Signal Memory** – Document corrections so future actors inherit learning.

This fourfold loop forms the *Feedback Engine*. Applied consistently, it keeps systems adaptive under turbulence. Applied personally, it converts ego into instrument.

Every collapse in history can be traced to a broken loop: warnings ignored, dissent silenced, lessons forgotten.

X.

Power Ethics for the Age of Collapse

As institutions decay, citizens will inherit more decision power by necessity. The line between ruler and ruled blurs. Thus, the ethics of power must democratize.

Three commandments for distributed authority:

1. **Do not hoard information.** Knowledge isolated becomes weaponized.
2. **Do not outsource conscience.** Algorithms optimize profit, not virtue.
3. **Do not command what you cannot explain.** Clarity is the new legitimacy.

In the age of collapse, legitimacy will flow from transparency, not titles. The next sovereigns will be those who hear deepest, not shout loudest.

XI ·

The Sovereign Dashboard

To operationalize these principles, each reader constructs a *Sovereign Dashboard*—a living map of feedback loops in their own sphere.

Inputs: people, data, rituals that deliver unfiltered truth.

Processors: meetings, reflection, analysis methods.

Outputs: decisions, statements, actions.

Sensors: metrics or mentors that confirm outcomes.

Audit it monthly. Strengthen weak sensors, reward truth-tellers, and reduce lag time between signal and response. The tighter the loop, the more alive the system.

Transparency is not a policy; it is metabolism.

XII ·

The Leader as Mirror

The mature sovereign realizes that leadership is reflective geometry. Every decision reveals the leader's inner architecture.

To manage others, one must manage attention; to manage attention, one must master perception.

In practice:

- Replace command language with inquiry.
- Replace secrecy with sequencing—releasing information at the pace people can integrate it.
- Replace certainty with clarity—admitting unknowns before they metastasize into lies.

Leaders who model uncertainty grant permission for collective intelligence to surface.

XIII ·

Case Reflections

- **The Tokugawa Shogunate (1603–1868)** preserved peace through strict feedback: local daimyos submitted reports and hosted alternate attendance in Edo, ensuring the center stayed informed.
- **Toyota's Andon Cord** allows any worker to halt production for safety—a physical symbol of reversible authority.
- **Wikipedia's edit history** demonstrates collective accountability; every change is visible, every mistake traceable.

Across centuries, the same geometry recurs: feedback decentralizes fragility.

XIV ·

The Inner Republic

Each individual carries a parliament within—desires, fears, ideals, instincts. Sovereignty begins when this internal assembly learns to debate honestly.

Meditation is the session; conscience is the opposition; reason is the chair.

The task is not to silence voices but to integrate them.

A person who governs self transparently cannot be easily governed by others.

XV·

The Covenant of Feedback

Write this as creed:

I will seek contradiction before confirmation.
I will measure impact, not intention.
I will listen downward as intently as upward.
I will design reversibility into every plan.
I will hold power as stewardship, not possession.

Recite it until it becomes reflex. Sovereignty is sustained not by control but by correction.

XVI·

Bridge

Imagine an empire where every palace wall is translucent, every policy leaves a traceable echo, every citizen can whisper truth upward without fear. That is the civilization beyond empire—the world where mirrors no longer distort but clarify.

Transparent power is not utopia; it is maintenance.

The work never ends, but the view clears.

XVII ·

Transmission

With feedback restored, power regains proportion. Yet structure alone cannot sustain meaning. After transparency must come purpose—the question of why to lead at all.

Next, in **Chapter 6: The Threshold of Meaning**, we descend from systems into soul—to explore how collapse births the hunger for purpose, and how meaning becomes the only currency that outlasts empires.

Key 26 · Historical Mirror · The Black Death and the Humanist Turn

I ·

A Silence That Swallowed Bells

In the spring of 1348, the bells of Florence stopped ringing. The plague took the ringers first. Within weeks the city was reduced to whispers—carts creaking over cobblestones, priests muttering last rites through cloth. Boccaccio wrote that fathers fled sons, lovers abandoned one another, and "every man thought to avoid death by fleeing from it."

From China's Gobi plains to the harbors of Marseille, the Black Death erased nearly half of Europe's population in four years. It was not merely biological annihilation—it was metaphysical collapse. The old coordinates of meaning – church, crown, and fate – failed at once. Faith offered no immunity; wealth bought no reprieve. Humanity was forced into an existential experiment: *what remains when the world's scaffolding falls?*

II ·

The Crack in Theology

Before the plague, salvation was collective. The Church mediated eternity; obedience ensured belonging. When whole monasteries perished praying, the promise cracked. Peasants began to suspect that virtue and survival were not correlated. Priests who survived charged for burials, and indulgence sellers multiplied.

The silence of God created a new sound: conscience. Ordinary men and women began interpreting scripture themselves. Literacy crept from cloister to market. This spiritual decentralization was the first whisper of modernity—the internalization of authority.

By the 1350s, sermons spoke of individual judgment and personal mercy. In the ashes of clerical collapse, the human soul discovered its singular worth.

III ·

The Art of Witness

Death made observers of everyone. Artists recorded what theology could not explain. The *Danse Macabre*—skeletons leading nobles and peasants in equal procession—spread across Europe's church walls. It was satire and solace at once: democracy of decay.

Yet within that morbidity lay a strange liberation. If death leveled all, life's value multiplied. Painters like Giotto turned from gold-leaf icons to human faces—creased, sorrowing, alive. The divine migrated from heaven into anatomy.

This was the aesthetic seed of humanism: attention to the real. To draw the curve of a hand became an act of reverence.

IV ·

Florence After Fever

When plague returned in waves through the 15th century, cities adapted instead of surrendering. Quarantine was invented in Ragusa; public health boards in Venice; payrolls for artists and architects in Florence to lure citizens back. Civic pride replaced feudal obedience.

The Medici, rising bankers of the time, built hospitals beside cathedrals, libraries beside markets. In their calculus, beauty could heal morale and trade simultaneously. Art became policy.

Out of this pragmatism emerged the first laboratories of Renaissance thought: universities teaching medicine from Arabic translations, workshops merging geometry with fresco. Survival turned curiosity into civic duty.

V.

The Shift in Psychology

Psychologists later called it *mortality salience*—awareness of death increasing the search for meaning. The plague compressed centuries of contemplation into a single generation. When half your acquaintances vanish, abstraction loses allure. People sought tangible virtue: kindness, craftsmanship, literacy, pleasure.

This pivot from piety to purpose mirrored what Viktor Frankl would later observe in concentration camps—that life endures only through meaning freely chosen, not decreed. The fourteenth century intuited this long before psychology named it.

VI.

Birth of the Individual

Petrarch, writing from Avignon amid pestilence, confessed in letters to the dead that he felt "a double exile—from the world and from myself." Yet his melancholy produced the modern diary. In confessing inwardly, he invented introspection as literature.

Where medieval chronicles cataloged kings, humanists cataloged consciousness. *Who am I* replaced *whose am I*. The map of salvation shifted from heaven's geography to the interior landscape.

This was not secular arrogance but adaptive necessity. When institutions fail, the self must become sanctuary.

VII ·

Economy of Absence

Labor shortages tripled wages. Serfs bargained with lords or walked away entirely, founding free towns. Property laws softened; guilds gained leverage. Power redistributed by demographic force, not decree.

Historians mark the end of feudalism here, but beneath economics ran psychology: people who buried half their world no longer feared masters. They had met the worst and survived. Confidence replaced compliance.

Collapse democratized dignity.

VIII ·

Science Through Suffering

Amid superstition, a few physicians broke precedent. Ibn Khatimah in Al-Andalus described contagion empirically, observing transmission patterns instead of divine wrath. In Italy, Gentile da Foligno dissected corpses despite bans. Each act of observation was heresy against despair.

From these violations emerged medicine as method—knowledge tested against death rather than dictated by doctrine. The Renaissance laboratory begins here: in the refusal to accept mystery as excuse.

IX ·

The Metaphor of Light

Plague winter forced shutters closed; when survivors reopened them, sunlight itself seemed reborn. Painters flooded canvases with illumination. The metaphor endured: enlightenment as recovery from darkness.

Across Europe, the *Ars Moriendi* manuals taught not how to die but how to live before dying—mindful, reconciled, unfinished but aware. This moral manual bridged to modern psychology's acceptance therapy: control the inner stance when outer control is gone.

The light was philosophical, not theological. It revealed the human as both fragile and sufficient.

X ·

The Humanist Equation

The equation was simple: if heaven's justice is uncertain, human justice must improve. Civic law, education, and art became tools of redemption. Bruni wrote histories praising citizens, not saints. Alberti designed facades for proportion, not penance.

Meaning migrated from eternity to excellence. To build well, to think clearly, to love wisely—these became new sacraments.

XI ·

Memory as Medicine

Communities that survived built ritual calendars of remembrance. Processions commemorated the lost; city archives preserved names of the dead. The act of listing became therapeutic—order wrested from chaos.

Neuroscience now confirms what those mourners sensed: naming grief integrates it. The civic record functioned as collective therapy, a neural rewrite of trauma into story.

Thus the archive was not bureaucratic—it was emotional architecture.

XII ·

Continuity Across Centuries

From the Black Death's void rose a chain of continuity:

– Personal literacy → introspection → literature.
– Public health → civic responsibility → secular governance.
– Artistic realism → scientific observation → modern empiricism.

Each link traced the same adaptive logic: meaning must evolve faster than mortality.

XIII ·

Echoes for Our Age

Pandemics return as pedagogy. COVID-19, like the plague, exposed institutional fragility and moral fatigue. Yet it also reignited craftsmanship, community gardens, mutual aid, remote learning—modern variants of the same Renaissance impulse.

History's gift is pattern recognition. The psyche that survived 1348 still lives within us, awaiting activation when collapse reappears.

XIV ·

Transmission

The fourteenth century proved that meaning is humanity's renewable resource. When every hierarchy failed, imagination rebuilt order from within.

Next, in **Key — Modern Parallel: Post-9/11 and the Digital Meaning Crisis**, we examine how another shock—less biological, more psychological—fractured the collective story of purpose, and how a generation raised on screens confronts the same void that once followed plague.

Chapter 6

The Threshold of Meaning

Part II — The Turning

Key 27 · Modern Parallel · Post-9/11 and the Digital Meaning Crisis

I ·

The Morning the World Split

At 8:46 a.m. on September 11, 2001, the first plane struck the North Tower.

Television anchors froze mid-sentence. Office workers stared at glass and smoke that seemed too cinematic to be real. When the towers collapsed, so did the myth of coherence.

For three decades after the Cold War, Western civilization had lived inside an illusion of permanence. Markets would rise, borders would soften, technology would liberate. The falling steel tore through that narrative as efficiently as the girders themselves. The twenty-first century began not with optimism but with dust.

What followed was not only geopolitical retaliation; it was an existential vacuum. For the first time since 1945, the West's faith in progress cracked.

II ·

Shock and Script

The human mind cannot process chaos without story.

In the first weeks, stories multiplied: freedom versus terror, democracy versus barbarism, good versus evil. Complexity simplified into slogan. The nation needed a mirror large enough to contain fear, so it projected it outward.

Psychologists studying collective trauma call this *narrative compression*—the shortening of nuance under emotional overload. The brain's limbic system demands clarity; ambiguity feels like threat. Hence the flags, the anthems, the mantras. Yet every oversimplified story extracts a cost: curiosity.

While firemen dug through ruins, Washington built new fortresses of certainty. The Patriot Act expanded surveillance; wars exported vengeance. The architecture of meaning turned defensive.

III ·

The Private Aftermath

Inside living rooms, the damage was quieter.

Families glued to screens replayed collapse loops until they blurred. Anxiety became background music. When the footage finally stopped, silence felt unsafe. Cable news filled it.

Sociologists observed a paradox: national unity rose as interpersonal trust fell. Americans volunteered, donated blood, waved flags—but also began suspecting one another. Fear of the outsider metastasized into policy. The collective story mutated into tribal scripts.

The psychologist Jonathan Haidt later called it moral polarization—tribes defining virtue by opposition. It was not terrorism that fractured society; it was the stories told afterward.

IV ·

The Digital Turn

As rubble cleared, a new infrastructure emerged: the internet's second age.

Blogs, forums, and nascent social platforms promised democratized voice. For a brief moment, meaning seemed participatory again. Citizens became publishers, communities formed across continents.

Then acceleration devoured reflection.

Algorithms optimized for engagement, not enlightenment. Outrage proved more clickable than nuance, fear more viral than fact. Within a decade, the network that promised connection engineered isolation at scale.

If 9/11 shattered physical towers, social media dismantled invisible ones—the slow institutions of deliberation, empathy, and shared attention.

V.

From Empire to Echo Chamber

By 2016, every citizen inhabited a private information empire. Feeds confirmed belief, banished contradiction.

The feedback deserts that once doomed monarchs now engulfed masses. Where kings once heard only courtiers, users now heard only themselves.

Cognitive scientists coined the term *epistemic closure*—a sealed loop of perception where new data cannot penetrate. The phenomenon that once isolated rulers now engulfed democracies.

In ancient myth, Babel fractured language; online, it fractured reality. Two people could inhabit the same street yet live in incompatible worlds of meaning.

VI·

The Currency of Attention

Economists once measured wealth in gold; today it is measured in focus.

Platforms discovered that outrage lengthens screen time by 30 percent. Thus the global advertising machine learned to mint conflict into profit.

The consequence was spiritual inflation: meaning debased by overproduction.

Each tweet promised revelation; each headline declared crisis. The sacred act of attention—the human capacity to dwell deeply—became commodified.

Neuroscientist Anna Lembke's research on dopamine shows why: every notification spike mirrors the addictive cycle of narcotics. Society became a lab rat pressing its own lever of distraction.

VII·

The Loss of Silence

After 9/11, airports adopted constant announcements: vigilance as background noise. The digital realm copied that soundtrack. Every ping said, *Stay alert*. A civilization that never pauses cannot metabolize grief.

In pre-modern rituals, mourning lasted forty days; silence was part of healing. The digital world replaced silence with scrolling. Grief outsourced to hashtags dissipates before integration.

The psyche, deprived of stillness, drifts toward nihilism—not the philosophical kind, but the physiological exhaustion of constant stimulus.

VIII ·

The Meaning Industry

Where religion once mediated purpose, the market stepped in.

Self-help titles, influencer sermons, branded mindfulness apps—all promise transcendence through subscription. Each sells the echo of the sacred without the discipline that once anchored it.

Sociologist Hartmut Rosa calls this *resonance collapse*: a world vibrating with signals but lacking depth. We sense everything, absorb nothing.

The result is paradoxical: technological omnipresence coupled with existential anemia. Humanity has never been more informed or less transformed.

IX ·

The Return of Mortality

Then came COVID-19.

Suddenly screens showed refrigerated trucks, graphs of exponential death. Mortality salience returned, this time global and simultaneous. For a few weeks the world rediscovered prayer, neighborliness, song from balconies. Then polarization reclaimed it.

Pandemic years mirrored plague years: faith in institutions eroded, local solidarities improvised. Once again meaning retreated to intimacy—to bread baking, gardens, shared music, acts of micro-care.

Collapse repeated its ancient instruction: simplify, slow, see.

X.

The New Humanism

Just as the Black Death birthed humanism, the digital plague is forcing a moral renaissance.

A generation raised on simulation now hungers for sincerity. Analog art resurges; craftsmanship returns; long-form writing revives. The pendulum swings from abstraction to embodiment.

This revival is embryonic but visible:

– Community libraries reopening as maker-spaces.

– Youth rejecting infinite growth for sufficiency.

– Spiritual seekers fusing science and mysticism without dogma.

It is the same pattern under new light: when the virtual exhausts, the visceral redeems.

XI.

Psychological Mechanism Revisited

Kahneman taught that minds seek coherence more than truth. After collective trauma, coherence becomes narcotic. The antidote is complexity embraced consciously.

To restore meaning, individuals must rebuild tolerance for ambiguity— the emotional muscle the modern era atrophied.

That means reading long texts, practicing silence, engaging people who contradict us. Each act expands the aperture of perception that fear once narrowed.

Meaning is not discovered; it is metabolized through attention.

XII ·

The Threshold

We stand where fourteenth-century Florence once stood: surrounded by data corpses instead of human ones, overwhelmed by signal instead of silence. The task is identical—to relocate the sacred within the human.

Art, science, and conscience must merge again. The next renaissance will not be painted on plaster but coded into conduct—ethical design, transparent media, compassionate economies.

The digital catastrophe, like the plague, is both wound and womb.

XIII ·

Bridge

Picture Times Square at midnight: screens blazing advertisements for freedom, luxury, purpose. Then imagine pulling the main switch. Darkness. Stars appear—forgotten constellations above the glare.

That darkness is not loss; it is the first moment of vision.

XIV ·

Transmission

When civilizations lose meaning, individuals must rebuild it from within. The next section enters the psychology of that reconstruction—how the mind converts chaos into coherence, and how purpose becomes the last immune system.

Key 28 · Psychological Mechanism · Viktor Frankl and the Will to Meaning in an Age of Collapse

I ·

The Prison and the Mind

When the Nazi guards tore the wedding ring from Viktor Frankl's hand, they did not know they were testing a hypothesis.

He had spent his medical career studying despair: why some patients succumbed while others endured. Auschwitz became his laboratory of last resort. Deprived of everything—family, manuscripts, freedom—Frankl observed that survival correlated not with strength but with significance. Those who located a reason to live—love, duty, unfinished work—outlasted the ones who lived only to avoid pain.

He wrote later, "Those who have a *why* can bear almost any *how*."

Meaning was not luxury; it was metabolism.

II ·

From Freud to Frankl

Freud saw human behavior as driven by pleasure; Adler, by power. Frankl added a third vector: purpose.

He called it the *will to meaning*—the innate drive to locate coherence between inner life and outer circumstance. Deny it, and the psyche sickens.

His insight inverted modern psychology's hierarchy. The search for comfort or control could never substitute for the need to matter. This hierarchy remains inverted in our consumer age: people anesthetize emptiness with distraction and call it choice.

Frankl's lesson is arithmetic for the soul: remove meaning, and the equation of existence collapses.

III ·

Existential Vaccination

In the camps, suicide was epidemic. Prisoners stepped into electric fences rather than endure another dawn. Frankl noticed that those who planned even one small future act—a conversation, a manuscript, a reunion—survived longer.

He began assigning "micro-missions" to the hopeless: care for a sick comrade, recall a line of poetry, envision telling the story afterward. Each act re-established time's arrow.

Modern neuroscience validates his fieldwork. Purpose regulates the brain's stress circuitry, lowering cortisol and restoring executive function. In trauma therapy this is called *meaning-making*: reorganizing chaos into narrative. Without that narrative, neurons loop endlessly through threat responses.

Meaning, then, is not philosophy. It is neurology.

IV ·

The Vacuum of Plenty

Frankl warned that when external threats vanish, the inner void expands.

He called it *existential vacuum*—a boredom born of safety. Postwar prosperity produced comfort but not contentment; modern technology multiplied this malaise. Anxiety disorders rose even as mortality fell.

The pattern is ancient. After every civilizational triumph comes psychological famine. Rome's citizens, freed from survival, turned to spectacle. Today's descendants scroll. Both seek stimulation to mask hollowness.

The modern epidemic of depression is not merely chemical; it is cosmological—a crisis of context. We have mastered how to live but forgotten why.

V.

Freedom and Responsibility

Frankl defined two kinds of freedom.

The first is external: the right to act.

The second is internal: the capacity to choose one's attitude.

The camps removed the first but could not touch the second.

He imagined a *Statue of Responsibility* to stand on America's West Coast balancing the *Statue of Liberty* on the East—freedom's twin.

In collapsing societies, both statues matter. Liberty without responsibility degenerates into chaos; responsibility without liberty ossifies into tyranny. The will to meaning requires both: room to act and reason to act well.

VI ·

Meaning as Immune System

Trauma scientists now describe resilience as psychological immunity. Like antibodies, meaning recognizes threat and organizes response.

Those with clear purpose experience shorter stress recovery times, stronger immune function, and reduced inflammatory markers. Purpose literally repairs tissue faster.

Communities exhibit the same biology. Nations with shared civic narratives recover from disaster more efficiently; those fragmented by distrust stagnate. The immune system of civilization is myth.

Frankl's discovery scales upward: individual purpose aggregates into collective coherence.

VII ·

The Crisis of Autonomy

Our century's malaise stems not from oppression but from overload. Choice without compass breeds paralysis.

The average person faces more daily decisions than a medieval monarch yet feels less in control. Algorithms suggest, corporations curate, governments nudge. Autonomy dilutes into option fatigue.

Frankl would call this *freedom without direction*. When everything is possible, nothing feels significant.

His cure: deliberate limitation. Choose a purpose and surrender lesser possibilities. Meaning emerges not from expansion but from exclusion.

Every "yes" worth living requires a thousand "no's."

VIII ·

The Triad of Purpose

Frankl mapped three paths to meaning:

1. **Creative Values** – what we give to the world through work or expression.
2. **Experiential Values** – what we receive from love, nature, or art.
3. **Attitudinal Values** – the stance we adopt toward unavoidable suffering.

Collapse threatens all three, but never simultaneously. When creation is blocked, experience remains; when both vanish, attitude endures. This triad ensures redundancy, like backup generators of significance.

In practice: write one honest page, witness one moment of beauty, endure one hardship with grace. The circuit stays alive.

IX ·

Suffering as Signal

Frankl refused to romanticize pain, yet he saw it as information.

Suffering without meaning is chaos; suffering interpreted becomes transformation.

The difference lies in framing. "Why me?" paralyzes; "What is this asking of me?" mobilizes.

Modern culture pathologizes all discomfort, seeking pharmacological anesthesia. But a civilization that abolishes pain abolishes depth. Without friction, no growth.

Meaning does not erase pain—it dignifies it.

X.

The Modern Clinic

Imagine Frankl alive today, walking through a modern metropolis.

He would diagnose not trauma but triviality. Neon signs shouting *enjoy* mask an epidemic of emptiness. Therapy markets self-esteem, not self-transcendence. The word *purpose* trends yet rarely costs anything.

He would remind us that purpose is not mood but sacrifice in service of value. The antidote to nihilism is not pleasure but devotion.

Where Freud asked, "What do you want?" Frankl asked, "What is life asking of you?" The second question saves civilizations.

XI.

The Collective Frankl

Communities, like individuals, must rediscover their *why*.

Post-industrial democracies built around consumption now face meaning deficits measured in suicides, polarization, and ecological apathy. To recover, nations must treat policy as psychotherapy—aligning economics with existential purpose.

Examples emerge:

– Bhutan's Gross National Happiness index valuing wellbeing over GDP.
– New Zealand's budget prioritizing child welfare and mental health.
– Cities adopting citizen assemblies as moral feedback loops.

These are Frankl's principles institutionalized: meaning as governance.

XII ·

Practical Reconstruction

To operationalize purpose, apply the **Frankl Protocol**—a modern exercise for readers rebuilding coherence amid collapse:

1. **Inventory Values** – List five things worth suffering for.
2. **Define Contribution** – Name one act that leaves the world better today.
3. **Confront Constraint** – Acknowledge limits honestly; design within them.
4. **Craft Narrative** – Write your experience as story, not complaint.
5. **Commit Ritually** – Anchor purpose through daily repetition.

Repeat weekly. The protocol rewires despair into design.

XIII ·

The Threshold State

Psychologists describe *liminality*—the space between old identity and new. Collapse is collective liminality.

Frankl's insight reframes it as incubation: meaning gestates in uncertainty. The task is to resist premature closure. Allow the unknowing. Purpose matures in silence.

The Black Death birthed humanism; the world wars birthed existentialism; our age of algorithms may yet birth conscious realism—a synthesis of data and dignity.

XIV ·

The Return of Faith

Frankl ended *Man's Search for Meaning* not with doctrine but with reverence. "What is demanded of man is not to endure meaningless suffering, but to find meaning in it."

Faith, stripped of institution, becomes trust in intelligibility—the conviction that life asks questions worth answering.

Such faith does not compete with science; it completes it. Empiricism explains mechanism; meaning explains motive. Both are needed for civilization to endure.

XV ·

Bridge

Picture the modern commuter on a packed subway, headphones sealing isolation. Across the carriage, a stranger smiles—small, unmonetized kindness. For an instant the noise recedes, and each remembers they exist in relation. That flicker is the will to meaning resurfacing: silent, stubborn, sacred.

Frankl would say the experiment continues. The human soul, cornered by chaos, still seeks coherence—and finds it whenever love outlasts fear.

XVI ·

Transmission

Meaning gives structure; myth gives language.

Next we descend into archetype—to the Phoenix that dies in fire and rises in light, the eternal emblem of renewal that links plague, war, and psyche into one continuum of rebirth.

Key 29 · Mythic Resonance · The Phoenix and the Alchemy of Renewal

I ·

Fire as Teacher

Every civilization worships something that burns.

The Greeks tended the eternal flame of Hestia; the Zoroastrians called it Atar, the visible presence of divine order; the Vedic hymns praised Agni, the messenger between gods and men. Fire consumes, but it also clarifies. It leaves no ambiguity between essence and excess.

From these fires rose one of humanity's most enduring symbols—the Phoenix. In Egyptian myth it was the Bennu bird, companion of Ra, reborn each dawn from sacred flame. In Greek retelling it lives five centuries, builds its own funeral pyre, and rises from the ashes singing. In Persian lore it is the Simurgh, feathers glinting with all colors of wisdom. Everywhere the story repeats: death is not the opposite of life but its maintenance cycle.

The Phoenix is the first metaphor of systems thinking. It teaches entropy not as tragedy but as renewal protocol.

II ·

The Anatomy of the Myth

The Phoenix myth survives because it encodes thermodynamics in spiritual language.

Every organism, every empire, every identity accrues residue—structures that once protected but now suffocate. When the cost of maintenance exceeds the value of meaning, the system must self-immolate.

The burn is not failure; it is optimization.

Just as forest fires germinate seeds that only open under heat, collapse releases dormant potential. The ash becomes substrate for regeneration.

Modern physics mirrors this. Ilya Prigogine's "dissipative structures" show that open systems maintain order by exporting entropy. Life survives by shedding. The Phoenix externalizes this law as story: what cannot transform must burn.

III ·

The Psychology of Ashes

Myth speaks in images, but its power is psychological. The Phoenix cycle mirrors the stages of human crisis.

1. **Combustion** – the breakdown of identity; loss of control.
2. **Ash** – the zero state; grief and emptiness.
3. **Ember** – faint awareness that something endures.
4. **Lift** – emergence of new orientation.
5. **Flight** – integration of past and future into purpose.

Therapists recognize this sequence as post-traumatic growth. Neuroscience confirms that under stress, the brain's default-mode network quiets, allowing rewiring of perspective. The fire of suffering, properly contained, burns neural pathways of despair into circuits of resilience.

Meaning, then, is ash transmuted into narrative.

IV.

The Collective Flame

When Florence emerged from plague, when Hiroshima rebuilt, when Rwandan artists carved memorial drums from shell casings, the same myth replayed at social scale.

Communities that ritualize remembrance without vengeance achieve what the Phoenix performs instinctively—conversion of memory into fuel.

Sociologists call this *collective effervescence*—the moment shared grief becomes shared strength. Memorials, festivals, revolutions—all are controlled burns preventing moral decay.

Without ritual fire, civilizations hoard their traumas. With it, they refine them.

V.

Alchemy and the Fire Within

The alchemists of the Renaissance borrowed the Phoenix as emblem of the *opus magnum*—the Great Work of transformation. Their furnaces were not factories but metaphors for conscience. To purify lead into gold meant to transmute ego into essence.

In Jung's psychology, this process became *individuation*: the confrontation with shadow that precedes integration. Fire, again, as catalyst.

Modern therapy echoes the same chemistry. Exposure treatment reintroduces fear in measured doses until the psyche reclaims mastery. Each session is a small controlled burn.

Across science and spirit the law holds: avoidance preserves suffering; contact transmutes it.

VI ·

The Age of Controlled Burn

Our century faces combustion on planetary scale—climate, economy, information. The temptation is to prevent all fires, yet suppression guarantees inferno. Forest ecologists now practice *prescribed burns* to restore ecological balance. Societies must learn the same: deliberate release before accidental destruction.

Digital detoxes, sabbaticals, moratoriums on growth—these are civic prescribed burns. They release accumulated stress, clear cognitive underbrush, and make room for new seeds of thought.

Without scheduled silence, entropy ignites elsewhere.

VII ·

The Phoenix as Governance Model

In political philosophy, the myth translates into cyclical renewal of legitimacy.

Democracies stagnate when incumbents fear turnover; monarchies rot when succession freezes. The Phoenix principle demands periodic self-dissolution.

The Roman *cursus honorum* rotated magistrates annually; the Iroquois Confederacy's councils renewed through condolence ceremonies; even corporate governance borrows the cycle through term limits and audits.

The health of a system is measured by how gracefully it allows rebirth.

VIII ·

Myth Against Nihilism

The Phoenix confronts nihilism with physics: destruction is never total.

Even the universe, expanding toward heat death, spawns new order through fluctuation. To believe in absolute annihilation is to misunderstand entropy's generosity.

Myth counters despair not with denial but with perspective. The bird dies singing because it understands sequence.

In personal collapse this knowledge becomes anchor: the worst moment is midpoint.

IX ·

The Symbolic Equation

Fire = Energy release.
Ash = Memory substrate.
Flight = Reorganization.
Applied to civilization:
Crisis = Resource redistribution.
Ruin = Cultural compost.
Rebirth = Innovation.

The Phoenix thus encodes the mathematics of sustainability long before ecology existed. It turns myth into management science.

X ·

Modern Re-incarnations

The symbol recurs everywhere once you know its signature:

– In literature: Mary Shelley's *Frankenstein* burns in pursuit of moral resurrection.
– In politics: South Africa's Truth and Reconciliation Commission as national rebirth through confession.
– In technology: open-source communities rebuilding failed software into stronger forks.
– In economy: Bitcoin emerging from the ashes of 2008's financial collapse, its genesis block quoting the headline "Chancellor on brink of second bailout."

Each is a Phoenix event: system purged by its own excess, reborn with altered DNA.

XI ·

The Inner Workshop

Every reader holds a personal furnace—the space where experience becomes essence.

To activate it, practice three rituals:

1. **Combustion Journal** – write what must die: habits, beliefs, fears. Burn or delete the page.
2. **Ash Meditation** – sit in silence visualizing the residue of loss; thank it for its instruction.
3. **Flight Plan** – design one small act embodying the new orientation within 48 hours.

These micro-rites translate myth into muscle memory. The point is not theater but thermodynamics: energy conserved through transformation.

XII ·

The Physics of Hope

Hope, stripped of sentimentality, is entropy management.

It is the decision to treat disorder as data.

When collapse arrives, the unprepared ask "Why me?" The prepared ask "What is this energy trying to release?"

Hope converts fear's heat into motion. That is why the Phoenix rises immediately—it wastes nothing.

XIII ·

The Flame and the Forge

Meaning forged through fire gains tensile strength. Metallurgy proves it: rapid cooling after heat, *quenching*, aligns atomic lattices. Societies and souls tempered by adversity exhibit the same resilience.

In this sense, the Phoenix is not bird but blueprint: a forge whose output is coherence.

Every age must pass through its kiln to remember what cannot burn—conscience, compassion, curiosity.

XIV ·

Bridge

At dawn the ashes shimmer. No trumpet, no audience—just a pulse beneath the gray. Then a feather moves.

The Phoenix rises slowly, not in triumph but in understanding. Flight is quieter this time, wings stronger, eyes older. It carries memory like heat within its breast.

Its message to the living: *Do not fear the fire. Fear the refusal to transform.*

XV ·

Transmission

The myth gives language; now we translate it into design.

Next comes **Key — Sovereignty Protocol: The Personal Creed and Daily Rituals of Purpose**—a practical manual for rebuilding meaning through behavior, anchoring the reader in practices that turn philosophy into continuity.

Key 30 · Sovereignty Protocol · The Personal Creed and Daily Rituals of Purpose

There comes a point when reflection must harden into rhythm.

Meaning cannot remain an idea; it must be scheduled into time. Every civilization that survived collapse learned to translate conviction into cadence—monks at prayer bells, farmers tracking stars, artisans repeating gestures until craft became meditation. The individual must do the same. Without ritual, belief dissolves; without creed, energy leaks. Sovereignty begins where the day acquires structure.

I ·

The Creed as Compass

A personal creed is not a list of affirmations. It is a private constitution: ten or twelve sentences that define what will not be compromised when the world tilts.

Write it by hand. Words born of ink acquire weight. Each line should answer one of three questions:

1. What do I serve that outlives me?
2. How will I behave when no one watches?
3. What am I prepared to lose in order to remain whole?

Ancient builders carved their oaths into stone so that storms could not erase them. You carve yours into behavior. When uncertainty multiplies—when markets convulse, networks vanish, reputations collapse—the creed functions as gyroscope. You do not need to know the destination; you need only to remain oriented.

Keep it visible: a card inside a wallet, a note taped to a mirror, a line whispered before sleep. A creed hidden is a creed unused.

II ·

The Ritual Architecture

Rituals are the software of meaning. They convert scattered intention into embodied memory.

To build them, follow a pattern older than empire: **dawn, labor, communion, closure.**

Dawn: Begin the day with stillness before contact. One minute is enough. Breathe, recall the first sentence of your creed, and visualize the smallest act that would honor it today. This single visualization trains the brain's reticular system to notice opportunities aligned with purpose; psychologists call it *implementation intention*, monks call it *vow renewal*.

Labor: Dedicate the first focused block of the day to creation, not consumption. No headlines, no feeds. The nervous system sets its tone from the first sensory input; choose authorship over reaction. Even thirty minutes of concentrated work on something tangible—a repair, a paragraph, a design—establishes agency that echoes through the remaining hours.

Communion: Midday is for connection without transaction. Share food, conversation, or silence with another human being expecting nothing in return. This simple practice counters the atomization that defines modern collapse. Communities begin when two people agree that time together is not wasted.

Closure: Before sleep, document three things: one you learned, one you improved, one you forgive. The act integrates memory and releases rumination, lowering physiological stress markers and strengthening continuity between days. Civilization itself began when nights ended with storytelling.

These four anchors—dawn, labor, communion, closure—form a day resilient enough to carry meaning through noise. When practiced for ninety consecutive days, they hard-code sovereignty into habit.

III ·

The Circle Method

Meaning decays in isolation. Create a **Circle of Twelve**: twelve names across your life who represent integrity in action—alive or dead, personal or historical. Review the list monthly. Ask, *Would my choices earn a seat among them?* This quiet accountability structure replaces the vanished moral scaffolding once supplied by guilds, monasteries, and extended families.

Sociological data confirm what ancient orders intuited: regular moral reflection with peers reduces anxiety, increases cooperation, and predicts higher creative output.

Purpose is contagious when witnessed.

IV ·

The Material Layer

The body must believe what the mind declares.

Feed it accordingly. A ritual of nourishment—clean food, water, movement—is a contract with tomorrow. Disrepair of body mirrors disrepair of spirit. Walk daily; exposure to daylight resets circadian chemistry and lifts the neurotransmitters of motivation.

Keep one object that symbolizes endurance: a stone from a river, a tool inherited, a photograph of those who endured worse. Touch it each morning. Neuroscience calls this *anchoring*; tradition calls it *sacrament*. Either way, it teaches the nervous system that continuity exists.

V.

Silence and Signal

Every creed requires intervals of silence to remain audible.

Schedule deliberate disconnection—one hour a day, one day a week—without devices, headlines, or commentary. Observe what remains. At first it will be restlessness; later it will be clarity.

The prophets of every faith, the scientists of every revolution, and the artists of every renaissance all reported the same phenomenon: revelation follows withdrawal. In an attention economy, silence is rebellion.

Use that silence to review alignment:

Did my actions today honor the creed?

If not, where did convenience replace conviction?

This is not self-criticism but calibration.

VI.

The Sabbath Principle

Civilizations collapse when they forget rest. Continuous extraction—of labor, data, or energy—creates the illusion of progress while hollowing the spirit. The Sabbath principle is universal: a periodic ceasefire between the self and its ambitions.

Choose any day. Step outside production. Read, repair, share a meal, walk without destination. Economists call this opportunity cost; wisdom traditions call it renewal. In rest, values re-emerge. A sovereign life balances intensity with pause.

VII ·

The Ledger of Gratitude

Keep a running ledger—not of possessions but of continuities. Each entry begins with *Still here is...*

Still here is breath.

Still here is a friend who answers.

Still here is morning light on concrete.

This practice transforms survival into awareness.

Frankl wrote that those who could locate gratitude in Auschwitz found freedom within captivity. Gratitude is not optimism; it is recognition of reality unmarred by despair. It trains perception to detect meaning amid entropy.

VIII ·

The Oath Renewal

Once each quarter, rewrite your creed from memory without looking. Compare versions. The changes reveal evolution or drift. If drift dominates, adjust behavior, not sentences. The goal is congruence between what is written and what is lived. The self that honors its own word becomes unbreakable.

When circumstances overwhelm, speak the first line aloud. Sound anchors intention; intention organizes chaos.

IX ·

Bridge

A creed matures when shared. Teach one element of your ritual system to another human being—a child, friend, or colleague. Transmission transforms belief into culture. Meaning replicated through relationship becomes civilization in embryo.

The monks who preserved Europe's memory did not plan a renaissance; they simply copied texts faithfully each day. Copy something worth continuing.

X ·

Transmission

Night returns. A candle flickers beside a page covered in handwriting. Outside, the city hums its sleepless song; inside, a human being reads the words they wrote months ago and still recognizes themselves.

Nothing grand has changed—no empire rebuilt, no system redeemed—yet the pulse of coherence is audible again. The light steadies.

The ascent has already begun.

Chapter 7

The Builders of the New World

Part III - The Builders

Key 31 · Historical Mirror · The Harlem Renaissance — Culture as Reconstruction

When a civilization's material scaffolding collapses, its imagination becomes the last factory still standing.

After the First World War, a generation of Black Americans carried the fragments of a broken republic northward. From the cotton rows of Mississippi to the alleys of Chicago and the docks of Norfolk, they packed instruments, Bibles, notebooks, and the memory of fields that had devoured their ancestors. The Great Migration was not merely demographic; it was an exodus from silence to self-definition.

By the winter of 1919, Harlem had become the densest concentration of Black intellect and art in world history. Thirty blocks pulsed with the sound of brass and ambition. The air itself seemed to vibrate with restoration. Landlords converted brownstones into rooming houses where poets slept two to a cot; bootblacks debated socialism; waiters recited verse between shifts. The apocalypse of Reconstruction had left the South hollow, but here, in uptown Manhattan, an invisible workshop began—the rebuilding of identity through language, rhythm, and light.

I ·

The City as Crucible

At dusk, the streetlights of Lenox Avenue flickered like neurons firing across a newborn mind. The Savoy Ballroom throbbed with a rhythm no empire could choreograph—syncopation as declaration. The body's movement became a manifesto: *we exist beyond your measure.*

Each step of the Lindy Hop carried centuries of forbidden joy. In those hours, dancers remade physics; gravity bent to resilience.

Yet beyond the music, another kind of architecture rose. Apartment parlors turned into salons where ideas fermented faster than any gin. Alain Locke, philosopher of Howard, declared that the "Old Negro" image had died in the trenches of France; the "New Negro" was being born here, hammering reality into art. Langston Hughes walked the avenues taking notes like a surveyor mapping a new continent of sound. Zora Neale Hurston collected folktales as if they were blueprints for endurance. Each writer added a brick to a cathedral of self-definition invisible to the city's skyline but stronger than its steel.

II ·

The Economic Underground

Harlem's glamour disguised scarcity. Beneath the jazz glow, unemployment and rent strikes rumbled. But scarcity sharpened invention. Beauty salons became credit unions; barbershops doubled as publishing houses; Pullman porters carried pamphlets of resistance under linen towels. Every transaction contained politics. When white galleries refused Black art, the community hosted its own exhibitions in church basements lit by kerosene lamps. The medium was survival, the message: *autonomy is the mother of elegance.*

In 1921, the NAACP's *Crisis* magazine printed Claude McKay's defiant sonnet "If We Must Die." The poem spread like voltage through a nation still burning from race riots. It was Shakespeare rewritten for the lynching tree, a reminder that language itself could become armor. When McKay later addressed the Comintern in Moscow, he carried Harlem's pulse into the very halls of empire, proving that even the marginalized could dictate theory to power. Culture had turned economic exclusion into moral export.

III ·

The Alchemy of Sound

To outsiders, jazz was entertainment; to its creators, it was code.

Improvisation mirrored social strategy: within constraint, infinite variation.

A horn section was a parliament where each voice demanded space yet listened to the others. The drummer's backbeat mocked the plantation clock; the soloist's break declared momentary freedom within shared time.

What philosophers later called complexity theory, Harlem musicians practiced nightly—self-organizing systems achieving order through rhythm.

By 1930, Duke Ellington's orchestra played at the Cotton Club under chandeliers reserved for white patrons, but the true audience was the Black working class outside listening through open windows. Ellington said little about politics, yet every modulation announced sovereignty: a people re-tuning Western instruments to African intervals, proving that structure could be re-coded without permission. Sound became syntax; syntax became identity.

IV ·

The Psychology of Creation

Historians call this decade a renaissance, but its psychology was closer to therapy. Trauma transmuted into art is civilization's oldest medicine.

W.E.B. Du Bois wrote of "double consciousness"—the fracture of seeing oneself through hostile eyes. Harlem turned that fracture into prism. Instead of healing by forgetting, artists healed by intensifying awareness. To write a sonnet under segregation, to compose a symphony in a language of mockery, was to assert moral physics: the oppressed revealing higher coherence than the oppressor.

Psychologists now recognize this as post-traumatic growth—the phenomenon where adversity catalyzes purpose. The Harlem generation enacted it collectively. They refused despair's monopoly on meaning. Each poem, painting, and melody was an act of neuro-cultural rewiring: pain rewritten as pattern.

V ·

The Silent Engineers

While jazz and poetry drew attention, another set of builders labored quietly—the educators, organizers, and publishers. Carter G. Woodson founded *Negro History Week* in 1926 to counter institutional amnesia; today it endures as Black History Month. A. Philip Randolph organized porters into unions that would later finance the Civil Rights Movement. Addie Hunton trained hundreds of Black nurses returning from the Great War. Their infrastructure of memory and skill outlasted the clubs and magazines. When the Depression hit, it was these systems that kept the lights on in Harlem kitchens.

Every renaissance needs both fire and scaffolding. The musicians lit the flame; the administrators ensured it did not burn out. Together they demonstrated that sovereignty requires rhythm *and* record-keeping—the dance floor and the ledger.

VI ·

The Empire Looks Back

By 1935, journalists in Paris and London wrote of "la Harlem noire" as if it were an independent state. European modernists borrowed its idioms; Picasso studied African sculpture through Harlem exhibitions; Sartre later admitted that Black Americans had revealed freedom's existential core before he named it. Influence had reversed direction. The colony of empire became its teacher.

But the price was fatigue. The Depression shuttered clubs; landlords reclaimed apartments; artists scattered to Chicago, Paris, Port-au-Prince. Yet dispersion was continuity, not death. Like spores, the creators carried Harlem's method wherever they landed: build culture first, economy later. Reconstruction begins in the imagination.

VII ·

Legacy and Blueprint

The Harlem Renaissance was not a decade of parties; it was an engineering project disguised as celebration.

Its formula can be written in four lines:

Memory + Art = Identity

Identity + Discipline = Economy

Economy + Ethic = Civilization

Therefore, Art = Civilization in Seed.

Every later movement of renewal—from Ghana's independence poets to Silicon Valley's garage inventors—follows this schema: imagination first, infrastructure second. Harlem proved that when systems deny participation, creation itself becomes governance.

VIII ·

Transmission

Morning after a night of rain. Steam rises from the asphalt; a trumpet echoes from an empty doorway. A woman opens her window and hums the last bars of a song she heard at the Savoy years before. The street is worn, the dream unfinished, yet the sound endures. It is the hum of a people rebuilding themselves note by note.

Key 32 · Modern Parallel: Regenerative Farmers, Repair Culture, and Makerspaces

When global supply chains broke in 2020, most people saw inconvenience. A few saw revelation. The empty supermarket shelves, the silence of grounded aircraft, the sudden fragility of comfort—these were not anomalies but messages. The system that fed half the planet on fossil calories and credit swaps had reached the edge of its own map. Out of that crack a new species of builder began to appear: the regenerative farmer, the repairer, the maker.

I ·

The Return to Soil

At dawn in Nebraska, Gabe Brown walks his fields without a plow. He presses a spade into dark earth that smells of rain and resurrection. Two decades earlier his land had been sterile from chemical dependency; today its carbon content has tripled. He calls it "biological capital." By mixing crops, grazing animals, and leaving soil unturned, Brown rebuilt fertility faster than any fertilizer ever could. His profits rose as inputs fell—a farmer's quiet rebellion against an economy of extraction.

Across the Atlantic, women in Andhra Pradesh practice zero-budget natural farming on micro-plots. They grow thirty species at once, share seeds freely, and record yields in chalk on mud walls. Their productivity per hectare rivals industrial farms, but their true yield is autonomy. No bank owns their future; no corporation sells their season. In every continent's corner, these small fields form the same equation Harlem once solved with jazz: creativity within constraint equals freedom.

II ·

Repair as Ritual

If industrial modernity worshipped the new, the twenty-first century's quiet counterculture reveres the repaired. In Amsterdam's **Repair Cafés**, retirees and teenagers sit side by side over broken toasters, threading new wires through old shells. They fix laptops, bicycles, and jackets while drinking coffee and sharing stories. A study from TU Delft found that ninety minutes in a repair session reduces anxiety more effectively than a mindfulness class. The hands teach the heart that nothing is beyond restoration.

In Japan, *kintsugi*—the art of mending pottery with gold—has become a metaphor for personal and civic healing. A cracked bowl, rejoined with luminous seams, is stronger than before. Cities adopt the principle: Rotterdam fills bomb-scarred facades with reflective glass rather than erasing the wound; Detroit converts abandoned auto plants into greenhouses and galleries. Repair is no longer maintenance—it is theology. The sacred act is to keep using what still has life.

III ·

The Makerspace Revolution

Beneath the flicker of 3-D printers, a new guild culture hums. From Nairobi's Gearbox Hub to Barcelona's Fab Lab, citizens now manufacture locally what empires once shipped globally. A pandemic ventilator shortage became a proving ground: open-source designs traveled faster than bureaucratic contracts. In 2021, a Kenyan engineer named Elizabeth Mutinda printed spare parts for hospital pumps on a $400 machine and kept an ICU running. The story spread through Telegram groups faster than any official directive. This is distributed civilization—Harlem's improvisation translated into hardware.

Economists once called such efforts hobbyist; today they call them resilience. A MIT study in 2023 estimated that small-scale fabrication could replace 25 percent of global shipping within a decade if regional networks align on standards. Each makerspace is a micro-forge of sovereignty, where learning merges with production and ownership loops back to the community.

IV.

Circular Economies and Ethic of Enough

In Copenhagen, architect Lendager Anders reuses entire walls from demolished buildings. In Ghana's Agbogbloshie scrapyard, artists sculpt from e-waste what corporations call junk. The shift is philosophical: value lies not in extraction but in extension. Where the twentieth century measured growth in tons mined, the twenty-first measures wisdom in materials saved.

Behavioral economists note that participants in circular economies report higher life satisfaction than those in linear consumption chains. The act of reusing reconnects humans with consequence. Each salvaged screw becomes an argument against despair. The circular ethic, like the blues, turns repetition into beauty.

V.

Community as Technology

The most advanced tool of the new builders is not digital; it is relational. Regenerative farms thrive through co-ops that share machinery; repair cafés depend on trust; makerspaces live by open-source reciprocity. Social scientists call this *bonding capital*, but its language is older: covenant. The same principle that sustained diasporas now powers peer-to-peer fabrication. A promise kept replaces a contract enforced.

In Porto Alegre, Brazil, neighborhood assemblies decide municipal budgets using participatory software. In Seoul, crowds of volunteers map wheelchair access through a civic app. These are governance prototypes arising from the same instinct as Harlem's salons: if institutions will not serve us, we will re-invent them at human scale.

VI ·

The Psychology of Making

Studies at Stanford's *Design Impact Lab* show that manual creation activates brain regions associated with agency and resilience. Depression scores drop when individuals shift from consumption to production. Neurochemistry confirms what craftsmen have always known: hands that make are hands that heal. The dopamine released by finishing a task—planting, soldering, carving—counteracts the learned helplessness that digital overload breeds.

When a community builds together, collective efficacy rises. A single restored tool or harvested crop becomes proof that effort still matters in a mechanized world. Meaning returns not through slogans but through sensation—the smell of soil, the hum of a motor revived.

VII ·

The Economy of Dignity

In 2025, a survey by the Schumacher Center found that regions with dense networks of local producers weathered inflation shocks twice as well as those reliant on imports. Dignity had measurable GDP value. Money circulated slower but stuck closer to home, amplifying communal wealth. Like jazz sessions funding future symphonies, micro-enterprises financed shared infrastructure: tool libraries, seed banks, cooperative insurance.

This is the builder's dividend—wealth that compounds in trust rather than speculation. Economists will give it formulas; history will remember it as common sense rediscovered.

VIII ·

The Bridge Between Ages

The Harlem artists and the regenerative engineers belong to the same lineage: each turned crisis into curriculum. One remixed language; the other reprograms matter. Both prove that creativity, when bound to community, outperforms conquest. The medium changed from brass and ink to soil and code, but the motive remained identical—to build worlds within ruins.

IX ·

Transmission

A workshop at twilight. A child watches her father weld the broken frame of a bicycle under a single hanging bulb. Sparks drift like fireflies; the air smells of metal and renewal. On a shelf rests a jar of soil from their garden—dark, alive, patient. Tomorrow they will ride that bicycle to the market where neighbors trade tomatoes for tools. No anthem plays, no flag waves, yet somewhere inside the hum of machines and the whisper of leaves, civilization exhales—alive again, built by its own hands.

Key 33 · Psychological Mechanism: Flow and Mastery as the Cure for Despair

Every collapse breeds two species of human: the spectator and the builder.

The spectator watches, comments, refreshes news feeds, measures ruin.

The builder picks up one fragment and starts shaping.

The difference is not talent but neurochemistry.

When Mihaly Csikszentmihalyi studied painters in the 1960s, he noticed that happiness was never their goal. They worked through hunger, ignored clocks, forgot status. Their reward was absorption itself—a state he called *flow*. Decades later, neuroscientists confirmed its pattern: dopamine for focus, norepinephrine for energy, endorphins for pain resistance, anandamide for connection. The mind in flow stops monitoring itself and begins merging with the act. It is self-transcendence achieved through doing.

Collapse deprives people of coherence; flow restores it from the inside out.

When systems fail, the brain still seeks pattern. In creation—writing, farming, soldering, repairing—it finds rhythm that mimics order. The hands remind the nervous system that cause and effect still exist. That reminder is survival.

I ·

The Anatomy of Flow

The conditions are universal: a clear goal, immediate feedback, difficulty balanced with ability, concentration free from distraction. When those four align, the brain's default-mode network—seat of rumination—goes silent. Anxiety dissolves because there is no self left to suffer. Monks reach this through meditation; builders reach it through work.

In post-industrial society, flow became rare. The average adult switches digital tasks every forty-seven seconds; each switch floods cortisol. Chronic fragmentation simulates collapse inside the skull. Flow reverses it, generating order where none exists. Psychologists now call it "autotelic activity"—the act that justifies itself. For a civilization in entropy, autotelic work is inoculation against despair.

II ·

Mastery as Meaning

Mastery differs from achievement. Achievement seeks applause; mastery seeks refinement. The master is perpetually unfinished. This mindset converts failure into feedback, delay into apprenticeship. The Japanese concept *shokunin*—craftsman as moral calling—captures it precisely: excellence as gratitude. A potter kneads clay until thought disappears, honoring ancestors through precision. Each imperfection becomes instruction.

In crises, mastery protects sanity because it provides continuity. A violin maker in Cremona shaping maple today follows a pattern four centuries old. A regenerative farmer tracking soil microbes joins a lineage of caretakers stretching to prehistory. Time compresses; identity stabilizes. The self that masters something, anything, reclaims authorship over experience.

III ·

The Neurology of Hope

Brain imaging shows that flow increases the density of white-matter tracts between attention, motivation, and emotion centers. Translation: repeated immersion rewires despair into capability. The more often a person enters flow, the more readily the brain shifts from helplessness to engagement. Even brief sessions—twenty minutes of repair, an hour of writing—leave chemical traces that counter learned helplessness.

Veterans in trauma programs who learn woodworking report 40 percent reductions in intrusive thoughts within three months. Depression scores fall not from talk but from touch—the tactile certainty of shaping matter. Each planed surface, each fitted joint, tells the limbic system: you still influence reality. That awareness is the opposite of collapse.

IV ·

Community Flow

Individual mastery matures into collective flow. Jazz ensembles, maker workshops, farming cooperatives—all achieve synchrony greater than their parts. Group flow demands trust and attention: eye contact, shared rhythm, sensitivity to others' signals. When achieved, language shortens, efficiency rises, and emotion synchronizes. Soldiers feel it in coordinated motion, surgeons in operating theaters, dancers in choreography. The same chemistry that knits neurons together can knit societies.

Harlem's jam sessions were neuro-civic laboratories. No hierarchy, no script, just listening until pattern emerged. Modern analogues thrive in hackathons, permaculture builds, disaster-relief crews. In each, collective absorption overrides fear. Collapse becomes choreography.

V.

The Builder's Mindset

To cultivate flow intentionally, psychologists suggest small rituals:

— Designate a space sacred to creation, however humble.
— Begin at the same hour each day to train anticipation.
— Remove metrics for the first hour; let curiosity, not comparison, steer.
— End with reflection: what worked, what resisted, what might evolve tomorrow.

Over weeks, these repetitions generate competence, competence breeds confidence, confidence births meaning. Purpose is not discovered but assembled—layer by layer like lacquer on wood. This is what the Harlem poets and modern makers share: an understanding that art and agriculture, coding and carpentry, are spiritual disciplines masquerading as labor.

VI.

The Antidote to Digital Despair

The modern mind lives in perpetual partial attention, its focus auctioned to algorithms. Flow reclaims attention as property. It demands slowness in a culture of speed. Neuroscientists now measure attention restoration in nature walks and manual crafts: fifteen minutes of gardening restores as much prefrontal capacity as an hour of rest. Meaning is metabolic; attention is its currency.

The dopamine loops of social media mimic flow but lack completion; they spike anticipation without resolution. Builders reverse the loop: exertion followed by tangible result, closure embedded in creation. Each finished task is a proof of existence. No feed provides that.

VII ·

From Therapy to Theology

Every culture that survived catastrophe sanctified craft. The Benedictine monks called labor *ora et labora*—work as prayer. Yoruba blacksmiths considered ironwork a dialogue with gods. Navajo weavers left one thread unfinished so that spirit could enter. Mastery became metaphysics: to align hand, mind, and matter was to align with creation itself. Flow is simply the scientific vocabulary for that ancient intuition.

In this light, despair is not a moral failure but a neurological imbalance—too much observation, too little participation. The cure is not more information but more incarnation. Touch what exists. Shape it until it answers.

VIII ·

Transmission

In a dim workshop, a woman sands a plank of walnut. The radio hums softly; dust floats in sunlight. For a moment the world's noise recedes. Grain by grain, the surface gleams beneath her fingers. She doesn't smile, yet something inside her steadies. Outside, the headlines scroll; inside, coherence returns. The board is smooth now, and so is her breath.

Key 34 · Mythic Resonance: Hephaestus and the Fire of Creation

Every civilization imagines a god of fire.

Some fear him, some revere him, but all understand that creation begins in heat.

In the Greek imagination, that force wore the face of Hephaestus — lame, soot-streaked, and indispensable. While Zeus ruled the sky and Poseidon commanded the sea, Hephaestus worked in the shadows beneath Olympus, forging the tools that made their power visible. His hammer shaped both thunderbolts and chains. His workshop was not temple but furnace.

Where the other gods spoke law, Hephaestus embodied process. He did not decree; he transformed.

And that difference matters, because the future will belong not to those who command but to those who build.

I ·

The Exile of the Maker

Hephaestus was thrown from heaven twice.

Once for defending his mother, Hera, once for daring to create without permission.

He landed in the sea, broken-legged, rescued by Thetis — the same goddess who would later birth Achilles. From that moment, he walked with a limp: the universe's reminder that creation carries injury.

But exile gave him perspective.

While the perfect gods debated order, Hephaestus learned resilience. He built his forge inside volcanic rock, the literal underworld of transformation. He gathered the discarded, melted the useless, reshaped the failed. In mythic language, he is the archetype of post-collapse civilization — the builder who turns ruin into resource.

His lameness is not flaw; it is proof of experience. The world's future architects will bear the same mark — not untouched, not immaculate, but refined by heat.

II ·

The Fire Beneath the World

Ancient poets described Hephaestus's forge as the heartbeat of the planet.

When mountains trembled, mortals said he was working.

To the Greeks, that was not superstition; it was cosmology. The earth itself depended on the labor of an unseen craftsman converting chaos into cosmos.

In every era, societies externalize this myth into technology. The Industrial Revolution was humanity's modern forge, turning coal into motion, ore into empire. But it also replicated the blindness of Olympus — worshipping power while scorning the worker. The true heirs of Hephaestus are not CEOs or engineers; they are those who reforge meaning from debris.

A regenerative farmer, a jazz musician, a maker soldering circuits in Nairobi — all are smiths at invisible anvils, working the molten edge between collapse and renewal.

Creation always begins underground, uncelebrated and unbearably hot.

III ·

The Marriage of Craft and Love

Hephaestus married Aphrodite, the goddess of beauty, and the union was a disaster in gossip but a triumph in symbolism.

Love without craft is indulgence; craft without love is tyranny.

Their marriage reminds builders that every act of creation must balance utility with grace. The Renaissance rediscovered this union when art and engineering merged in the hands of da Vinci — the modern echo of Hephaestus marrying Aphrodite again through geometry and aesthetics.

Psychologically, the story encodes integration: the masculine principle of order meeting the feminine principle of allure. To forge is not merely to assemble but to harmonize. The smith's fire softens metal; beauty softens the builder.

IV ·

The Invisible Artisans

In the *Iliad*, when Achilles receives his new armor from Hephaestus, the poet spends fifty lines describing the shield.

It depicts cities, oceans, seasons, festivals, war — a miniature cosmos. The detail is the point: creation is holy when it reflects the world it serves.

Every artisan today stands in that lineage.

The mechanic restoring an old engine, the coder writing open-source software, the mother cooking with care after a day's exhaustion — all build worlds that function because they mirror understanding.

Hephaestus never led armies or issued decrees. Yet without his forge, Zeus's thunderbolts would have remained imagination. Creation, not command, is civilization's spine.

V.

The Fire Within

In Jungian psychology, Hephaestus represents the archetype of sublimation — transforming pain into productivity. The forge is the psyche's furnace.

Depression, humiliation, rejection — these are the ores of the inner world. Unworked, they poison; heated, they illuminate.

Modern builders experience the same alchemy. The artist who channels grief into sculpture, the survivor who invents a tool to prevent others' suffering — both enact the myth in real time. The forge burns not to destroy but to purify.

Heat is information; endurance is intelligence.

Hephaestus teaches that the soul's worth lies in its ability to bear temperature without losing shape.

VI.

The Guild of Fire

In medieval Europe, blacksmiths were half feared, half revered. They were exempt from certain taxes and bound by secret oaths. Sparks were believed to contain spirits; the ring of hammer on anvil warded off evil. Every village revolved around a forge. When plague or famine struck, the smith repaired what could be repaired, melted what was ruined, and remade the tools of survival. The forge was both temple and laboratory.

Today, that role migrates to workshops, community labs, digital studios. The hum of 3-D printers and the clang of metal are echoes of the same liturgy: transformation through repetition. Each spark a prayer, each line of code a hymn.

Hephaestus has many hands now, scattered across continents, all anonymous.

VII ·

The Builder's Wound

The archetype also warns.

Hephaestus, humiliated by his peers, built traps to capture them. He forged golden thrones that bound the sitter, nets that ensnared adulterers. The lesson: creation without empathy becomes revenge. Every innovator risks this — the seduction of control through craft.

Technology can heal or humiliate, depending on the heart that guides it.

To build the new world, the builder must temper mastery with mercy.

Every hammer blow should echo a question: *Does this liberate or enchain?*

VIII ·

The Modern Forge

In 2025, the earth's literal core burns at 5,500 degrees Celsius — a permanent reminder that the world endures because fire never sleeps. Humanity's outer systems may flicker, but within, the same molten persistence continues.

That is Hephaestus: the element that refuses entropy.

Regenerative farms, repair cultures, and makerspaces are micro-forges where this cosmic heat translates into civic action. Their sparks may look small, but they carry the same energy that keeps continents alive. Each hammer strike of creation—be it seed planted, circuit soldered, or story written—is the planet remembering itself.

IX·

The Hand and the Flame

There's an ancient belief that Hephaestus's apprentices were automata—metal beings animated by divine breath. In mythic logic, they were precursors of machines, proof that the divine resides in design.

But the secret is simpler: the moment a human shapes matter with intent, something living enters the object. A chair built with care outlasts a factory product because attention has frequency. Meaning binds atoms more tightly than glue.

To build with purpose is to bless with presence.

X·

Transmission

A forge at twilight. Sparks fall like constellations across stone. A figure leans over the anvil, sweat running through soot, face lit from below by the orange pulse of molten iron. Outside, the city sleeps, unaware that its future is being tempered in silence. The hammer rises again. The air trembles. Each strike is a heartbeat. Each heartbeat says the same word: *Build.*

Key 35 · Sovereignty Protocol: The Skill Tree Map — Ten Timeless Crafts That Rebuild Civilizations

When the music fades and the myths cool, every renaissance still depends on hands.

Empires collapse in speeches; they are rebuilt in workshops.

The future will not belong to ideologues but to the competent—those who can repair, cultivate, construct, teach, and compose coherence from raw material.

This is the **Skill Tree**, the civic DNA of renewal.

I ·

The Logic of Skill

A skill is sovereignty translated into muscle memory.

It cannot be censored, confiscated, or defaulted.

Money may vanish, institutions may crumble, but knowledge embedded in nerve endings travels intact.

A mason in ancient Egypt, a weaver in Benin, a coder in Lagos share the same grammar: deliberate practice yielding autonomy.

Psychologists call it procedural memory; civilizations call it survival.

The tree grows in four roots—food, shelter, energy, and meaning—and ten branches that cover every layer of renewal.

Master one deeply, understand three broadly, and you become civilization-proof.

The Ten Branches of Builder Sovereignty

1. Food Alchemy — Soil to Sustenance

Learn to feed ten people from one plot.

Compost, seed-save, ferment.

Food is politics rendered edible.

A person who can grow calories from waste becomes an economy unto themselves.

In psychological terms, gardening re-links action with outcome; serotonin levels rise, anxiety falls.

The body learns that effort still matters.

2. Water and Energy — The Right to Light

Rain capture, filtration, small-scale solar.

Energy independence begins with modest wattage: one panel, one pump, one light that works when the grid fails.

Each watt produced locally reduces geopolitical dependence by a fraction.

Every builder of the new world is, by definition, a micro-utility.

3. Shelter Craft — Structure as Integrity

Carpentry, masonry, design that breathes.

A house built with your own hands becomes a psychological fortress; maintenance becomes meditation.

Relearn proportion, airflow, joinery.

Vernacular architecture outlives real-estate bubbles because it obeys climate, not fashion.

4. Fabric and Fiber — The Weaver's Revolution

Textiles shaped civilization before metal.

To spin, knit, or stitch is to assert continuity.

Each thread counters disposability.

Communities that regain textile autonomy reduce global shipping emissions and reclaim aesthetic identity.

Weaving circles are ancient social networks—therapy disguised as craft.

5. Metal and Machine — The Forge Renewed

From bicycle repair to 3-D-printed prosthetics, metalwork restores feedback between idea and matter.

Every community needs at least one smith—the person who keeps motion alive.

In crisis, the ability to fabricate or fix determines the speed of recovery.

Noise of hammer on anvil: the sound of hope made tangible.

6. Code and Circuit — The Digital Hammer

Coding is today's carpentry.

Open-source literacy equals political agency.

A citizen who can audit an algorithm resists manipulation.

Learn to script, to solder, to protect data.

Software is simply logic expressed through electrons; the wise builder writes logic aligned with ethics.

7. Medicine and Maintenance — Healing as Infrastructure

Basic first aid, herbal knowledge, water sanitation.

Health systems collapse first and rebuild last.

Every household trained in care shortens catastrophe.

To know how to stop bleeding or grow antiseptic herbs is to possess civilization's first obligation: compassion operationalized.

8. Story and Symbol — The Cultural Forge

A civilization without storytellers forgets why it should continue.

Writing, music, visual art, ritual—all are pattern languages of identity.

Record local history, teach myth, compose songs.

When empire noise fades, story keeps coordinates of meaning.

Every builder must also be a bard.

9. Teaching and Transmission — The Replicators

Skill that is not shared dies in one generation.

Educate horizontally: peer-to-peer, apprentice-to-master, child-to-elder.

Learning accelerates when curiosity replaces hierarchy.

Every builder should maintain an open notebook—a visible record of process.

Transparency becomes lineage.

10. Finance and Stewardship — The Ethic of Enough

Understand money as stored intention.

Use community currencies, mutual credit, cooperatives.

Keep ledgers simple, visible, honest.

Measure wealth by resilience: how many days can your circle endure without outside supply?

That metric is the real GDP of the future.

II ·

The Ladder of Mastery

Each branch has four rungs: **Curiosity → Competence → Contribution → Teaching.**

A society ascends when its members climb together.

Curiosity keeps humility; teaching completes the circuit.

Track progress monthly: one new skill explored, one mastered, one passed on.

The data of renewal is apprenticeship multiplied.

III ·

The Ritual of Hands

Set aside an hour each day for tangible creation.

Schedule it like prayer.

Phone off, hands on.

The nervous system, once trained to finish, recalibrates the mind toward optimism.

Anthropologists note that cultures with daily manual rituals—kneading dough, carving, weaving—exhibit higher resilience indices during upheaval.

Creation is cognition.

IV.

The Commons Ledger

Form local guilds: ten people, ten skills, mutual obligation.

List assets—tools, seeds, knowledge—and share.

Digitize later; begin on paper pinned to a wall.

When crises come, the list becomes lifeline.

Trust grows by visible reciprocity.

V.

The Moral Clause

Skill divorced from ethic re-creates empire.

Every craft carries a vow: to repair more than one destroys, to teach without hoarding, to balance mastery with mercy.

Write that clause at the top of your workshop wall.

The line between creator and exploiter is intention.

VI ·

The Temporal View

Measure progress not by speed but by depth.

Ancient cathedrals took centuries; a loaf of sourdough takes a day—both obey patience.

Builders of the new world think in cycles, not quarters.

A good tool lasts thirty years; a good custom lasts generations.

VII ·

The Neural Dividend

Skill learning increases brain-derived neurotrophic factor—the molecule of resilience.

Every mastered motion strengthens cognition against decay.

Civilizations that teach crafts extend collective intelligence.

The hand educates the brain; the brain informs the hand.

Feedback between the two is consciousness in practice.

VIII ·

Building Your Tree

1. Draw a trunk on paper.
2. Label the ten branches.
3. Circle one branch that calls you this year.
4. Map weekly steps from novice to mentor.

5. Record one sentence of reflection each Sunday.
6. Within ninety days, patterns emerge: capability replacing anxiety, rhythm replacing distraction.
7. This becomes your personal Sovereignty Dashboard—the operating system of independence.

IX.

The Community Threshold

Invite neighbors.

Teach one workshop a month.

Trade service for service—plumbing for tutoring, web design for vegetables.

Within months, the neighborhood becomes micro-civilization.

Economists call it import substitution; elders call it taking care of each other.

Both mean the same thing: freedom localized.

X.

Transmission

Twilight settles over a town square.

A circle of lamps glows inside an old warehouse where people work—hands moving, voices low, laughter rising like sparks.

A teenager planes a piece of oak while her grandmother threads a loom.

Outside, wind rattles empty billboards that once sold distraction.

Inside, the hum of creation continues, steady as breath.

Civilization is back on its feet, not with fanfare but with practice.

Chapter 8

The Economy of Integrity

Part III - The Builders

Key 36 · Historical Mirror · Post-WWII Japan and the Reconstruction of Quality

When Tokyo burned in March 1945, the firestorm erased forty square miles and a million homes. From the ashes of that furnace, Japan faced an emptiness deeper than defeat—a nation without tools, factories, or faith in its own hands. The miracle that followed was not luck, not aid, not even policy. It was a moral decision: to rebuild value through integrity instead of abundance.

I.

The Zero Point

In the first winter after surrender, steel was rationed, paper scarce, and hunger chronic. Families dismantled rail tracks for scrap; children lined up for American cornmeal. Yet in the small town of Ueda, a textile technician named Toyoda Kiichiro wrote a single sentence to his staff: *"Build the loom as if your family will depend on it for a hundred years."* That sentence became the germ of Toyota's production philosophy.

Across the islands, similar awakenings flared. Potters in Mashiko repaired kilns with broken bricks; carpenters reused the nails of burned houses; seamstresses unstitched worn garments to study their geometry. Every gesture carried the same vow: if we cannot be rich, we will be precise. The catastrophe stripped away decoration until only discipline remained.

II ·

The Birth of Kaizen

When American statistician W. Edwards Deming arrived in 1950 to lecture on quality control, he expected bureaucracy. Instead, he found hunger for purpose. Factories still roofless took notes by lantern light. Deming's central message—that workers closest to the process hold the knowledge of improvement—fell on soil already prepared by centuries of craft humility.

The Japanese called it *kaizen*: continuous, participatory refinement. Unlike Western efficiency, which measures output, *kaizen* measures conscience. A worker who notices a defect and stops the line honors the group more than one who hides it. Integrity became productivity. By 1960, Toyota's *andon* cord—the right of any employee to halt production—was spiritual engineering: an industrial translation of the samurai code.

Kaizen was less technique than theology: excellence achieved through honesty.

III ·

The Moral Aesthetics of Monozukuri

The term *monozukuri* means "the art of making things," but its kanji roots imply devotion—*mono* (thing) plus *zukuri* (to give birth). Every object is a moral event. When a craftsman polishes steel for an unseen surface, he testifies that virtue does not depend on witness. This ethic resurrected national dignity more effectively than propaganda.

In 1955, a journalist visiting a Hitachi radio plant asked why workers bowed to machines before shifts. The foreman replied, "We greet the tools that allow us to feed our children." Respect for the instrument produced respect for the outcome. Faults fell, exports rose, but the deeper change was metaphysical: work regained sanctity.

Within twenty years, "Made in Japan" transformed from warning label to global guarantee. Yet the true product was not cars or electronics—it was trust.

IV·

The Invisible Guild

This moral economy required structure. Networks of small suppliers, many family-run, formed vertical guilds around larger firms. Loyalty replaced contract; mastery replaced margin. When a part failed, the supplier's shame outweighed financial loss. Engineers spoke of *gemba*—the actual place where value is created—and managers were expected to stand there daily. The executive's presence among workers dissolved hierarchy into mentorship.

Such systems contradict modern abstraction. They depend on proximity, patience, and repetition—three virtues algorithmic capitalism erodes. Yet during Japan's postwar ascent, they generated compound integrity: quality became self-enforcing.

V·

The Aesthetics of Restraint

Consumer desire in the 1960s exploded worldwide, but Japanese designers practiced minimalism born of scarcity. The transistor radio, the bullet train, the Walkman—all compact, elegant, efficient. Their grace came from constraint. The West pursued scale; Japan pursued silence between forms. The result was beauty without waste.

This discipline extended beyond design into finance. Lifetime employment, mutual obligation, and modest executive pay created stability through self-limitation. Critics later called it rigidity; for a generation, it was civilization's backbone.

VI ·

Integrity as National Strategy

By 1980, observers called it the "Japanese miracle." Yet the miracle was moral arithmetic: cumulative honesty multiplied by time. Nations measure power by GDP, but cohesion is a stronger metric. The industrial sociologist Robert Bellah wrote that Japan's success stemmed from a "functional equivalent of religion"—a civic faith that sincerity in small acts supports cosmic order. A rivet placed true becomes a prayer.

When competitors imitated Japan's methods without its ethos, the results faltered. Tools transfer easily; integrity does not. Copying efficiency without conscience is counterfeit progress.

VII ·

The Cracks in Perfection

No resurrection is pure. By the 1990s, the same discipline hardened into inflexibility. Salarymen collapsed from overwork; innovation slowed under conformity's weight. The lesson is cyclical: integrity must evolve, not fossilize. The builder's creed requires self-correction as much as precision. A system too proud to change forgets the humility that birthed it.

VIII ·

The Universal Pattern

Across history, every durable culture converges on this equation:

Integrity → Quality → Trust → Prosperity.

Break any link and the chain rusts.

Athens lost it through hubris, Rome through luxury, Weimar through deceit. Japan restored it through accuracy. The sequence holds because it mirrors human psychology: trust reduces transaction cost, freeing energy for creation.

A civilization that prizes honesty in the smallest motions generates abundance as a side effect. The next civilization will need this law more than technology.

IX ·

Transmission

Dawn over Yokohama Bay. A worker in a spotless uniform checks a single screw on an assembly line before the siren sounds. Outside, cherry blossoms drift against factory windows. He inhales, adjusts the torque by a fraction, nods once. The gesture takes three seconds and seventy years of history. The city wakes to the quiet rhythm of integrity reinventing wealth.

Key 37 · Modern Parallel - Circular Economies, Bitcoin, and the Return of Censorship-Resistant Value

In 2008 the world's monetary architecture cracked. Banks froze, currencies wavered, and confidence—the invisible glue of civilization—evaporated. Out of that silence appeared a nine-page document signed only Satoshi Nakamoto. Its promise was simple: a system of value without trust in authority. Behind the mathematics hid a moral question older than money itself—how do you preserve integrity when institutions no longer deserve it?

I ·

The Genesis of Resistance

Bitcoin's first block carried a message from The Times of London:

"Chancellor on brink of second bailout for banks."

That headline was the scar on its birth certificate. The code embedded it forever, a digital monument to betrayal. Each coin mined afterward became a fragment of protest forged into math. Yet the brilliance of Satoshi's design was not technology but ethics: transparency through code, scarcity through discipline, consensus through voluntary verification.

It was the first currency to turn honesty into protocol. No priest, no president, no central banker—only cryptographic proof. Integrity rendered executable.

II ·

The Moral Physics of Hard Value

Throughout history, civilizations have collapsed when their mediums of exchange detached from truth. Roman silver was diluted; Weimar paper multiplied; 21st-century credit inflated beyond comprehension. Each era rediscovered the same law: value depends on verifiable limits.

Bitcoin reinstated that law by binding economics to thermodynamics. Every coin requires energy, every transaction requires consensus. Wasteful? Only to those who forget that entropy is the price of order. In a universe ruled by scarcity, proof-of-work is proof-of-reality.

To critics it was code; to believers it was covenant—a social contract without signatures, enforced by physics itself.

III ·

The Circular Counter-Current

While digital scarcity spread online, another revolution took root in the soil: the rise of circular economies. From Amsterdam's De Ceuvel district to Costa Rica's regenerative zones, designers began closing loops that industrial modernity had left open. Waste became input, output became nourishment. In 2022, the Ellen MacArthur Foundation estimated global circular initiatives could cut resource use by 39 percent and create 4.5 trillion USD in net benefit by 2030.

Yet beneath the metrics lies morality. Circular design re-centers responsibility. When a company owns its materials for a product's entire life, it must build for repair instead of disposal. Integrity migrates from slogans to supply chains. The economy turns monastic—nothing wasted, everything redeemed.

IV.

From Transparency to Traceability

Blockchain's core idea—distributed verification—now extends into material production. Coffee beans, diamonds, vaccines, and carbon credits travel with digital fingerprints. This is not surveillance; it is confession. Every transaction recorded is a statement of conscience: this came from here, this caused this, this can be trusted.

For centuries, merchants required reputation; now they require data with the same purity. When traced supply chains meet circular design, an ancient virtue returns—accountability visible to all participants. The marketplace becomes moral space.

V.

The Shadow and the Light

Integrity attracts corruption like light attracts moths. Speculation, fraud, and excess energy consumption followed Bitcoin's rise, echoing Japan's later rigidity. The corrective will not come from prohibition but from evolution: systems that pair cryptographic honesty with ecological humility.

Projects like Chia's proof-of-space, Ethereum's proof-of-stake, and community micro-grids link energy generation to digital value. They hint at a new synthesis: the Economy of Integrity 2.0, where each watt spent yields both currency and carbon accountability. The forge and the garden finally share current.

VI ·

The Psychology of Ownership

Behavioral research from Cambridge shows that holders of decentralized assets display higher long-term planning scores than average investors. To self-custody wealth requires patience, literacy, and self-discipline—the very traits eroded by instant credit. Circular producers report similar mental patterns: satisfaction derived from maintenance rather than consumption. Both groups rebuild temporal perspective, the missing dimension of collapsed cultures.

Integrity, it turns out, rewires time perception. When value depends on stewardship, the mind extends its horizon.

VII ·

Local Ledgers and Micro-Commons

In Detroit, a neighborhood co-op runs its own token to reward recycling; in Kenya, solar villages exchange energy credits through mobile wallets; in Barcelona, the Rec currency circulates among small businesses to keep money local. Each experiment shrinks distance between effort and reward. Trust returns not through ideology but through participation.

This is civic money: designed to strengthen reciprocity rather than speculation. Where national currencies inflate abstraction, local tokens embed context. A transaction becomes a handshake with memory.

VIII ·

The New Merchant Ethic

Medieval trade once relied on oaths sworn before gods; the modern builder swears before code and community. Both demand the same principle: do not falsify measure. Whether measuring gold, kilowatts, or data, precision is piety.

Corporate cultures adopting this ethic now publish open ledgers of emissions, wages, and waste. Integrity becomes competitive advantage. Patagonia's lifetime repair policy, Fairphone's modular design, and Bitcoin's immutable record are facets of one renaissance: honesty rediscovered as profitability.

IX ·

The Circle and the Chain

The circular economy's loops and the blockchain's chains seem opposites—organic versus digital—but together they describe the full geometry of renewal. The circle ensures continuity; the chain ensures memory. Combine them and you get civilization's new nervous system: transparent, regenerative, antifragile.

It is the same pattern that Japan embodied through kaizen—incremental improvement through visible process. Only the medium changed from assembly lines to algorithms.

X ·

Transmission

A hydro-powered data center hums beside a valley of terraced rice fields. One produces encrypted blocks, the other harvests grain; both run on the same sunlight refracted through time. In a nearby workshop, a teenager repairs a smartphone using parts ordered with digital currency earned from composting waste. The circuit closes—the planet's metabolism and its money share rhythm again.

No anthem, no leader, just systems quietly telling the truth.

Key 38 · Psychological Mechanism: Integrity Over Expedience — Identity-Based Habits and the Inner Economy of Trust

Civilizations do not corrode all at once; they corrode in micro-choices.

Every shortcut taken under pressure—every quiet compromise—becomes a small defection from truth. Integrity, whether national or personal, is the compound interest of thousands of kept promises. Once that rate turns negative, collapse is not dramatic; it is incremental.

I ·

The Currency Within

Psychologists call it self-signaling: the brain watches its own actions to decide who we are.

Each time a person honors a small obligation—pays a bill on time, keeps a secret, finishes a repair—the nervous system updates its internal ledger: trustworthy. Each evasion writes the opposite entry: fragile.

Over years, those entries determine resilience far more than income or IQ.

Martin Seligman's early work on learned helplessness showed that people lose motivation when outcomes feel disconnected from effort. Integrity reconnects them. When cause and effect are visible, agency returns. The habit of honesty is therefore not moral decoration but cognitive architecture: it restores coherence between act and result, which is the foundation of sanity.

II ·

The Dopamine Loop of Expedience

Modern economies engineer the opposite loop. Instant rewards—notifications, debt-fuelled consumption, algorithmic validation—teach the brain that gratification precedes effort. The prefrontal cortex, responsible for planning and inhibition, weakens under such conditions; impulse becomes policy.

Neuroscientists at the University of Hamburg (2020) found that chronic multitaskers exhibit reduced gray-matter density in the anterior cingulate cortex, the region linked to error detection. A society built on distraction thus loses its neurological ability to notice deviation. Expedience becomes invisible, which is why integrity must now be trained deliberately, as a muscle once taken for granted.

III ·

Identity as Behavior, Not Belief

James Clear's behavioral research reframed habit change through a single insight: "Every action is a vote for the type of person you wish to become."

Identity, then, is not declared; it is accumulated. The Japanese engineers of kaizen knew this long before psychology quantified it: repetition engraves character.

When Toyota standardized the practice of pausing the assembly line to correct errors, it institutionalized humility. Workers learned that stopping for truth costs less than proceeding in illusion. The same applies internally. Integrity is the act of stopping the line within oneself—of halting momentum to verify alignment between value and behavior.

IV.

Cognitive Dissonance and the Moral Budget

Leon Festinger's 1957 studies on cognitive dissonance revealed that humans experience measurable stress when behavior conflicts with belief. We resolve it either by changing behavior or rewriting belief. In times of decline, entire societies choose the latter: they rationalize.

We tell ourselves that corruption is necessary, that small lies are survival, that everyone cheats. But dissonance, like debt, accrues interest. The longer it compounds, the harsher the eventual correction.

Integrity interrupts this inflation of self-deception. To admit error is to default early—to clear the moral balance sheet before collapse. That act, repeated collectively, is how nations reform before failure.

V.

The Neuroeconomics of Trust

Functional MRI studies from Zurich's Laboratory for Social and Neural Systems Research show that trust activates the same dopaminergic reward circuits as monetary gain. Betrayal, conversely, lights up the anterior insula—the region associated with disgust. Our biology therefore encodes morality as homeostasis: cooperation feels right because it stabilizes internal chemistry.

This discovery reframes ethics as energy management. Lies cost more ATP than truth because they require cognitive suppression, memory load, and emotional monitoring. Honesty is literally metabolically cheaper. Integrity conserves glucose; deceit burns it. In energetic terms, virtue is efficiency.

VI ·

Cultural Myopia and the Short Game

Economist Ernst Fehr demonstrated that societies with higher long-term orientation scores—measured by the willingness to sacrifice immediate gain for future stability—show greater GDP per capita and lower corruption indices. Integrity, scaled, becomes competitiveness.

Yet post-industrial culture trains myopia: quarterly profits, election cycles, algorithmic engagement. Expedience is rewarded publicly even as it corrodes privately.

When Japan's craftspeople refused to outsource precision to cheaper regions, they preserved not only jobs but identity. When a modern corporation ignores that lesson for a transient stock price bump, it mortgages its soul for liquidity. The invisible loss is culture's credit rating.

VII ·

Shame Versus Guilt: Two Moral Engines

Anthropologists divide moral regulation into shame cultures and guilt cultures.

In shame systems (e.g., classical Japan), behavior is governed by external perception; in guilt systems (e.g., post-Reformation Europe), by internal conscience. The healthiest societies synthesize both—public transparency reinforcing private accountability.

Digital life, however, distorts this balance: it amplifies shame while eroding guilt. Viral outrage replaces reflection; performance substitutes repentance. To rebuild integrity we must invert the dynamic—quiet self-correction over public spectacle. The moral revolution will be private or it will not last.

VIII ·

The Integrity Threshold Effect

Psychologists studying organizational behavior at Harvard (2021) found that once corruption passes roughly 15 percent of visible transactions, the perception of honesty collapses system-wide. People stop reporting misconduct because they believe "everyone does it." Restoring integrity then requires symbolic resets—public audits, leadership purges, truth commissions.

For individuals, the same threshold exists at smaller scale. Once daily self-betrayals exceed a certain density—missed commitments, broken routines—the identity ledger flips from credit to deficit. Recovery demands not punishment but ritual: one consistent act of honesty repeated until trust resumes compound growth.

Integrity, therefore, has a tipping point, just like liquidity. It evaporates slowly, returns suddenly.

IX ·

The Mirror Exercise

A simple discipline emerged from behavioral therapy and Stoic journaling alike: before sleep, replay the day backward and note where action diverged from intention. No judgment—only ledger entry. Over weeks the mind begins to anticipate the audit and self-correct in real time. This is identity-based budgeting: attention as accounting.

When practiced collectively—families, teams, even small communities—the mirror exercise becomes civic infrastructure. Shared reflection replaces surveillance. A society that can admit error nightly never reaches collapse; it recalibrates daily.

X ·

Integrity as Freedom

Expedience feels like liberty but functions as dependence. The liar depends on forgetfulness; the addict on supply; the fraud on opacity. Honesty, by contrast, severs those cords. Viktor Frankl wrote that freedom is not from conditions but from responses. Integrity is that inner margin of choice expanded through practice.

To live without deceit is to reduce uncertainty. To reduce uncertainty is to reduce fear. The most radical freedom left in a surveilled world is to need no disguise.

XI ·

The Feedback of Virtue

Jonathan Haidt's concept of "moral elevation" describes the physiological warmth people feel when witnessing acts of integrity. The emotion triggers oxytocin release, increasing trust and cooperation among observers. Virtue, then, spreads epidemiologically. Each honest act is a broadcast signal that recalibrates others' expectations upward.

In decayed cultures where cynicism reigns, such signals are antiviral. They rebuild the moral immune system, one honest transaction at a time.

XII ·

Transmission

A craftsman locks his workshop after midnight. On the bench lies a watch he could have sold hours earlier had he ignored the microscopic flaw no one would see. He chose correction over convenience. The city outside sleeps in artificial glow; his lamp burns with an older light—the kind that powered civilizations before currency existed.

He smiles, knowing no algorithm can counterfeit the feeling of work aligned with worth.

That is integrity's dividend: peace without permission.

Key 39 · Mythic Resonance: The Reversal of Midas — Value Through Restraint

Gold gleams brightest before it blinds.

Every empire learns this too late.

The Greeks told it as warning, not wonder: the tale of a king who mistook abundance for divinity and turned his own daughter into metal.

I ·

The Gift That Devoured

In the oldest version of the story, Midas is no villain. He is generous, cultured, a patron of Dionysus' musicians. When the god grants him one wish, Midas asks for the power to turn all he touches into gold. At first the palace fills with laughter; even the roses glitter. Then hunger comes. Bread becomes metal, wine solidifies, love freezes mid-embrace. What began as mastery over matter becomes exile from life.

The moral was never greed alone; it was *instrumental blindness*—the inability to distinguish means from ends. Money was invented as a tool for exchange, yet when a tool becomes the measure of all value, it reverses purpose. Midas was not punished; he was granted the logical conclusion of his own desire.

II ·

The Economic Mirror

The twentieth century replayed the myth with spreadsheets instead of scrolls. Nations learned to measure success by GDP, not well-being;

corporations by quarterly profit, not durability. In 2008, the global financial system froze for the same reason Midas starved: liquidity without nourishment. Derivatives multiplied like golden dust, detaching wealth from work until the system could no longer taste reality.

Historians will say it was leverage; psychologists will say it was denial; poets will say it was the old curse wearing a tie. Every chart since has confirmed what the myth predicted: excess turns to entropy when unmoored from meaning.

III ·

The God of Boundaries

In later retellings, Dionysus tells the repentant king to wash in the river Pactolus. When Midas does, the gold flows from his body into the water, birthing Anatolia's first gold-bearing sands. The curse becomes resource. The key is *release*—letting value flow again.

Restraint, therefore, is not deprivation; it is re-entry into circulation. Economists call it the velocity of money; mystics call it right relation. Systems—biological, financial, or ecological—remain alive only when exchange exceeds accumulation. The hoarded becomes the haunted.

IV ·

The Alchemy of Enough

The Stoics taught *metriotes*—the art of the sufficient. Epictetus, born a slave, owned nothing yet claimed complete freedom: "He is rich who limits his desires." In modern behavioral terms, this is hedonic calibration. Neuroimaging studies show that satisfaction peaks not at abundance but at the moment of proportional fit between effort and reward. Beyond that, dopamine levels drop, attention diffuses, and boredom returns.

Midas' touch was therefore not reward but overstimulation—a neurological short circuit. His salvation required a reset of sensory thresholds, exactly what fasting, silence, and voluntary simplicity achieve for the modern psyche. Each practice lowers stimulus to recover sensitivity, converting restraint into pleasure.

V.

The Ecology of Restraint

Ecologists describe carrying capacity—the limit beyond which ecosystems collapse. Civilizations ignore it by externalizing cost. Yet the biosphere enforces accounting. Carbon, plastic, debt: all are forms of delayed recognition. The Anthropocene is Midas at planetary scale—oceans glittering with the refuse of prosperity.

But reversal is still possible. When Iceland's bankers triggered their country's bankruptcy in 2008, the citizens refused bailouts and rewrote the constitution by assembly. They washed their economy in their own Pactolus. Similarly, Bhutan's choice to measure *Gross National Happiness* over GDP was not naivety but mythic literacy—the understanding that enough is the threshold of sacred.

VI.

The Inner River

Every person carries a Pactolus within: the capacity to transmute excess back into flow. It begins with audit. What in my life has turned to gold but no longer nourishes me? Which habits glitter but numb? Each identified and released restores motion.

Buddhist psychology names this *non-attachment*, but it is closer to *right possession*: holding without clutching. In neuro-behavioral terms it rewires reward circuits from craving to appreciation. The paradox holds—only what we can release do we truly own.

VII ·

The Craftsman's Paradox

Contrast Midas with Hephaestus, the divine smith. Both work with metal, but Hephaestus tempers fire through patience. Every hammer stroke is restraint in motion: force paused, redirected, refined. The forge succeeds because it accepts boundary. This is the builder's wisdom: perfection requires friction; creation requires containment.

Modern creators—coders, farmers, engineers—face the same test. Speed and scale seduce, but endurance comes from rhythm. Restraint is the unseen ingredient in quality, whether in code elegance or crop rotation. The master stops one iteration before excess heat warps the whole.

VIII ·

Cultural Reversal

Japan's *wabi-sabi* aesthetic, born from Zen monks repairing cracked bowls with gold lacquer, inverted Midas entirely. Instead of turning clay to gold, they turned gold into humility. Kintsugi does not hide fracture; it glorifies repair. The imperfection becomes inheritance. Through it, value arises from continuity, not novelty—the true antidote to disposable culture.

A society practicing *kintsugi economics* would measure prosperity by the beauty of its mended systems: rivers restored, crafts revived, trust repaired. The act of mending becomes currency.

IX ·

The Modern Pactolus

Today's Pactolus is digital. Attention is the new gold, mined from consciousness. Each scroll, click, and feed prolongs the curse of endless conversion—human time into data, data into capital, capital into isolation. The antidote again is release. To log off is to wash the hands of Midas dust. To return attention to one's craft, garden, or child is the modern ritual of purification.

Neuroscientists studying mindfulness show that attention trained on single-task presence increases default-mode network efficiency by 15 percent and lowers anxiety markers. Reclaiming focus is not luxury; it is metabolic necessity.

X ·

The Covenant of Restraint

Civilization's renewal will hinge on rediscovering sacred limits: consumption capped by regeneration, technology bound by ethics, ambition yoked to stewardship. The covenant is not with gods but with time. Future generations are the unseen shareholders of every present decision. To honor them is to refuse the Midas impulse in policy form.

Economist Herman Daly called this "steady-state economics": growth measured in wisdom, not volume. The builders of the new world will recognize progress not by speed but by silence—the absence of waste, noise, and needless motion. Their wealth will be the continuity of breath between generations.

XI ·

Transmission

At sunset, the old king kneels by the river. His hands, once gilded, tremble as the current strips them clean. Gold flecks swirl downstream, catching light for a moment before sinking into silt. The water runs clearer with each passing second. On the far bank, reeds whisper the sound of tools being forged anew. The age of possession ends; the age of creation begins.

Key 40 · Sovereignty Protocol: The Household Value Stack — Defining What Cannot Be Debased

Every civilization keeps two ledgers: one for its currency, another for its conscience. When the first collapses, the second decides if the people survive or vanish. Money can be reissued; meaning cannot. The sovereignty of a household begins where its values cannot be printed, inflated, or hacked.

I.

The Inner Treasury

A family that has no shared definition of value becomes an annex of empire. Advertising, politics, and social media fill the vacuum. But when households articulate their own metrics of worth—what they will defend, what they will forgo—they re-mint civilization at the smallest scale.

The "Household Value Stack" is the counter-architecture to a collapsing market. It replaces the GDP of distraction with a personal balance sheet of integrity.

Its layers mirror the macroeconomy but invert its logic:

Layer	Conventional economy	Sovereign household
Monetary	Income and consumption	Savings and stewardship
Temporal	Scheduling by demand	Rhythm by design
Emotional	Stimulation and novelty	Presence and calm

Layer	Conventional economy	Sovereign household
Cultural	Trend adoption	Heritage and creation
Ethical	Compliance	Conscience

When the outer system debases, this inner stack appreciates.

II ·

Audit of Worth

The protocol begins with inventory. Over seven days, list every recurring expense, subscription, and dependency. Mark each as *survival, comfort,* or *signal.*

Most find that 30 percent of their spending serves only to announce identity. Cancelling these is not austerity; it is sovereignty reclamation. The freed attention becomes capital.

Next, conduct the *time audit.* Track hours as if they were currency units. How many are spent on production versus reaction? On creation versus consumption? Studies from the American Time Use Survey show that reassigning just one reactive hour daily to deliberate practice yields a 20 percent boost in life satisfaction scores over six months. Time is the true reserve asset; the rest is derivative.

III ·

Establish the Ethical Peg

Fiat currencies collapse when trust erodes; lives collapse when ethics drift. To stabilize both, you need a peg—a fixed moral standard not subject to convenience.

Write one sentence that defines it. Example: *"Our wealth is measured by what we can give without fear."*

Post it visibly. Every decision—financial, relational, vocational—must clear that exchange rate. This peg transforms abstract morality into operational policy.

IV.

Build the Reserve Assets

Resilience requires holdings that no inflation can touch:

1. **Skill Capital** – what you can do with your hands and mind independent of permission. Cook, repair, teach, grow, code, heal. Skills are inflation-proof because they appreciate with use.
2. **Social Capital** – relationships of reciprocity. A neighbor who lends tools is worth more than an interest-bearing account.
3. **Moral Capital** – reputation for reliability. In every crisis, trade routes reroute around trust; those who keep their word become the new banks.
4. **Cultural Capital** – songs, stories, rituals, recipes. These carry identity through collapse; they are the continuity layer of civilization.
5. **Physical Capital** – food, tools, shelter, health. Not hoarded but maintained.

Together they form a balanced portfolio where each asset hedges another's loss.

V.

The Family Council

Once a month, gather all members—elders, partners, children—and review the stack aloud. What did we earn? What did we erode? Let the youngest speak first. This inverts hierarchy and trains succession.

Anthropologists studying intergenerational resilience note that families who hold regular narrative councils exhibit 40 percent higher recovery rates after economic shocks. The ritual teaches continuity of meaning, not merely of property.

Record decisions in a single notebook kept beside the household altar or desk. This becomes the *Book of Worth*—a living constitution more binding than wills.

VI.

The Practice of Debasement Detection

In collapsing systems, lies enter through language. The phrase *"It's just business"* once excused slavery; *"It's just content"* now excuses manipulation. The household's defense is linguistic vigilance.

Create a glossary of integrity—five words you will never use loosely: *truth, trust, freedom, love, time*. Define them precisely and revisit yearly. Semantic clarity precedes moral clarity.

When external narratives distort these words, the glossary acts as firewall. Children raised within clear definitions of value resist propaganda naturally; their neural pathways for moral reasoning strengthen through repetition, just as muscle fibers do under steady load.

VII ·

Micro-Rituals of Preservation

Ritual converts intention into rhythm. Three daily acts preserve the value stack:

1. **The Threshold Pause** – before entering the home, stop for one breath. Leave the world's noise outside; cross the line consciously. Neurologically this resets the amygdala, reducing cortisol levels by up to 25 percent.
2. **The Table Gratitude** – one minute of silence before meals, acknowledging the chain of life behind each bite. Anthropologists trace this simple act to higher prosocial behavior and lower consumption.
3. **The Evening Reconciliation** – before sleep, settle any unresolved tension or debt within the household. Integrity resets overnight only when accounts close clean.

These habits compound. Within months, the atmosphere of a house thickens into trust—the most luxurious scent civilization ever made.

VIII ·

Reinvesting Surplus

When the basics stabilize, surplus should not seek speculation but stewardship. Direct excess energy—money, attention, knowledge—into local repair: a garden, a library shelf, a neighbor's project. Economists call this "import substitution at micro scale." Spiritually it is reciprocity.

The return on such investment is not percentage yield but participation. Each restored square meter of soil or friendship increases communal antifragility.

IX.

Transmission Protocol

Wealth that cannot be transmitted is vanity. Teach children not only what to earn but what to preserve. Replace allowance with apprenticeship: link pocket money to skill contribution. A teenager who repairs a household item or plants a tree adds measurable capital to the stack.

Record these acts in the Book of Worth as entries of lineage. The next generation thus inherits not entitlement but competence.

X.

Sovereign Metrics

To evaluate progress, replace GDP with four metrics:

1. **Integrity Index:** number of promises kept divided by promises made.
2. **Attention Dividend:** hours spent in creation divided by hours in consumption.
3. **Trust Liquidity:** number of reciprocal favors outstanding.
4. **Cultural Continuity Rate:** rituals maintained this month versus forgotten.

These metrics may seem poetic, but they quantify what the future will prize when fiat graphs fail. In the coming century, the most valuable data will not be monetary but moral.

XI ·

Transmission

At dawn a woman kneels in her kitchen, not to pray but to mend a cracked bowl. Sunlight catches the hairline seam of gold glue as coffee brews quietly behind her. Outside, the city hums with numbers she no longer fears. Her wealth sits in the calm of her breath, the warmth of her child's laughter, the repaired bowl cooling on the counter. Value, she knows now, is anything that survives the silence.

Chapter 9

The Cultural Rebirth

Part III - The Builders

Key 41 · Historical Mirror: Ireland's Post-Famine Revival · Memory as Resistance

Civilizations rarely die from hunger alone. They die when their stories starve.

Ireland in the mid-nineteenth century was both: a nation stripped of food and narrative, its language outlawed, its songs censored, its faith mocked as superstition. Yet from that void rose a quiet rebellion of words. While empires measured progress in railways and rifles, Ireland began to measure it in poems, presses, and classrooms. This is how a culture rebuilds when its fields are bones.

I ·

The Silence After the Wind

In 1847—the "Black '47" of folk memory—sailors in Cork watched ships of grain depart the harbor while emaciated families collapsed on the docks. Over a million would die; another million would sail. The famine was not only ecological; it was structural. Absentee landlords exported produce for profit even as tenants perished. Economist Amartya Sen would later call it an "entitlement failure"—food existed, but access was severed.

In that silence after the wind, when the potato rows lay black and the last Gaelic prayers faded from the parishes, something else germinated: remembrance. Survivors began to treat memory as a crop that could not be taxed. Granny tales, keening songs, and whispered proverbs became seedstock for identity's second harvest.

II ·

The Return of the Word

By the 1880s, Ireland was literate in English but starved for Irish soul. Scholars such as Douglas Hyde and Eoin Mac Neill launched the Gaelic League (*Conradh na Gaeilge*) in 1893. Its mission was not mere translation but re-enchantment—reviving a worldview encoded in syntax itself. The Irish language, with its mutable verbs and absence of possessive "have," expressed relationship rather than ownership. To restore it was to decolonize grammar.

Village halls became classrooms; emigrant letters became textbooks. Within a decade, over 600 branches sprouted across the island. Teenagers who might once have fled to Liverpool now debated etymology by candlelight. The League's motto, *Tír gan teanga, tír gan anam*—"a country without a language is a country without a soul"—was less slogan than survival algorithm.

III ·

The Theatre as Forge

Culture cannot resurrect itself in silence; it needs stage and song. In 1899, W. B. Yeats and Lady Gregory founded the Irish Literary Theatre, soon renamed the Abbey. Its plays reframed folklore as prophecy. *Cathleen ni Houlihan* presented Ireland as an old woman who transforms into a young queen when her sons sacrifice for her. Audiences wept, not from nationalism but recognition—they were seeing their hunger mythologized into purpose.

Through theatre, tragedy acquired structure; through structure, despair found dignity. The Abbey became both shrine and school for imagination, teaching that empire could be resisted not by musket but by metaphor.

IV.

Songs of the Reaper

While Dublin intellectuals debated style, the western counties kept pulse through music. The fiddle and uilleann pipes carried encoded history: each reel, a ledger of endurance. The tune "The Harvest Home" survived even in diaspora because it disguised grief as celebration. Ethnomusicologists later traced modal shifts in famine-era songs showing oscillation between major and minor keys—an audible record of resilience oscillating with loss.

Psychologists would recognize it as "emotional regulation through ritualized expression." Singing allowed trauma to breathe without speech. The body kept the rhythm that politics forbade.

V.

Education as Insurrection

After the famine, British administrators imposed the *National School* system to anglicize the next generation. Yet in small stone cottages from Kerry to Connemara, hedge-schoolmasters taught subversively. They blended catechism with arithmetic, Irish poetry with Latin grammar. Lessons were traded for butter, turf, or a prayer. The pupils sat on sod benches, reciting lines of *Aisling* verse where Ireland appeared in dreams as a captive woman awaiting release.

These clandestine classrooms were the prototypes of later independence movements. By 1916, nearly every signatory of the Easter Proclamation had once sat in such a circle. The hedge schools proved that education need not be licensed to be legitimate; sovereignty begins wherever knowledge passes hand to hand.

VI ·

The Emigrant Archives

Exile, paradoxically, became archive. From New York to Melbourne, emigrants founded societies, newspapers, and temperance halls that preserved accent and idiom. The *New York Irish World* mailed editorials back across the Atlantic, fueling land-reform campaigns. Money earned on American railroads funded Gaelic presses in Galway. Diaspora thus inverted dependence: capital flowed from colony to colony, bypassing the metropole.

In sociological terms, it was a "transnational feedback loop of identity." In mythic terms, it was diaspora as diaspora's cure—home rebuilt in echo.

VII ·

The Psychological Turn

By the century's end, Ireland's famine generation had transformed mourning into mission. What began as elegy became agency. The collective psyche discovered what Viktor Frankl would later articulate: suffering ceases to be tragedy when it gains meaning. Every revival meeting, every folk festival, was a small act of logotherapy—a community asserting that purpose could redeem pain.

The colonized mind healed not through denial but through narrative coherence. Storytelling became therapy before psychology had the word.

VIII ·

The Continuity of Hearth

Inside cottages, grandmothers still lit turf fires with a coal carried from an ancestor's hearth. To outsiders it seemed superstition; to those who knew, it was continuity protocol. The ember symbolized unbroken lineage—heat transferred across generations despite famine, eviction, and migration. Anthropologists later recorded similar practices among Polynesian voyagers who carried sacred firestones between islands. Cultures that move yet keep flame survive; those that forget the fire's name do not.

IX ·

Bridge

By 1922, Ireland emerged politically independent but spiritually unfinished. The next struggle would be not for sovereignty of land but for sovereignty of story: how to remember without freezing in victimhood.

That challenge, reborn in the twenty-first century, reappears wherever communities seek renewal after devastation—whether post-genocide Rwanda, post-apartheid South Africa, or post-lockdown societies searching for coherence. The pattern endures: trauma metabolized into art, grief translated into governance.

X ·

Transmission

A boy walks a coastal road at dusk, clutching a worn primer of Irish verse. The sea below is black glass; each wave recites a forgotten vowel. From a cottage ahead drifts a reel on fiddle—minor key, then major. He smiles, not understanding the words yet, but feeling them take root. Behind him lies famine; before him, language. Between them, the thin eternal thread of song.

Key 42 · Modern Parallel: Indigenous Australian Art Revival · Re-Rooting Identity Through Creation

Civilizations remember through pigment long after words are erased.

In the heart of Australia, where ochre dust meets ultraviolet sky, memory did not vanish under colonization—it went underground, coded into color. What began as forbidden ceremony has become one of the most profound acts of cultural resurgence on Earth: a renaissance of painting that turned survival itself into art.

I ·

The Canvas of Silence

For almost a century after European settlement, Aboriginal people were painted out of the national story. Languages were banned in schools, ceremonies criminalized, children taken under assimilation policies that sought to bleach culture from memory. Yet the land kept whispering. Dreaming tracks—the invisible pathways connecting sacred sites—continued to hum beneath bulldozers and barbed wire.

By the 1960s, as the civil rights movement spread worldwide, elders in the remote desert community of Papunya carried a question heavy as thirst: how to transmit Dreaming law to children growing up between mission and dust? The answer would come not from politics but from pattern.

II ·

The Birth of Papunya Tula

In 1971, art teacher Geoffrey Bardon arrived at the Papunya settlement, 240 kilometers northwest of Alice Springs. He noticed children sketching circles and lines in the dirt—symbols of ancestral journeys. Encouraging them to paint these forms on walls, he soon found local elders joining in. Men like Kaapa Tjampitjinpa and Clifford Possum began translating sand stories onto masonite boards using schoolhouse acrylics. Within months, the walls bloomed with cosmology: concentric circles for waterholes, dotted lines for tracks, u-shapes for people sitting in council.

When authorities ordered the murals painted over, fearing "paganism," the artists retreated indoors and founded the **Papunya Tula Artists Cooperative**. From those secret gatherings emerged a new genre—**Western Desert Painting**—a fusion of ancient cartography and modern abstraction. Each canvas was a satellite image of spiritual geography centuries before Google Earth.

III ·

The Market and the Meaning

By the late 1970s, these works reached galleries in Sydney and New York. Critics hailed them as avant-garde; collectors saw investment. But for the painters, money was secondary. Every dot was covenant. Each piece carried encoded law—who could tell which story, which symbols required permission, which could never be sold. Elders created "inside" and "outside" layers: surface beauty for outsiders, sacred narrative for those initiated.

This dual language protected integrity within exposure. It was the opposite of appropriation: a controlled revelation where survival depended on secrecy disguised as generosity. In behavioral terms, it was a perfect adaptation to colonial gaze—sharing without surrender.

IV.

The Circle Returns

As exhibitions toured Europe, Aboriginal artists visited Paris, London, and New York—cities built on stolen aesthetics. Yet instead of feeling dwarfed, they recognized something ancient mirrored in modern form. Abstract expressionism, minimalism, and pointillism suddenly looked like echoes of Dreaming art's logic: pattern as cosmology. The colonized had unknowingly prefigured the avant-garde.

Anthropologists began mapping this reversal: the periphery teaching the center. The **Great Circle of Culture** had closed—art once dismissed as "primitive" now defined the future of global visual language. This was not assimilation; it was asymmetrical enlightenment.

V.

Healing Through Creation

Clinical studies by the Cooperative Research Centre for Aboriginal Health (2010) show that community art programs correlate with 25 percent reductions in depression and substance abuse in remote settlements. Neuroscientists attribute this to the *flow* state described by Mihaly Csikszentmihalyi: deep immersion aligning body and attention. In these painting circles, trauma becomes rhythm; despair converts to design. The brush becomes a neural prosthetic connecting grief to meaning.

Women's collectives such as the **Tjala Arts Centre** extended the renaissance into textile, weaving, and ceremonial song. Each new medium functioned as therapy and testimony. A pattern repeated across trauma studies worldwide: when words fail, art rewires.

VI ·

From Margins to Museums

By 2019, Aboriginal and Torres Strait Islander art accounted for nearly 25 percent of Australia's visual art market, generating over $200 million annually and anchoring hundreds of remote livelihoods. The **National Gallery of Australia's Indigenous Art Triennial** became a global event. Works by Emily Kame Kngwarreye and Rover Thomas entered the canon beside Monet and Pollock. The shift was not tokenistic; it was tectonic. For the first time since colonization, Indigenous cosmology shaped national aesthetics rather than the other way around.

Prime ministers now quote songlines in speeches. Corporations commission dot paintings for lobbies—but the true victory lies not in decoration but in definition. The culture no longer asks to be seen; it decides how.

VII ·

The Ethics of Revival

Every renaissance risks consumption by the very systems it critiques. As tourist markets grew, some communities faced counterfeit mass production. In response, Indigenous lawyers and elders developed protocols of consent and attribution, forming the **Indigenous Art Code (2010)**—a moral contract restoring agency to artists. Each authentic piece now carries provenance, story, and fair compensation. Integrity, once oral, became legal.

The pattern repeats the mythic structure of all sovereignty work: first survival, then self-expression, then governance. Beauty matures into law.

VIII ·

The Global Resonance

The desert paintings have since inspired movements in Canada's First Nations, the Māori renaissance, and Pacific weaving revivals. Their success revealed a universal principle: cultural health is measurable not by uniformity but by the number of living languages and art forms. Diversity is the immune system of civilization.

As environmental crises deepen, Indigenous art offers more than color—it offers cosmology. Dreaming maps remind humanity that land is not property but relation, that ownership without reverence is starvation of the spirit. The world listens again to the oldest teachers on Earth.

IX ·

The Myth Beneath the Paint

Every Papunya Tula canvas is a fragment of the Dreaming—stories where ancestors traveled as lightning, serpents, wind. In Jungian terms, these are archetypes of transformation: chaos condensed into order, fire into pattern. The painters externalize collective unconscious the way ancient shamans once did in caves at Lascaux. Their dots are neurons in the earth's own brain, connecting myth to geology.

Psychologically, the viewer experiences coherence—the same calm that desert silence induces. What science calls "aesthetic arrest," myth calls revelation: to behold the pattern is to remember belonging.

X ·

Bridge

The Indigenous art revival reveals the mechanism by which all cultures regenerate: **creation as re-connection**. When a people translate pain into pattern, they restore coherence between memory and meaning. The same dynamic governs individuals seeking recovery from loss, addiction, or alienation. The psyche heals when expression re-links experience to identity.

Next, we explore that psychological mechanism directly—the process by which collective storytelling repairs internal fracture and transforms trauma into continuity.

XI ·

Transmission

In the desert near Yuendumu, an elder finishes a canvas at dusk. She blows gently across the final dots, sealing them with breath. The sun sinks, igniting the sand in crimson light; the painting seems to glow from within. Children laugh nearby, their footprints circling hers like constellations. The Dreaming continues, not in myth but in motion—each heartbeat another dot on the endless map of return.

Key 43 · *Psychological Mechanism: Narrative Therapy and the Collective Repair of Meaning*

Civilizations are stories people agree to inhabit.

When those stories break, the psyche fragments with them. The twentieth century's wars, famines, and displacements shattered not only infrastructure but internal coherence—the sense that life forms a continuous thread. To rebuild it, individuals and cultures alike turn instinctively to narrative. Telling becomes healing. Listening becomes architecture. Meaning, reassembled sentence by sentence, becomes civilization's invisible scaffolding.

I ·

The Shattered Self

Psychologists define trauma not as pain but as interruption—an experience too intense to integrate into the normal flow of memory. The event freezes; time stops. The mind protects itself by dissociation, exiling the fragment. Whole societies perform the same defense: they erase what cannot be borne. After the Great Famine, after genocides, after pandemics, archives fill with silence.

Narrative therapy begins where silence ends. Developed by Michael White and David Epston in 1980s Adelaide, it emerged partly from working with communities scarred by colonization. White noticed that patients spoke in deficit stories: *I am broken. I failed. I have no control.* His insight was radical—identity is a story told about the self, not a fixed essence. Change the story, and healing follows.

II ·

Externalization: Separating the Problem from the Person

The first move in narrative therapy is linguistic surgery. The therapist helps the client rename the problem as something external: *the depression, the violence, the hunger.* This subtle shift reclaims agency. The person becomes protagonist rather than symptom. In cultural form, this is what Ireland did by personifying the nation as *Cathleen ni Houlihan* or what Aboriginal artists did by painting loss as pattern. They transformed paralysis into plot.

Neuroscientist Dan Siegel later found that when subjects reframed trauma through storytelling, neural integration increased between the amygdala (emotion) and prefrontal cortex (reason). The act of naming reorganizes the brain. Myth has known this for millennia: to name the demon is to limit its power.

III ·

Re-authoring Identity

The second principle is *re-authoring*: expanding a person's story beyond the trauma script. Instead of *I survived famine,* the narrative becomes *I learned endurance and generosity from famine.* The event remains, but its meaning changes direction. This mirrors Viktor Frankl's logotherapy insight that suffering ceases to be suffering the moment it gains purpose.

Cultures re-author themselves through festivals, art, and education. When Ireland revived Gaelic or when Papunya painters translated Dreaming into acrylics, they weren't aesthetic movements; they were collective therapy sessions. The new story did not erase the old wound—it metabolized it. Pain, integrated, became wisdom.

IV.

Witness and Resonance

Trauma isolates; narrative reconnects. For healing to complete, someone must listen. The listener is the mirror in which coherence reforms. South Africa's Truth and Reconciliation Commission functioned as national therapy precisely because it provided structured witnessing. People recounted horror, but in the presence of acknowledgment rather than denial.

Psychologically, empathy from others reactivates the brain's mirror-neuron system, reestablishing social belonging. This is why storytelling circles, twelve-step meetings, and oral histories remain more effective than solitary journaling. The human nervous system heals relationally or not at all.

V.

The Physics of Coherence

In systems theory, coherence describes the alignment of oscillating parts into stable pattern. Heart-rate variability studies show that when individuals enter coherent emotional states—gratitude, compassion—their physiological rhythms synchronize with others nearby. Groups literally entrain each other. Storytelling performs the same synchronization at the cognitive level.

When a family recounts its shared past, internal clocks align; uncertainty decreases. Economies and nations function on the same principle. Collapse begins when narratives diverge beyond resonance—when citizens no longer agree on meaning. Thus, rebuilding coherence is not sentimental work; it is strategic infrastructure.

VI ·

The Narrative Immune System

Just as the body recognizes pathogens, the mind recognizes falsehoods that threaten coherence. Repeated exposure to contradictory or cynical stories weakens this immunity, leading to societal cynicism. Restoring a truthful collective story is therefore akin to vaccination. Each honest testimony strengthens the antibodies of trust.

Researchers at Stanford (2016) found that people who regularly practice autobiographical storytelling show higher resilience scores under stress. The act of connecting events to a personal through-line inoculates against despair. Cultures practicing daily or weekly communal storytelling—Indigenous yarning circles, Sabbath reflection, family meals—show similar protective effects against fragmentation.

VII ·

Myth as Narrative Therapy

Myth operates as premodern psychology. In the Greek underworld, Orpheus descends to retrieve Eurydice—the soul lost to death—but fails when he turns back too soon. The story encodes the rule of integration: trauma can be revisited only with forward vision. Looking back in doubt collapses coherence again.

Modern trauma therapy mirrors this: exposure must be titrated, paced, forward-facing. Myth translates neurology into parable. When Irish poets revived famine songs or Aboriginal painters depicted ancestral journeys, they practiced mythic neuroscience—structured revisiting without collapse.

VIII ·

The Collective Journal

At the community level, narrative therapy becomes cultural journalism. Post-conflict societies that document atrocity—through museums, archives, oral histories—achieve lower relapse into violence. Psychologists call it *meaning maintenance.* When experience is symbolized, it stops haunting.

Projects like Rwanda's *Gacaca* courts or Chile's *Museo de la Memoria* serve this function. The medium varies—courtroom, canvas, or song—but the neurocognitive outcome is constant: chaos encoded into sequence, sequence into sense. A culture that writes remembers; one that refuses, repeats.

IX ·

The Ritual of Continuity

The deepest mechanism is ritual repetition. Storytelling must not be singular catharsis; it must become liturgy. In narrative therapy, clients retell updated stories until the new identity feels natural. Societies do the same through annual remembrance days and artistic revivals. Each retelling reinforces neural and social pathways of meaning, preventing regression.

When Irish families gather to sing famine songs not in mourning but pride, when desert painters teach grandchildren to dot ancestral maps, the nervous system of culture stabilizes. The wound becomes rhythm. The scar, design.

X.

Integration and Action

True narrative repair ends with behavior change. A person who re-authors their story begins to act from new scripts—helping others, mentoring, rebuilding. The feedback loop completes: meaning creates motion, and motion sustains meaning. At societal scale, this becomes civic renewal: communities that control their stories invest more in shared institutions because they see themselves as protagonists, not victims.

This is why education reform, local journalism, and community arts funding are not luxuries but resilience infrastructure. They maintain the narrative economy that underwrites all others.

XI.

Transmission

In a town hall after dark, the power flickers. A circle of people remain, candles between them. One woman finishes reading her family's story of loss and survival. For a moment no one speaks. Then an elder nods and says, "That happened to us too." The room exhales; the air steadies. Outside, the streetlights hum back to life. The story, told and heard, has repaired the grid.

Key 44 · Mythic Resonance: Orpheus and the Descent into Memory · Retrieving Lost Songs

When language fails, music waits beneath it.

In every age of ruin, a singer walks into the dark carrying only sound.

The Greeks called him Orpheus: poet, prophet, the one who could move stone with tone.

His lyre, strung with gut and grief, was civilization's first therapy instrument.

I ·

The Original Descent

The myth begins at the threshold between worlds. Eurydice, Orpheus' beloved, dies from a serpent's bite. Refusing finality, he descends into Hades armed with nothing but melody. The guardians—Cerberus, Furies, even the stern king himself—pause as song dissolves the air around them. For the first time, death listens.

Orpheus sings of memory stronger than oblivion. Moved, Persephone grants his plea: Eurydice may return if he walks ahead and never looks back until sunlight touches her face. He agrees, but near the exit turns in doubt. In that instant she fades. The music stops; silence reclaims the world.

The ancients heard warning in this: when faith fractures, resurrection falters. Psychologists hear mechanism: trauma revisited too soon collapses integration. Every myth is a user manual disguised as tragedy.

II ·

The Psychological Translation

In modern terms, Orpheus represents consciousness re-entering the unconscious to retrieve the lost parts of the self. Eurydice is memory—what the mind buries to survive. The underworld is the limbic system, repository of raw emotion. The song is narrative coherence: patterned vibration binding chaos into form.

Jung called this the descent into the *shadow*. Freud called it abreaction. Neuroscience calls it reconsolidation. Different vocabularies, same path: healing requires visitation of pain without possession by it. Turn back too early, and the ghosts reclaim you.

III ·

Cultural Echoes

Every civilization has sung this journey. In the Egyptian *Book of the Dead*, the soul chants passwords to pass gates of night. In Sumer, Inanna descends through seven doors, shedding ornaments of ego until she stands bare before darkness. In the *Bhagavata Purana*, Krishna plays flute to draw consciousness back from despair. The pattern holds: sound as guide, faith as bridge, restraint as law.

Ireland knew it in the *Aisling* poems—visions of a woman nation glimpsed then lost; Aboriginal Dreaming knows it in the songlines traced between stars and waterholes. The same archetype migrates through millennia: the artist as psychopomp, retrieving coherence from entropy.

IV.

The Lyre and the Brain

Modern research on music therapy completes the circle. Functional MRI shows that melody integrates hemispheres: rhythm activates motor cortex, harmony recruits emotion, lyrics stimulate language centers. When survivors of trauma sing their stories, neural networks reconnect across divides that speech alone cannot bridge.

This is Orpheus at work inside gray matter. The lyre's strings are axons; the song, electrical pulse. Where medicine sedates, melody synchronizes. Hospitals now use rhythmic auditory stimulation to restore gait after stroke; veterans hum to regulate breathing. The myth, it turns out, was empirical.

V.

The Ethics of Return

Orpheus' failure was not weakness but curiosity. He needed proof that love endured outside the song. The lesson: healing requires trust in unseen process. Therapy, art, and faith all demand the same discipline—walk forward without certainty. The instant one demands evidence, the enchantment dissolves.

In civilizational terms, this warns reformers: new orders collapse if built on suspicion of the very imagination that birthed them. A nation that doubts its myth cannot resurrect it. The builder must believe long enough for structure to self-support.

VI ·

The Song as Map

Each generation re-composes the descent. Blues arose from bondage, flamenco from exile, reggae from displacement. Every genre begins with descent and ends with return. The scales themselves mirror the journey: down into minor tension, up into major release. To sing is to trace the topography of loss and homecoming simultaneously.

Musicologists note that cultures under oppression favor call-and-response forms—dialogue across void. The pattern functions neurologically like bilateral stimulation in EMDR therapy: alternating tones move trauma between hemispheres until equilibrium returns. The ancestors encoded neuroscience in rhythm centuries before scanners confirmed it.

VII ·

Modern Orpheus

In 1989, cellist Mstislav Rostropovich stood before the fallen Berlin Wall and played Bach while crowds wept. In 2015, Syrian pianist Aeham Ahmad wheeled his piano through bombed Damascus streets, performing amid rubble until militias burned the instrument. Both acts repeated the archetype: descent into chaos, retrieval of beauty. Sound as defiance of entropy.

Psychologists call this *aesthetic courage*: creating meaning within destruction to prevent psychic collapse. The musician does not deny darkness; he tunes it.

VIII ·

Collective Descent and Return

When whole cultures undergo trauma—famine, genocide, environmental loss—the Orphic pattern scales upward. Museums, choirs, commemorations become collective underworlds where society revisits its dead. The return requires artistry, not policy. Policy remembers statistics; art remembers souls. Only the latter prevents repetition.

Ireland's post-famine revival, Aboriginal painting circles, South Africa's choirs after apartheid—each enacted musical archaeology. Melody carried what prose could not bear.

IX ·

The Discipline of Listening

To retrieve the lost, one must listen at frequencies beneath speech. Silence is half the ritual. Orpheus' true instrument was not the lyre but attention. Modern life, drowning in noise, has lost this faculty. Cognitive-load studies show average attention span shrinking to eight seconds—shorter than a goldfish's. Restoring deep listening is therefore moral work.

When two people truly listen—without interruption, correction, or performance—the brain releases oxytocin, synchronizing heart rhythms. This is the measurable physiology of empathy, the scientific face of love songs.

X.

Rewriting the Ending

Ancient myths fix Orpheus' death—torn apart by Maenads who cannot bear his refusal to sing for anyone but ghosts. Yet every retelling is a chance to re-author. In this age of narrative therapy, the story can end differently: he returns, teaches, and hands the lyre to others. Each listener becomes new singer; each song, new descent.

Cultures that survive learn to hand down instruments rather than idols. Music becomes method, not monument.

XI.

Transmission

A musician stands in an empty subway at midnight. Trains rumble like distant thunder, lights flicker against tile. He lifts a violin and begins to play—a slow lament that fills the tunnel with echo. Commuters pause on the platform; someone begins to hum. The notes rise, circle, return. For a moment the city forgets its exhaustion. The underworld listens, and life keeps walking toward the light.

Key 45 · Sovereignty Protocol: The Family Ritual Kit · Practices for Cultural Continuity

Every empire falls, but a family that keeps ritual never truly collapses.

States may govern by policy, markets by price, religions by creed—but civilizations endure only through domestic ceremony. The smallest unit of culture is not the citizen or consumer; it is the household gathered around a repeated act that says: *we still remember.*

I ·

The Architecture of Continuity

Anthropologists studying cultural survival—from Navajo clans to Jewish diasporas—find one constant: ritual density predicts longevity. The more shared gestures a community performs, the stronger its internal coherence. Ritual acts as a mnemonic circuit—encoding values in motion so that memory bypasses decay.

Every civilization that survived conquest, famine, or exile did so because its daily life contained rehearsals of meaning: lighting lamps at dusk, reciting names of ancestors, breaking bread before speech. These gestures are the muscle memory of civilization.

The Family Ritual Kit is not a product but a pattern: a set of repeatable, portable acts that maintain coherence when systems fail. Each is small enough to perform without permission, powerful enough to recalibrate identity.

II.

The Morning Alignment

The day begins with a single breath taken before screens, news, or tasks. The household faces the light—window, flame, or sky—and says aloud one sentence that encapsulates purpose. *We are here to build, to care, to endure.*

Psychologists call this "implementation intention." Neuroscientists measure it as a 20 percent improvement in executive function throughout the day. Spiritually, it is covenant renewal: the dawn as contract. No empire can legislate what one whispers to sunrise.

III.

The Table as Temple

In stable societies, the meal table replaces the altar; in unstable ones, it becomes the last altar standing. Anthropologist Mary Douglas called food "the language of holiness." Every shared meal reasserts belonging.

Establish a ritual of **The Unhurried Meal** once a day—no devices, no rushing. Begin with gratitude for specific things within reach: the farmer, the cook, the rain. Gratitude synchronizes parasympathetic response, lowering blood pressure and conflict frequency. In practice, it is the simplest peace treaty a family can sign.

IV.

The Weekly Circle

Once a week, create a 30-minute council. Light a candle, pass an object—stone, feather, cup—and let each person speak without interruption. The rule: respond only after a full breath.

This reintroduces what most democracies lost—ritualized listening. Anthropological data from the Okanagan and Balinese subak councils show that ceremonial listening structures reduce community disputes by over 40 percent. Within families, they preempt resentment before it festers.

Record insights in a simple notebook titled *The House Chronicle*. Over time it becomes a sacred text—not of doctrine but of experience. The Chronicle will outlive social media feeds and one day guide descendants through their own storms.

V.

The Festival of Repair

Choose one day each month as *Repair Day*. Fix what is broken—objects, relationships, promises. Children mend toys or clothes; adults resolve old emails, debts, or arguments. The point is symbolic restoration: entropy reversed by attention.

Sociologists note that communities which institutionalize maintenance outperform those obsessed with innovation. Repair sustains trust because it demonstrates care. In Japan, the tradition of *kintsugi*—mending pottery with gold—taught that fracture adds beauty. In the household, the same principle redefines success: not perfection, but continuity through care.

VI.

The Ancestral Table

Once a season, gather images, names, or objects of ancestors—biological or chosen—and retell their stories. This is not nostalgia; it is neural architecture. Children who know at least three generations of family history show 23 percent higher emotional resilience, according to Emory University's "Do You Know?" study. The ritual teaches that identity extends backward and forward simultaneously.

If ancestors are unknown, adopt symbolic ones—writers, saints, or local builders whose values align with the family covenant. The point is lineage of principle, not blood.

VII ·

The Ritual of Silence

Each household needs one hour weekly where no one speaks or consumes media. Silence recalibrates auditory sensitivity, improving empathy and creativity. Monastic communities measured increased cooperative behavior after collective silence sessions, even without doctrinal unity.

Light a candle at the start; extinguish it at the end. The boundary marks time as sacred. Within that hour, meaning settles like dust undisturbed.

VIII ·

The Transmission of Craft

Every culture anchors its continuity in a skill: weaving, cooking, carving, storytelling. Choose one craft per generation and teach it deliberately. Skill becomes the vessel of philosophy. The child who learns to mend wood also learns patience; the teenager who gardens learns time's law.

This is pedagogy by gesture. The craft's function matters less than its repetition. The goal is to embed virtue in muscle memory so that when words and institutions fail, hands still know what integrity feels like.

IX ·

The Closing of Day

At dusk, gather for **The Candle Sentence**—one line spoken together while lighting or dimming a lamp. It can change with seasons:

We built what we could today.

We forgive what we could not.

Tomorrow we begin again.

The rhythmic closure releases accumulated tension and gives children temporal security. Sleep quality improves; arguments fade. It is a micro-litany against chaos.

X ·

The Sabbath of Attention

Once every seven days, abstain from one habitual dependency—screen, purchase, or noise. This voluntary restraint mirrors the economic Sabbath embedded in every pre-industrial society, a systemic reset of consumption. Studies from the University of British Columbia show that digital sabbaths reduce anxiety markers by 30 percent and increase interpersonal satisfaction by half.

The deeper purpose is metaphysical: to prove to oneself that worth exists independent of output. A civilization that cannot pause eventually burns its circuits.

XI ·

The Covenant Renewal

At year's end, review the House Chronicle and re-write the family covenant. Ask: *What values proved true under pressure?* Delete the rest. Like pruning a tree, this ensures vitality. Every revision keeps the covenant alive rather than fossilized.

Then, seal the year with a shared act of generosity—a donation, a feast, or a letter to someone forgotten. Cultures rise by generosity's compounding interest.

XII ·

The Continuity Principle

When performed regularly, these rituals build what sociologists call "cultural homeostasis": the ability of a group to self-regulate identity through repetition. The family becomes an organism that remembers. In collapse, that memory functions as software for reconstruction. Each household thus becomes an ark, carrying story, skill, and sanity through the flood.

XIII ·

Transmission

Night settles over a small home at the edge of a restless city. Inside, four candles flicker on a wooden table. The family finishes its circle; the youngest closes the Chronicle. Outside, sirens echo; the grid hums. Inside, time slows. The flame steadies, mirrored in each pair of eyes. Beyond currency, beyond politics, civilization endures—right here, in the quiet repetition of care.

Chapter 10

The Sovereign Future

Part IV · The Future

Key 46 · Historical Mirror: Ghana's Cooperative Movement and the Architecture of Local Power

When empire fades, the first builders are rarely soldiers.

They are farmers who decide to count grain together.

I ·

After Independence, Before Memory

In 1957 Ghana became the first sub-Saharan colony to shake free from European rule. Kwame Nkrumah stood beneath the new black-star flag and promised a self-governing destiny: "Seek ye first the political kingdom, and all else shall be added." But the harder question lingered—*added by whom?* The empire's exit left hollow ministries, half-built railways, and a people trained to obey distant accountants.

Across cocoa farms from Koforidua to Kumasi, smallholders knew that independence meant little without economic muscle. Prices were still set in London; shipping was controlled by foreign firms. So, they organized—not as parties, but as cooperatives. By 1962 there were over 1 500 registered co-ops in Ghana, weaving together farmers, carpenters, fishermen, and market women. Theirs was not theory but survival: pooling credit, bulk-buying fertilizer, sharing trucks when fuel ran thin.

Nkrumah recognized the power. In 1960 he told Parliament, *"Our cooperatives are the schools of socialism."* What he meant was that democracy without daily cooperation would collapse back into patronage. He imagined each co-op as a micro-republic—self-governing, transparent, disciplined. For a brief decade, it worked.

II ·

The Cocoa Commons

Cocoa was Ghana's lifeblood, accounting for 60 percent of exports. Under colonial rule, individual farmers had been crushed by fluctuating London prices. The Ghana Cooperative Cocoa Marketing Union (GCCMU) reversed the equation. Thousands of growers pooled harvests, negotiated collectively, and built local storage depots to bypass middlemen.

Archival data from the Bank of Ghana shows that between 1958 and 1965 co-op members received 15–20 percent higher net income than independent sellers. That margin built schools, clinics, and rotating credit funds—the invisible infrastructure of sovereignty.

Each cooperative used a ritual meeting called *the weighing*. At dawn, farmers gathered to measure beans on a communal scale, watched by elected record-keepers. The scale was both tool and symbol: justice visible in kilograms. When corruption rumors spread, they checked the weights again, in public. Trust became a measurable unit.

III ·

Women of the Market

Beneath the headlines of cocoa and nationalism worked another network—market women known as *makola*. Denied formal banking, they built their own rotating savings groups, called *susu*. Each week, every trader contributed a coin; each week, one received the pot. It was finance without institutions, enforced only by reputation.

Anthropologist Christine Okali's fieldwork later showed repayment rates above 98 percent—higher than commercial banks. The *makola* controlled flow: when the city faltered, they extended credit; when inflation hit, they anchored prices through solidarity. Economists now call such groups "informal safety nets," but in truth they were shadow governments—resilient, adaptive, and profoundly female.

IV.

The Political Crosscurrent

By 1966, Ghana's optimism cracked. Global cocoa prices slumped, debts piled, and Cold War pressures mounted. A military coup toppled Nkrumah while he toured Asia seeking industrial partners. The new regime accused co-ops of party loyalty and dissolved many. Trucks were impounded; funds seized. Within months, thousands of farmers reverted to private selling. The network frayed.

Yet even under repression, cooperative habits persisted underground. Villagers still met to repair roads or share fertilizer, now under the name "self-help groups." Like root systems after fire, they waited for rain. In 1971 a new Cooperative Societies Decree legalized them again, and by 1978 membership surpassed one million. Sovereignty, once practiced, is difficult to unlearn.

V.

Education as Empowerment

The co-ops did more than market crops—they taught literacy and accounting. Many members learned to read through tally books. The slogan was simple: *If you can count your beans, no one can cheat you.* Education shifted from charity to strategy.

By the 1980s, as IMF structural adjustment cut public services, co-op training centers quietly filled the gap. In Volta Region, artisans built low-cost housing cooperatives; in Northern Ghana, shea-butter producers exported directly to European buyers. Each initiative replaced dependence with design.

VI ·

The Moral Geometry of Participation

A cooperative works only if its members practice disciplined trust. Anthropologist David Apter called this "moral geometry"—a balance between self-interest and collective duty. At meetings, every voice carried weight proportional not to wealth but contribution. Decisions were by consensus. Transparency was ritualized: ledgers read aloud, profits divided publicly. Such acts built what economists later modeled as "social capital," but within villages it was simply good manners elevated to governance.

VII ·

Collapse and Continuity

When Ghana entered the 1983 drought, food shortages triggered rural exodus. State farms failed, yet local co-ops revived food distribution. Their informal logistics delivered grain where ministries could not. During the famine, survival often depended less on the state than on one's membership card.

These networks became laboratories for future decentralization. By the 1990s the government's new constitution recognized cooperatives as legitimate development partners. What began as colonial resistance matured into national backbone.

VIII ·

Lessons in Micro-Sovereignty

The cooperative movement demonstrates that sovereignty is scalar: it can exist simultaneously in a nation and in a neighborhood. Political independence without economic interdependence is illusion. Ghana's farmers understood this intuitively. Their autonomy was not declared in constitutions but practiced in ledgers, meetings, and shared risk.

Modern analysts now see Ghana's 1950s–60s co-ops as early prototypes of decentralized governance—systems where accountability emerges from participation, not surveillance. When every member counts beans together, power disperses naturally.

IX ·

Echo Across Time

Today, Ghana's credit unions hold assets exceeding $3 billion. Digital platforms like Esusu and Chama adapt the same rotating-savings model with smartphone apps. The architecture persists: cooperative DNA evolving through new tools. The lesson travels far beyond West Africa—into crypto collectives, mutual-aid networks, and local-currency experiments.

The principle remains constant: sovereignty grows where trust is structured.

X ·

Transmission

Dawn in Koforidua. Farmers gather around a rusted scale balanced on a wooden crate. One pours cocoa beans into the pan; another adjusts the counterweight until equilibrium settles. Numbers are recorded, jokes exchanged, coins passed hand to hand. No flags wave, no anthem plays—yet here, in this precise alignment of trust and measure, a nation renews itself quietly. The weight holds steady. The light strengthens. Sovereignty begins again, one kilogram at a time.

Key 47 · Modern Parallel: Rojava's Local Governance and the New Experiments in Distributed Power

I ·

The Desert That Governed Itself

In 2012, as Syria tore itself apart, a stretch of desert on the country's northern frontier began to hum with an improbable order. Amid the chaos of civil war, three Kurdish-majority cantons—Afrin, Kobane, and Jazira—declared not a state, but a *system*. No new flag, no anthem, no presidential palace. What emerged was something rarer: *autonomy without domination.*

They called it the Autonomous Administration of North and East Syria, known colloquially as **Rojava**—"the West," in Kurdish, referring to the western part of Kurdistan. Its foundation was not conquest but coordination. Local councils sprang up in bombed-out towns; committees for education, agriculture, women's rights, and security formed overnight. When asked who gave them permission, one elder answered simply, *"No one. The world was busy, so we governed ourselves."*

What began as survival evolved into one of the most radical experiments in democratic decentralization in modern times.

II ·

The Philosophy Beneath the Rubble

The architecture of Rojava did not appear from vacuum. Its blueprint had been imagined decades earlier by **Abdullah Öcalan**, leader of the Kurdistan Workers' Party (PKK). From his prison cell in Turkey, Öcalan read and reinterpreted the work of American anarchist **Murray Bookchin**, who envisioned "libertarian municipalism"—a form of grassroots democracy built through networks of self-governing communities rather than centralized states.

Öcalan's synthesis—**democratic confederalism**—became Rojava's north star. It held three tenets:

1. Power should rise from the bottom, not descend from the top.
2. Women's liberation is inseparable from social freedom.
3. Ecology, not extraction, must guide economics.

The result was a polity closer to a living organism than a bureaucracy—thousands of local councils linked by coordination committees but not bound by coercion. Decisions flowed horizontally, like capillaries carrying consent.

III ·

A New Kind of Defense

No sovereignty survives without defense, yet Rojava's model inverted the traditional chain of command. The **People's Protection Units (YPG)** and the **Women's Protection Units (YPJ)** fought not as state armies but as federated militias accountable to local assemblies. When ISIS advanced on Kobane in 2014, these militias—largely volunteers—held the city through 134 days of siege, with coordination achieved by radio, consensus, and unbroken will.

After the battle, an elderly commander explained, *"We defended not land but principle."* It was the first war in modern history fought explicitly in the name of decentralization. Their victory was improbable, their cost staggering, but their example reshaped global imagination: a society without a state had defended itself against the most brutal centralizers of all.

IV.

The Communes

At the core of daily life were **communes**, small assemblies of fifty to one hundred households. Each elected two co-chairs—one man, one woman—and formed committees for security, economy, education, and justice. Every month, delegates met in neighborhood councils, which then linked upward into district and regional assemblies.

A teacher in Qamishli described it this way: *"Before, we waited for orders. Now, we wait for each other."*

In practice, that meant conflict mediation replacing police, cooperatives replacing corporations, and deliberation replacing decrees.

By 2018, there were more than 4,000 functioning communes across Rojava's regions. Even amid war, they managed bread distribution, electricity, and schooling. Harvard researcher Thomas Schmidinger called it "the most advanced example of participatory democracy operating under active bombardment."

V.

The Women's Revolution

No modern polity has placed women's liberation so centrally in its constitution. The **YPJ** became both shield and signal: an army of women fighting for autonomy in every sense. In the commune system, every administrative role required gender parity; any decision made by a male-only committee was automatically invalid.

Village schools began teaching *Jineology*—"the science of women"—linking history, ecology, and philosophy to reconstruct social thought beyond patriarchy.

One fighter summarized it: *"We do not take power from men. We remove the idea that power belongs to them."*

Sociologists later noted measurable social shifts: child marriage rates halved between 2014 and 2018; literacy among girls rose by 40 percent despite wartime conditions. In a region where empire and extremism had long fused, this was nothing short of civilizational surgery.

VI ·

Economics Without a Center

Rojava's economy operated through **cooperatives**, echoing the Ghanaian movement half a century earlier. Every neighborhood had work co-ops—bakeries, textile workshops, farms—owned collectively and managed by rotating committees. Profit was capped; surplus reinvested locally. A 2016 study by the London School of Economics estimated that cooperatives produced roughly 70 percent of the region's food supply during the war years.

Critics called it naïve socialism; supporters called it ethical pragmatism. In truth, it was adaptation: sanctions, sieges, and war had already destroyed conventional markets. People either collaborated or starved.

The cooperatives succeeded not because they rejected trade but because they localized it. Transactions were personal; reputation replaced regulation. Every loaf of bread carried both the price of flour and the proof of solidarity.

VII ·

Fracture and Survival

No utopia lasts unchallenged. Turkish invasions in 2018 and 2019 seized parts of Rojava, displacing tens of thousands. The region's oil fields became bargaining chips between competing powers. Yet the councils continued—smaller, poorer, stubborn.

When international journalists asked how they still functioned without state protection, a councilwoman from Amuda replied: *"We learned that waiting for rescue is another form of slavery."*

Even as borders shifted, the practice of self-governance became irreversible. Villages reconstituted councils in exile; diaspora networks organized remittances through encrypted platforms. In effect, Rojava's idea escaped its geography—*a sovereignty that travels.*

VIII ·

The Global Reflection

Scholars now cite Rojava alongside the Zapatista communities of Chiapas and the Gandhi-inspired panchayats of India as living examples of **post-state governance**. The model resonates in climate movements, open-source projects, and digital collectives seeking autonomy without isolation.

The irony is that while nation-states still debate what democracy means, a region born of war quietly demonstrated it. The Rojava Charter of 2014 contains a line worth engraving in every parliament: *"The right of self-determination belongs to the community."*

That sentence is the political equivalent of oxygen. Once tasted, it is impossible to forget.

IX ·

Bridge to the Builders

Rojava's councils prove that freedom can be designed as a process, not declared as a monument. Like Ghana's farmers, they showed that sovereignty grows horizontally—through consensus, craft, and courage.

But every experiment demands inheritance. Ideas must be encoded, not merely lived. The next section distills the psychological logic that either sustains or sabotages this autonomy—the mind of stewardship, the tension between collective purpose and fatigue.

For civilizations to rise again, they must learn not only how to build systems, but how to **feel responsibility across time**.

X · Transmission

Night in Kobane. The city hums on solar lanterns and whispers. In a courtyard, twelve neighbors sit in a circle under a fig tree, papers spread across the ground—tonight's agenda: water rations, school repairs, one unresolved dispute. The youngest member, a girl of fifteen, speaks; the oldest, a widow, nods in agreement. A cat walks through the lamplight; somewhere beyond the hills, artillery murmurs. Yet the meeting continues, steady as breathing. The minutes recorded by hand. The decision made together.

This, too, is a parliament. The air itself holds the vote.

Key 48 · Psychological Mechanism: Stewardship and the Long Time Horizon

I ·

The Mind of the Builder

Every empire collapses for the same reason: the loss of long-term memory.

Its citizens stop planting trees whose shade they will never see.

Stewardship is the antidote—the quiet rebellion against short-term thinking. It is not maintenance but inheritance: the capacity to hold responsibility for outcomes that extend beyond one's lifespan. The cognitive engine of stewardship is rare, because it resists both apathy and ambition. It is the psychology of patience in an age of acceleration.

Neuroscience gives this virtue a location. The prefrontal cortex—responsible for planning and impulse control—activates when we imagine distant futures. Yet functional MRI studies (Berns et al., 2007) reveal that most people treat their "future self" as a stranger; the brain's empathy network disengages when we picture ourselves decades ahead. Stewardship, then, begins as an act of intimacy—recognizing the future self and the future community as kin.

II ·

The Collapse of Temporal Vision

Modern civilization suffers from *temporal myopia*: the inability to perceive consequences that unfold slowly. Stock markets reward quarterly returns; governments cycle every four years; social media accelerates outrage by the minute. The economist John Maynard Keynes once said, *"In the long run, we are all dead."* The statement became prophecy—a civilization of short horizons, optimized for consumption rather than continuity.

Anthropologists call this *temporal collapse*. Civilizations that survived longest—Egyptian, Chinese, Andean—engineered cultural mechanisms to extend perception: ancestor worship, dynastic cycles, agricultural calendars that forced multigenerational planning. Their rituals were cognitive prosthetics, reminding each generation that they were both seed and soil.

Today, digital culture fragments that awareness. The average human attention span has shrunk to eight seconds (Microsoft study, 2015). Our technologies make us gods in power but infants in perspective. Stewardship is the forgotten muscle.

III ·

The Steward's Trance

Psychologists studying master craftspeople describe a peculiar state of mind—a blend of absorption, humility, and devotion. Mihaly Csikszentmihalyi named it **flow**, but in the context of stewardship it becomes something slower: *devotional flow*.

A Japanese carpenter restoring a temple beam will polish joints hidden from sight, whispering, *"The gods can see."* A Ghanaian farmer plants cocoa knowing that only his grandchildren will taste full yield. A Syrian council member in Rojava revises a charter clause that may guide towns long after her death.

In all these acts, time thickens. The present expands to include the unborn. Neuroimaging links such long-horizon thinking to reduced amygdala activity—less fear—and greater activation in the medial prefrontal cortex, associated with meaning and narrative integration. The steward's trance, neurologically, is serenity through significance.

IV.

Cognitive Architecture of Stewardship

1. **Temporal empathy** — the ability to feel for future beings as vividly as for current ones.
2. Experiments by Hal Hershfield (UCLA, 2011) found that when participants viewed aged avatars of themselves, retirement savings doubled. The visualization collapsed psychological distance.
3. **Delayed reward circuitry** — dopamine modulation through effort rather than impulse.
4. Long-term projects trigger smaller but more sustained dopaminergic responses (Schultz, 2015). The steward learns satisfaction through trajectory, not climax.
5. **Systemic self-concept** — identity fused with environment.
6. Indigenous philosophies encode this as relational ontology: "I am because we are." Stewardship internalizes ecology as ego, reducing destructive externalities without moral policing.
7. **Narrative continuity** — the ability to locate oneself within an ongoing story rather than a discrete life.
8. Viktor Frankl called it *logos*: purpose that outlives the individual. Neuroscience now confirms that storytelling literally lengthens temporal focus by binding events into sequence (Hasson, Princeton 2010).

These four traits form the neuropsychological blueprint of sustainable civilization. When absent, collapse accelerates; when restored, ascent begins.

V.

The Antidote to Apathy

The opposite of stewardship is not greed—it is despair. Studies after the 2008 financial crisis showed that populations exposed to prolonged uncertainty experienced *decision fatigue*: people stopped planning altogether. In Weimar Germany, hyperinflation shortened the psychological future horizon to mere days. Savings vanished; so did meaning.

Stewardship counteracts despair through *constructive repetition*. Routine—tending a garden, repairing a tool, teaching a child—creates continuity even when systems fail. Neuroscientist Andrew Huberman notes that repetitive, goal-linked motion stabilizes the brain's locus coeruleus, reducing anxiety and reactivating focus. In plain terms: movement with purpose repairs temporal coherence.

Every great renewal begins with a small repetitive act performed in faith that tomorrow exists.

VI.

Intergenerational Reciprocity

In evolutionary terms, humans are unique for investing heavily in offspring long after birth. Biologists call this *kin altruism*, but stewardship extends it beyond bloodlines. When a community plants mangroves or archives language, it behaves as a single organism spanning centuries.

The Haudenosaunee Confederacy articulated this principle in the **Seventh Generation** rule: leaders must make decisions considering their impact seven generations ahead. Modern governance, by contrast, operates on a four-year horizon—seventy times shorter. The cognitive load of thinking in centuries is immense, but cultures that ritualize it—

through proverbs, songs, or ceremonies—keep the mental pathway open.

Rojava's councils echo this wisdom. Their charters require ecological assessment before any construction. In the desert, that means imagining rainfall fifty years hence—a political act of imagination as sacred as prayer.

VII ·

The Economics of Care

Economist Kenneth Boulding once observed that capitalism, socialism, and communism all failed to define a "love economy"—systems sustained by care rather than coercion. Stewardship is precisely that missing economy. Its currency is continuity; its profit, endurance.

Empirical research supports this. Companies that prioritize *environmental, social, and governance* (ESG) goals outperform peers over 10-year periods by 20–30 percent (Harvard Business Review, 2022). In communities, participation in cooperative projects correlates with higher life satisfaction (World Values Survey, 2020). The data converge on one insight: care compounds like interest.

The steward does not reject wealth; they redefine it as relational capital—trust, soil fertility, memory. In a collapsing world, these assets inflate in value as others decay.

VIII ·

Temporal Discipline as Freedom

Time is the final frontier of sovereignty. A person who cannot control attention cannot control destiny. Stewardship trains temporal discipline—the ability to act today for outcomes invisible tomorrow.

Stoic philosophers called it *prohairesis*, the internal faculty of choice immune to circumstance. Modern cognitive science calls it *executive control*. Either way, it is the spine of agency.

When citizens synchronize this discipline collectively—through calendars, rituals, or work cycles—they form a temporal commons. Cathedrals once took centuries to complete because time itself was considered communal property. To reclaim sovereignty is to reclaim time as a shared medium, not a market commodity.

IX ·

The Return of the Long View

Future-oriented cultures leave markers for successors. The Japanese maintain **ikebana schools** that trace lineages of instruction back 500 years. The **Long Now Foundation** in Nevada is building a clock designed to tick for 10,000 years. In the Nordic countries, **forest bonds** tie investors to tree growth cycles exceeding a human life. These are modern cathedrals of time—acts of faith measured in centuries.

Their psychological function mirrors that of ancient rituals: they externalize the long view, allowing mortal minds to think immortally. Stewardship, when institutionalized, becomes culture itself.

X ·

Transmission

Night in the desert again, but quieter now. A Rojava teacher seals a glass jar containing seeds, letters, and a child's drawing of a tree. She buries it near a school rebuilt from rubble. "For whoever finds this," she writes, "the soil remembers." Years later, the jar will surface after rain, its paper faded but intact. The tree it describes will already be there—grown from the same seeds, tended by hands she will never know.

This is stewardship: a conversation between centuries conducted in roots and light.

Key 49 · Mythic Resonance: Atlantis Rebuilt and the Archetype of Lost Wisdom Restored

I.

The Dream That Sank

Long before satellites mapped coastlines and empires carved borders, there was a story about a city that vanished beneath the sea. Plato wrote it down in the *Timaeus* and *Critias*, perhaps as allegory, perhaps as warning. Atlantis, he said, was an island kingdom blessed with wisdom, wealth, and technological power beyond its age. Yet as arrogance replaced virtue, the gods withdrew their favor. One night of quakes and waves erased it from the earth.

The myth is older than Plato. Archaeologists trace fragments of similar tales across continents: the Mesopotamian flood, the Indian *Mahapralaya*, the Mayan deluge, the Norse drowning of Ymir's world. Each encodes the same truth—that civilizations drown not because of nature alone but because of dissonance between power and conscience.

Atlantis is not a place. It is a recurring psychological state: *a society that outpaces its soul.*

II.

The Memory Beneath Water

Every culture inherits its own version of Atlantis, and each generation must decide what to salvage from the ruins. Beneath the literal flood imagery lies a deeper pattern—the rhythm of excess, collapse, and renewal. Mythographers call this *catabasis*, the descent into darkness before ascent. Jung called it the night sea journey. It is the archetypal process of regeneration through loss.

When civilizations fall, their wisdom rarely dies; it submerges, waiting for retrieval. Sumerian mathematics reemerged in Greek geometry; Mayan calendar logic informs modern astronomy; Alexandria's lost manuscripts survive in fragments through Arab scholars. Knowledge behaves like coral—it rebuilds on the skeletons of its predecessors.

Thus the legend of Atlantis survives because the human psyche senses the necessity of submersion. The flood cleanses corruption and compresses memory into seed form. Collapse is conservation disguised as catastrophe.

III ·

The Hidden Code of the Myth

Read symbolically, Atlantis represents a cycle every intelligent society must endure. The myth unfolds in five archetypal movements:

1. **Harmony** — alignment of power and principle.
2. **Overreach** — hubris born of mastery.
3. **Disconnection** — moral systems lag behind technological ones.
4. **Deluge** — the self-correction of imbalance.
5. **Renewal** — wisdom recovered, reframed, and dispersed.

In Plato's account, the survivors of the flood scatter across the world, founding new cities and teaching remnants of the old arts. It mirrors what historians now call *knowledge diaspora*—the diffusion of genius after collapse. When Byzantium fell, scholars fled to Florence, igniting the Renaissance. When Germany expelled Jewish scientists, quantum mechanics migrated to Princeton. Every Atlantis, once destroyed, seeds ten new lights elsewhere.

IV.

Atlantis as Cognitive Map

Psychologically, Atlantis symbolizes the tension between ego and ecosystem. The Atlanteans represent the rational mind unmoored from empathy—the intellect pursuing control over connection. In Jungian terms, they are the *inflated conscious ego* that forgets its origins in the collective unconscious. The flood is the unconscious reclaiming balance.

Modern parallels are obvious: AI without ethics, economies without ecology, networks without narrative. Each carries Atlantean DNA—brilliance without humility. When the sea rises, it is not punishment but *re-equilibration.*

To rebuild Atlantis rightly, we must restore the missing symmetry between knowledge and wisdom, between speed and stillness. True sovereignty is not escape from nature but participation in her intelligence.

V.

The Builders' Covenant

In every post-flood story, survivors make a covenant with the divine or with time itself. Noah's rainbow, Utnapishtim's tablet, Manu's seed boat—all declare a vow: *we will remember.* This is the archetypal essence of stewardship reframed through mythic language.

The covenant's function is psychological. It externalizes guilt and encodes gratitude, transforming trauma into ritual. Survivors need a visible symbol to bind them to responsibility. In Rojava, it is a charter written in war. In Ghana, it was a scale balanced at dawn. In our era, perhaps it is a ledger that tracks not profits but planetary repair.

Every civilization must choose its rainbow—its visible proof that memory will not sink again.

VI ·

The Rebuilders' Blueprint

If the Atlanteans fell for worshiping their own power, the new builders must worship process. Myth tells us the secret: the city was circular. Concentric rings of land and water surrounded its temple. Scholars debate the geometry, but the symbol is unmistakable—a self-similar pattern, like an atom or a galaxy. The circle represents recursion: systems nested within systems, all reflecting one another.

To rebuild Atlantis, therefore, is to design recursive governance—small councils mirroring larger assemblies, feedback flowing both directions. Ghana's co-ops, Rojava's communes, blockchain networks, and citizen assemblies all unconsciously echo this shape. Decentralization is myth made structural.

The true Atlantean rebirth is not vertical like a tower; it is concentric like a ripple. Power radiates outward, soft but continuous.

VII ·

Archetypes of the Return

Across cultures, the flood hero never rebuilds the same city. He or she carries fragments—laws, seeds, songs—into new soil. Gilgamesh fails to retrieve immortality but returns with wisdom. The Hopi emerge from underground after the third world's destruction to inhabit the fourth. The Greeks imagine Deucalion and Pyrrha repopulating the earth by casting stones that transform into humans.

The archetype of the *Returner* reminds us that survival is not preservation; it is transformation. To rebuild Atlantis is to rebuild differently—to carry forward essence, not architecture. Every reborn world is smaller, humbler, wiser.

VIII ·

The Modern Atlantis

If Atlantis exists anywhere today, it is digital. The internet is our shimmering island—vast, interconnected, radiant with knowledge, yet sinking under waves of noise. Its creators dreamed of universal enlightenment; its users drift between wonder and surveillance. The same imbalance that drowned the mythic city—hubris without harmony—threatens this one too.

But the tools for restoration also lie within it. Open-source projects, decentralized ledgers, and cooperative digital commons are attempts to encode humility into code. They are the new temples rising from data rather than stone. The question is whether we can remember the covenant—to align intelligence with integrity before the next flood is algorithmic rather than oceanic.

IX ·

The Sovereign Imagination

Rebuilding Atlantis requires not blueprints but imagination disciplined by ethics. Stewardship alone sustains; imagination renews. The philosopher Alfred North Whitehead wrote, *"The art of progress is to preserve order amid change and to preserve change amid order."* That sentence could have been etched above Atlantis' gates.

To live as a sovereign individual is to hold both: structure and flow, mastery and mercy, reason and reverence. In mythic language, sovereignty is Poseidon's trident recast as compass rather than weapon—a tool to measure depth, not to dominate it.

X.

Transmission

In the depths, the lost city glows again—not of stone, but of memory. Columns shimmer like coral, inscriptions pulse with bioluminescent code. From the seabed rise builders not of marble but of consciousness—crafting new circles, weaving new vows. Above, on the surface, a storm calms. The ocean reflects starlight as if remembering its own design.

Atlantis is no longer lost; it is distributed. Every act of care, every council meeting, every child taught to imagine centuries—these are its rebuilt walls. The city breathes through us now, quiet and alive.

Key 50 · Sovereignty Protocol: The Blueprint for a Micro-Commons · How to Build a Local Co-operative, CSA, or Timebank in 90 Days

I ·

The Return of the Small Republic

Every civilization that endures does so through miniature republics—villages, guilds, cooperatives—that act as living organs within the larger body. When empires fracture, survival begins in the neighborhood. The sovereign future is not imagined through ideology but through design: groups of five to fifty people mastering the art of interdependence.

A *micro-commons* is any locally governed system that shares resources, responsibility, and reward. It may grow food, circulate credit, exchange labor hours, or manage renewable energy. Its scale is human; its logic, ecological. It is the modern descendant of Ghana's cocoa unions and Rojava's communes—the smallest unit of freedom that can feed itself.

The goal is not utopia. It is reliability. A system that can still function when power blinks, banks freeze, or algorithms vanish is worth more than rhetoric.

II ·

Phase One: Foundation (Weeks 1–4)

1. **Assemble a circle of trust.**
2. Begin with three to ten people who share geography and values. Diversity of skill is crucial: one logistician, one communicator, one craftsperson, one record-keeper. What matters most is reliability. A small group that meets deadlines will outlast a visionary crowd that doesn't.

3. **Define the resource focus.**
4. Choose one tangible flow: food, tools, knowledge, or time. Start narrow. A CSA (community-supported agriculture) may organize a single crop or garden bed. A timebank may track just five recurring tasks—childcare, repairs, tutoring, cooking, transport. The principle is early proof of function.
5. **Draft the Covenant.**
6. One page, handwritten or typed. It states purpose, decision method, and contribution rule. Example:
7. *"We agree to meet weekly, contribute two hours or equivalent value, decide by 75 percent consensus, and record all exchanges publicly."*
8. This paper is your moral firewall. Without it, friendship collapses under pressure; with it, community survives disagreement.
9. **Choose the ledger.**
10. A notebook, spreadsheet, or open-source platform such as Holochain or Mutual Credit Services. Transparency prevents corrosion. Ledger visibility is the secular equivalent of sacred witness.
11. **Secure a meeting place.**
12. A living room, café, temple hall, or library room. Physical presence stabilizes trust. The first four weeks should prioritize rhythm over result—meeting at the same hour trains reliability into habit.

III ·

Phase Two: Operation (Weeks 5–8)

1. **Launch the exchange.**
2. Begin circulation. In a CSA, collect pre-season contributions and distribute produce boxes weekly. In a timebank, log hours using one-to-one parity—every skill equal in credit. Equality in unit value prevents hierarchy from reforming.
3. **Measure trust quantitatively.**

4. Track attendance, delivery, and fulfillment rates. A group maintaining above 80 percent completion is resilient. Anything lower demands diagnosis—usually unclear roles or uneven load. Trust is not mystical; it is measurable reliability over time.
5. **Institute rotating roles.**
6. Every month, rotate coordinator, treasurer, and communicator. Rotation dissolves hidden power and trains redundancy. It also surfaces latent talent. Ghanaian cooperatives thrived because every member could run the meeting if needed.
7. **Document everything.**
8. Keep minutes, decisions, and ledgers open. In crises, documentation is collective memory; it allows newcomers to integrate fast and prevents myths of betrayal.
9. **Celebrate the cycle.**
10. Ritualize success. A shared meal, a tree planting, a harvest song—anything that marks continuity. Joy is logistical lubrication; groups that celebrate last longer than those that only labor.

IV.

Phase Three: Expansion (Weeks 9–12)

1. **Establish external linkages.**
2. Connect to adjacent commons—another CSA, a local credit union, a repair café. The goal is not merger but federation. Two linked groups sharing data and surplus achieve economies of scale without centralization.
3. **Create a resilience fund.**
4. Contribute a small monthly share—1 to 3 percent of earnings or time—to a mutual-aid pot. Use it only for emergencies or expansion tools. This fund transforms charity into insurance.
5. **Codify conflict resolution.**
6. Borrow from Indigenous and restorative models: structured listening, summary by mediator, 24-hour cooling-off period.

Conflict, when ritualized, becomes calibration rather than corrosion.
7. **Audit energy and supply chains.**
8. Trace where inputs come from. Replace one external dependency each quarter with a local or renewable source. This incremental substitution builds sovereignty the way compound interest builds wealth.
9. **Publish an annual report.**
10. One page listing contributions, outcomes, lessons. Transparency converts effort into inspiration for replication elsewhere. Civilization scales by imitation, not decree.

V.

Governance Model

Level	Purpose	Size	Decision Rule
Circle	Core participants	5–15	Consensus or ¾ majority
Cluster	Federation of 3–6 circles	30–90	Delegated consensus
Commons Council	Network of clusters	150–300	Consent with veto rights

The architecture mirrors natural scaling laws: complexity grows logarithmically, not exponentially. Decision cost remains linear while capacity multiplies. In this geometry, freedom becomes fractal.

VI ·

Metrics of Vitality

- **Participation rate** > 75 percent
- **Diversity index** ≥ 0.4 (occupation or gender)
- **Reciprocity balance** ± 10 percent
- **Cash or time reserve** ≥ 4 weeks operations
- **Emotional cohesion** — survey trust score ≥ 7/10

These numbers are not bureaucracy; they are diagnostics of morale. A commons that measures its own heartbeat rarely flatlines.

VII ·

Economic Mechanics

1. **Credit loop.**
2. Every contribution—labor, produce, expertise—earns credit redeemable within the circle. Surplus can trade externally at negotiated exchange rates. Currency is memory; keep it honest.
3. **Local reserve.**
4. Hold physical or digital reserves equal to one-month turnover. In crisis, liquidity preserves cooperation.
5. **Reinvestment.**
6. Allocate one-third surplus to maintenance, one-third to innovation, one-third to education. This triad sustains continuity, creativity, and capacity.
7. **Transparency ledger.**
8. Post transactions publicly. Sunlight is cheaper than audits.

VIII ·

Culture and Ritual

A commons survives on rhythm more than rule. Establish repeating ceremonies:

- **Opening Circle** — each voice shares intention.
- **Harvest Moment** — acknowledge contributions aloud.
- **Quiet Hour** — monthly silence or reflection period to prevent burnout.

Anthropologists note that rituals increase serotonin and oxytocin in groups, strengthening empathy and cohesion. A commons that prays or sings together can survive disagreement without fracture.

IX ·

Failure Modes and Antidotes

Failure	Symptom	Antidote
Centralization creep	One leader hoards decisions	Enforce rotation + ledger visibility
Entropy	Meetings stop producing action	Re-define single deliverable per session
Moral fatigue	Loss of meaning or resentment	Re-articulate covenant; renew ritual
External capture	Donors or politicians co-opt agenda	Diversify income; publish decisions

The micro-commons must remain antifragile—able to gain strength from shock. When crisis strikes, record what worked, and teach it. Resilience is collective hindsight operationalized.

X ·

The 90-Day Arc Summarized

Week	Action	Outcome
1–2	Form circle, choose resource	Trust base + purpose
3–4	Draft covenant, ledger, space	Governance installed
5–6	Launch exchange	Proof of concept
7–8	Rotate roles, refine systems	Distributed skill
9–10	Link externally, create fund	Network effect
11–12	Audit + celebrate	Continuity secured

Ninety days to sovereignty. Not absolute, but functional—the kind that feeds, funds, and focuses people when institutions falter.

XI · Transmission

Evening settles over a small town. Inside a converted garage, ten people count jars of honey and handwritten IOUs. A child adds the numbers on a chalkboard; her laughter punctuates the sums. No minister, no algorithm, no invisible hand—only hands visible, exchanging promise for promise. Outside, the streetlights flicker; inside, the light holds steady. The circle adjourns. The micro-republic breathes.

Chapter 11

The Testament of the Builders

Part IV · The Future

Key 51 · Historical Mirror: Monastic Rules as Operating Systems of Moral Order

I ·

Silence Before Structure

At dawn in Monte Cassino, 529 CE, a bell tolls three times—metal on stone in a world without electricity. In the half-light between Roman decay and medieval dawn, a former soldier named Benedict of Nursia writes his Rule. It is neither manifesto nor sermon but a manual: seventy-three chapters of logistics for souls. Sleep schedules, meal portions, discipline, humility, leadership rotations—all specified with engineering clarity.

What Benedict inaugurated was not merely a religious order but the first sustained organizational operating system of post-imperial Europe. When Rome's bureaucracies collapsed, monasteries became repositories of continuity: scriptoria, clinics, libraries, granaries, schools. The Rule was their firmware.

Every great collapse requires a protocol that teaches how to live when central authority dies. The monastic movement was that protocol—distributed, redundant, self-healing.

II ·

The Architecture of Obedience

The Rule of St. Benedict begins not with creed but with command: *"Listen, my son, to the precepts of the master, and incline the ear of thy heart."* It demands obedience, but of a peculiar kind—listening obedience, attentive rather than authoritarian.

Each monastery was a miniature republic governed by an abbot, yet accountability flowed through ritual and rotation. Offices changed regularly; no monk could hoard power or possessions. Even the abbot was subject to council. The monastery thus balanced hierarchy and consensus long before modern management theory.

Daily life ran on precise intervals: eight canonical hours of prayer, three of labor, two of study, one of reflection. The bell was their clock and constitution. Where Rome measured time by imperial edict, monks measured it by discipline. The sound of that bell was the heartbeat of civilization resetting its rhythm.

III ·

Stability and Conversion of Manners

Benedict's Rule required three vows: obedience, stability, and conversion of manners. The second was revolutionary. Monks could not wander; they belonged to place. In an age of marauding tribes and shifting lords, stability was resistance. To root oneself was to defy entropy.

"Conversion of manners" meant ongoing recalibration—a lifetime debugging of ego. Every task was liturgy. Cleaning latrines held equal dignity with illuminating manuscripts. By sacralizing maintenance, the Rule converted labor into prayer and eliminated status asymmetry. Sociologists now call this flattened hierarchy "role rotation." In Benedict's logic, it was simply justice.

The psychological effect was profound: when every action is ritual, burnout becomes meaningful effort. The Rule prefigured modern cognitive-behavioral therapy: behavior shapes belief.

IV.

Copyists as Coders

Within the cloisters, scriptoria buzzed with quills. Each letter copied was checksum against oblivion. Over five centuries, monks duplicated nearly all surviving Latin literature and large parts of Greek science. Their marginalia reveal debugging habits: notes flagging errors, cross-references, version control. In effect, they invented peer review and information redundancy.

The Abbey of Lindisfarne, Monte Cassino, and Cluny functioned as distributed servers synchronizing knowledge across Europe. When Vikings burned one, others restored from backup. No king ordered this; the Rule itself encoded the network. It was the first resilient information infrastructure of the post-Roman world.

V.

Time as Commons

In monastic life, time was shared property. The bell divided hours not for efficiency but equity: no monk could hoard hours as wealth. This temporal commons became Europe's first social safety net. Where peasants lived by seasonal chaos, monks lived by steady predictability. Hospitals, guesthouses, and schools sprang from this abundance of ordered time.

Economic historians credit monasteries with founding proto-capitalism, yet their true innovation was moral accounting. Ledgers recorded alms and grain, but also virtue and penance. Every transaction was spiritualized, keeping greed subordinate to grace.

VI ·

Cistercians and The Industrial Mind

By the 12th century, the Cistercian Order refined Benedict's Rule into precision engineering. Their abbeys spread like fractal patterns across Europe—uniform layout, standardized workflow, water power for mills and furnaces. Economic historians note that Cistercians were Europe's largest producers of iron and textiles before the Industrial Revolution.

Their Rule-driven standardization was open-source. Any new monastery could request plans and advice. Cistercians redefined efficiency as piety and turned spiritual discipline into mechanical innovation. In their water channels and work schedules we find the DNA of modern operations management.

VII ·

Resilience Through Recursion

When the Black Death decimated Europe, monasteries absorbed orphans and preserved medical knowledge. When wars burned fields, they replanted. The Rule's strength was recursion: each monk trained a novice, each abbey founded a daughter house. Like self-replicating code, the order grew by copying essence not appearance.

Because obedience was to principle, not person, failure of a leader did not collapse the system. Leadership rotation and documented ritual ensured institutional memory. That is why the Benedictine Order has persisted for fifteen centuries without a CEO.

VIII ·

Psychological Mechanics of The Rule

Modern neuroscience would recognize in the Rule three psychological technologies:

1. **Predictability and safety.** Regular schedule reduces cortisol levels and stabilizes mood—documented in studies of ritual behavior (Oxford, 2014).
2. **Purpose coupled to action.** Every task justified by divine intent sustains dopaminergic motivation without burnout.
3. **Communal mirroring.** Chant and shared rhythm synchronize breathing and heart rates, amplifying empathy and cohesion.

In neural terms, the monastery was a regulated collective nervous system—precisely what modern organizations struggle to engineer digitally.

IX ·

Legacy of The Rule

The Rule of Benedict outlived empires because it balanced three axes: stability, discipline, and adaptability. Charlemagne used it to reorganize education; Francis of Assisi softened it with joy; Ignatius of Loyola weaponized it for mission. Every subsequent order modified the source code but kept the core: a written standard plus daily iteration.

Modern constitutions owe their durability to this template. The U.S. Founders read translations of Benedict's Rule; corporate charters mirror its checks and balances. Even software engineering borrows its language—*version, iteration, release*. The monk was the first project manager of Western memory.

X.

Transmission

Midnight in a stone cloister. Candles flicker against vellum. A monk leans over a page, writing the final line of a psalm: *Ut inam dirigantur viae meae* — "Let my ways be directed." Outside, barbarians move through the forest; inside, a heartbeat of ink keeps time. The empire is gone, but the Rule remains—steady as breath, ready for the next builders to inherit.

Key 52 · Modern Parallel: Mutual Aid Playbooks and Open-Source Models in the 21st Century

I ·

The New Monks of Crisis

When the pandemic struck in 2020, supply chains broke faster than faith in institutions. Supermarket shelves emptied; hospitals rationed masks; governments floundered in spreadsheets. In that vacuum, a quiet network of civilians began to organize without permission. They called their groups **Mutual Aid**—a phrase borrowed from the Russian anarchist Peter Kropotkin, who a century earlier argued that cooperation, not competition, was the engine of evolution.

Within weeks, more than 6 000 mutual-aid collectives appeared across the United States alone. In London, 3 500 neighborhood WhatsApp groups mapped who had medicine, who needed groceries, who could drive. In Manila, jeepney drivers built roadside "community pantries" stocked by strangers. In Nairobi, slum dwellers pooled savings for hand-washing stations when the state ignored them.

No single leader called them into being; no one owned the brand. The model propagated like mycelium—self-similar, humble, unstoppable. Every spreadsheet was a monastery of empathy, every volunteer a monk of logistics.

II ·

The Playbook of Survival

What these groups shared was not ideology but architecture:

1. **Open communication.** Public channels replaced gatekeepers. Slack, Signal, Telegram, Google Sheets—modern scriptoria of coordination.
2. **Transparent accounting.** Donations tracked in real time; every dollar a line in the open ledger.
3. **Distributed leadership.** No presidents, only moderators; no charisma, only consistency.
4. **Rapid iteration.** Feedback loops compressed to hours; needs assessed, routes redrawn, deliveries confirmed.
5. **Moral code.** Aid without hierarchy: anyone could ask, anyone could give.

Sociologists later compared these cells to Benedictine monasteries. Each had rhythm (daily check-ins), ritual (packing shifts, debrief circles), and Rule (guidelines pinned at the top of chat threads). Their obedience was to need itself.

A volunteer in Brooklyn said, *"We don't wait for permission because hunger doesn't."* That single line captured the essence of decentralized ethics: authority as responsiveness.

III ·

From Mutual Aid to Open Source

The same logic governed another invisible cathedral rising at the same time: the **open-source software movement**. Long before COVID, coders had been building commons of code that anyone could use and improve. By 2023, more than 90 percent of global digital infrastructure depended on open-source libraries maintained mostly by volunteers.

The parallels are exact. A repository on GitHub is a digital monastery: shared Rule (license), shared rhythm (commit cycles), humility before collective intelligence. Pull requests echo the Benedictine vow of correction—every contribution reviewed by peers, every error confessed and repaired.

Where medieval monks copied scripture to preserve knowledge, modern maintainers copy repositories to preserve function. Redundancy is salvation. When one server fails, mirrors restore from backup; when one maintainer burns out, another forks the code. The ethos is recursive mercy.

IV.

The Psychology of Contribution

Why do people work for free in crises or in code? Behavioral economics offers clues. Studies by Harvard's Public Goods Lab (2021) show that altruistic collaboration triggers dopamine and oxytocin surges comparable to monetary reward. The brain's reward system responds more strongly to *visible impact* than to income.

Mutual-aid groups and open-source communities optimize for visibility: every task, every contribution recorded publicly. This transparency converts effort into feedback, feedback into meaning. In turn, meaning produces endurance.

Participants describe "collective flow"—a shared trance of purpose similar to what Csikszentmihalyi observed in jazz ensembles or surgical teams. The mind expands beyond ego; time compresses. It is the secular analog of monastic devotion.

V.

The New Rule of Digital Commons

Across these networks, certain unwritten laws recur—modern successors to Benedict's Rule:

1. **Show up.** Reliability outranks genius.
2. **Document everything.** Memory is communal property.

3. **Distribute authority.** Leadership rotates; credit diffuses.
4. **Default to trust, verify through transparency.**
5. **No profit without purpose.**

These maxims stabilize trust at planetary scale. They also inoculate against hierarchy creep—the disease of every empire. When everyone can read the ledger, corruption suffocates for lack of shadow.

In 2022, the volunteer developers of the Linux Kernel formalized a *Code of Conduct* explicitly citing "mutual respect and shared stewardship." That phrase could have been carved above any monastery gate a millennium earlier.

VI ·

Case Study — The Mask Makers

In the first pandemic spring, textile workers from Porto Alegre to Pune converted living rooms into micro-factories. Designs for fabric masks traveled through Telegram in minutes. The pattern repository "Open Source Mask Project" logged 2 million downloads by May 2020. No patents, no royalties. Hospitals later traced thousands of saved lives to those designs.

One participant said, *"We were never alone; we were connected by thread."* The metaphor was literal and spiritual: fiber as data, cloth as code, humanity woven line by line.

VII ·

Case Study — Open Insulin and the New Bio-Commons

In a garage lab in Oakland, a collective of scientists called **Open Insulin** works to produce low-cost insulin outside pharmaceutical monopolies. Their principle: life-saving knowledge should not be property. Their lab notebooks are online; their formulas open.

This is molecular mutual aid—science democratized through the same ethic that copied manuscripts in stone cloisters. As medieval scribes preserved theology, these volunteers preserve biology. Both acts defy scarcity as destiny.

VIII ·

Resilience as Protocol

When disasters multiply—pandemic, cyber-attacks, climate shocks—systems built on hierarchy fail first. Mutual-aid networks prove antifragile: they gain coordination from stress. Each failure becomes training data.

Data from MIT's Center for Collective Intelligence (2022) show that decentralized groups outperformed centralized relief agencies by 30 percent in speed and 40 percent in coverage during early COVID months. The reason: information moved horizontally, not bureaucratically.

Resilience, therefore, is not redundancy of supply but redundancy of compassion.

IX·

From Aid to Architecture

After the immediate crises faded, many mutual-aid groups evolved into lasting institutions: tool libraries, cooperative groceries, community Wi-Fi networks. The transition from relief to design marks the civilizational hinge—the moment when empathy learns engineering.

Open-source communities follow the same trajectory. What begins as volunteerism becomes infrastructure. Linux now powers 96 percent of the world's servers; Wikipedia, written by millions, functions as the planet's reference library. We live inside the cathedrals they built without marble.

These are the Testament's heirs—orders of builders bound not by creed but by code.

X·

Transmission

Night in a coworking loft, routers blinking like votive lamps. A dozen volunteers review pull requests, others pack food parcels in the same room. Screens glow; so do faces. Someone reads aloud a new line in the charter: *"All knowledge is for repair."* The group nods, commits the change, saves the file. Outside, rain drums against glass; inside, another monastery of the future hums quietly into dawn.

Key 53 · Psychological Mechanism: Moral Elevation and the Contagion of Virtue

I ·

The Invisible Current

Every civilization depends on invisible electricity—trust, admiration, and imitation flowing between people. When that current falters, laws multiply and hearts cool. When it surges, movements ignite without orders.

In 2010, social psychologist Jonathan Haidt described a state he called **moral elevation**—a warm, rising sensation in the chest when witnessing acts of courage or compassion. MRI scans show synchronized activation in the ventromedial prefrontal cortex and vagus nerve: biology echoing reverence. It is awe translated into physiology.4

The monasteries of old engineered this current through ritual and story. The mutual-aid collectives of the present do it through transparency and witness. Each good deed publicly seen becomes a neuron firing in the social brain. Virtue spreads by mirror.

II ·

The Physics of Example

Haidt's lab found that subjects shown footage of altruism—firefighters running into buildings, strangers shielding others—reported stronger prosocial intent for hours. Follow-up experiments by Simone Schnall at Cambridge (2013) proved the effect behavioral: participants who watched virtuous acts were twice as likely to help with tedious tasks afterward.

Moral elevation is emotional contagion harnessed for coherence. In collective settings—choirs, protests, volunteer shifts—the feeling compounds. Heart-rate studies of group singing reveal synchronization within seconds; collective dopamine spikes make virtue briefly addictive.

Every builder order, from Benedictines to open-source maintainers, has unconsciously cultivated this physics: visible integrity raises voltage; others align.

III ·

The Descent of Cynicism

The opposite current is cynicism—a self-protective numbness. It spreads faster because it costs nothing. In decaying institutions, exposure to hypocrisy erodes empathy receptors; repeated disappointment teaches detachment. Psychologists call it **learned amoralism**—the belief that sincerity is naïve.

Digital culture amplifies cynicism through performative outrage. Algorithms reward derision over devotion. Each sneer is a micro-cut in the connective tissue of trust. Civilizations die when their citizens can no longer believe in decency without irony.

The work of the builder, therefore, is to re-enchant the moral imagination—not with slogans but with consistent proof that cooperation still functions.

IV ·

The Architecture of Elevation

Across centuries, communities have encoded elevation into architecture and ritual. Gothic cathedrals lifted the gaze vertically; Zen gardens pulled it inward; Benedictine chant synchronized breath across bodies.

Modern equivalents exist: disaster-relief warehouses organized like sanctuaries, hackerspaces glowing with collaborative concentration.

The essential components are identical:

1. **Visibility** — goodness must be seen to be believed.
2. **Participation** — spectatorship converts to service.
3. **Repetition** — ritual fixes virtue into muscle memory.
4. **Story** — narrative gives moral data emotional storage.

Neuroscience confirms what monks intuited: repetition under emotional charge rewires moral circuits. The daily office, the nightly code review, the routine grocery delivery—each is practice in sustained empathy.

V.

Virtue as Network Effect

In 2009, Nicholas Christakis and James Fowler mapped altruism across social networks. A single act of generosity inspired three degrees of imitation: the friend, the friend's friend, and the friend's friend's friend. Statistical modeling showed clusters of moral contagion persisting months after the original event. One act could influence hundreds through invisible chains.

They called it **"the ripple of goodness."** Economists later reframed it as *positive externality*. In truth, it is civilization's immune system. Every moral act strengthens adjacent cells. When enough nodes radiate integrity, corruption finds no host.

VI.

The Mirror Neuron Republic

Functional MRI studies (Rizzolatti et al., 1996 → present) identified **mirror neurons**—cells that fire both when performing an action and when observing it. These are empathy's hardware. They also explain moral elevation: witnessing courage activates the same neural pattern as enacting it.

Societies become what they repeatedly watch. When entertainment glorifies cruelty, empathy atrophies; when it dramatizes decency, compassion rehearses itself. The Rule of the Builders must therefore include curation—guarding attention as sacred resource. Each screen is a cathedral or a coliseum depending on what it displays.

VII.

Designing for Decency

If vice can be engineered—through addictive interfaces and outrage loops—so can virtue. The builder civilization will design **interfaces of conscience**.

- **Feedback loops** showing collective benefit ("you saved 12 kg CO_2") convert morality into measurable pleasure.
- **Transparent dashboards** of community contribution mimic monastic ledgers.
- **Narrative dashboards**—stories of beneficiaries—sustain empathy through specificity.

Behavioral scientists at MIT's Human Dynamics Lab demonstrated that adding small "empathy cues" to digital collaboration tools—faces, progress bars, gratitude prompts—increased cooperation by 35 percent. The future monastery glows from screens, not candles.

VIII ·

The Psychology of Witness

Moral elevation requires audience. Not fame, but fellowship. When people witness integrity in real time, mirror circuits synchronize. This is why livestreamed rescue efforts or transparent ledgers inspire more donations than abstract appeals.

Ancient monastics understood witness as confession; modern builders enact it as **public accountability**. Open-source commits, community budgets, live-streamed assemblies—all are digital confessions of work. Transparency is humility operationalized.

The paradox: privacy breeds pride, while visibility breeds care. When one's effort is seen, it becomes sacred again.

IX ·

Renewing Faith in Each Other

Despair tells moderns that human nature is selfish. Yet evolutionary biology dismantles the myth. Cooperative behaviors appear in every species that survives stress: ants, whales, primates. Survival favors empathy clusters. Humanity's problem is not moral weakness but narrative amnesia—we forget our cooperative lineage.

Re-storying civilization means narrating altruism as power. Historians rarely write of kindness because it leaves fewer ruins. The new chroniclers must document builders the way old ones documented kings. The archive of decency must grow until it outweighs cynicism in collective memory.

X.

Transmission

A night market after a storm. Generators hum; puddles mirror lanterns. Strangers pass food to strangers, each motion wordless, efficient, tender. A boy hands his umbrella to an old woman and runs off laughing into rain. For a moment the crowd feels the same small warmth rise through the chest—a pulse shared across hundreds. No anthem plays, yet something sacred circulates. The city breathes in unison, illuminated from within.

Key 54 · Mythic Resonance: The Rule of Builders and the Ten Vows of Renewal

I ·

The Silence After the Hammers

When the last stones of empire cool, silence takes the shape of prayer.

Out of that hush the Builders emerge—calloused hands, soot-streaked faces, eyes lit not by victory but by endurance. They speak no new creed at first; they listen to what the ruins whisper. In every age of reconstruction—from Benedict's cloister at Monte Cassino to a flooded village on the Ganges—someone hears the same instruction: *Begin again, but begin clean.*

Myth remembers these moments as dawns. The Egyptians named them *Zep Tepi*, the first time; the Sumerians called them *Udug hul temen*, the day the foundations were cleared of evil. Every civilization keeps a record of its restart. Each record begins with vows.

II ·

The Archetype of the Rule

Long before constitutions, there were Rules.

Benedict's *Regula Monachorum* (530 CE) guided men who wished to live neither in chaos nor in tyranny. Its genius lay not in theology but in rhythm: pray, work, rest, repeat. The Rule was a metronome for meaning.

In the mythic imagination, such Rules descend from higher sources. Moses receives tablets, Manu writes cosmic law, Hammurabi inscribes order on basalt. The pattern is identical: revelation translates into routine. Law becomes the bones of resurrection.

The Builders of this century inherit that lineage. They are neither monks nor revolutionaries; they are custodians of coherence. Their Rule must be simple enough to memorize and deep enough to steer worlds.

III ·

The Ten Vows of Renewal

The new Rule is not written on stone but on conscience.

It arises wherever hands rebuild with humility. Its ten vows echo through ages, adaptable as water yet firm as oak.

1. **The Vow of Presence**
2. To show up fully in every task, refusing distraction as the new idolatry.
3. For the absent mind cannot shape matter.
4. **The Vow of Craft**
5. To perfect one thing each day—bread, code, beam, sentence—until mastery becomes meditation.
6. **The Vow of Honesty**
7. To speak what is true even when silence is safer. Truth is the mortar between stones.
8. **The Vow of Stewardship**
9. To leave each tool, plot, and system stronger than found. Ownership is replaced by guardianship.
10. **The Vow of Mutuality**
11. To measure success by the strength of the circle, not the size of the throne.
12. **The Vow of Learning**
13. To treat ignorance as forgivable but stagnation as sin. Every library is a seed vault.
14. **The Vow of Silence**

15. To pause before reacting, allowing wisdom to surface through stillness. Noise builds nothing.
16. **The Vow of Beauty**
17. To weave grace into utility, for what is ugly within soon decays without.
18. **The Vow of Courage**
19. To defend the fragile—ideas, children, beginnings—against entropy and fear.
20. **The Vow of Joy**
21. To celebrate labor and laughter as twin sanctities. A civilization that cannot sing cannot last.

Together these vows form the Rule's pulse: presence, craft, honesty, stewardship, mutuality, learning, silence, beauty, courage, joy. Break one, and the cadence falters. Keep them, and time itself bends toward coherence.

IV.

The Mythic Weavers

In Norse legend, the Norns spin fate from three wells. In Greek memory, the Moirai measure life by thread. In Yoruba cosmology, the orisha Obatala molds humanity from clay each dawn. Across mythic continents the act of creation is always repetitive, never finished. The Builders stand in that continuum.

Their weaving is literal—fiber, circuit, social fabric—and metaphysical. Each vow adds a strand; together they form the **Loom of Continuity**. Where empire wrote edicts in marble, the Builders inscribe rhythm in behavior. They understand what the ancients knew: that culture is rehearsal, not monument.

V.

The Trial of Fire

Every Rule is tested by the element it ignores. Benedict's monks faced sloth; industrial builders faced greed; digital builders face distraction. The myth calls this trial *Agni-pariksha*—the ordeal by fire.

When the networks burn with misinformation, the Builder holds silence.

When systems tempt speed over substance, the Builder chooses craft.

When cynicism sneers, the Builder answers with beauty.

Virtue here is not ascetic denial but sustained alignment under pressure. The Rule's purpose is calibration. Fire proves metal.

VI.

The Hidden Reward

No hero's medal awaits these vows. The reward is resonance—the quiet sense that one's actions rhyme with the deeper order of things. In Sanskrit this harmony is *Rta*, in Chinese thought *Li*, in physics coherence. The Builder feels it when tool meets timber, when idea meets need.

Psychologists would call it *flow*; mystics would call it grace. Both point to the same neural symphony: attention merged with intention. That state is civilization's heartbeat.

VII ·

The Return of the Sacred Ordinary

Modernity exiled sanctity from labor, dividing holy from useful. The Rule erases that line. To sweep a floor attentively is liturgy. To debug code ethically is prayer. The myth of the Builders reinstates what medieval craftsmen called *opus dei*—the work of God hidden in work of hands.

When enough people live this way, temples are unnecessary. The city becomes the cloister. The marketplace hums in tune with the monastery bell.

VIII ·

Transmission

Every Rule requires apprentices. The vows survive only when spoken aloud, taught through imitation. In monasteries, novices learned by watching elders. In the coming century, mentorship returns as moral technology. Each Builder must train three: one younger, one older displaced worker, one peer. This triad closes the loop of knowledge and compassion.

Thus the Rule multiplies not through evangelism but through example. It spreads quietly, like yeast through dough.

IX ·

The Eternal Ledger

In mythic vision, the gods keep ledgers not of wealth but of intention. The Egyptian *Weighing of the Heart* judged balance, not obedience. The Rule revives that accounting: did your work add order or noise? Did your words heal or corrode trust? Such introspection replaces surveillance with conscience.

When conscience governs, oversight becomes unnecessary. Civilization reverts to self-regulation—the highest form of freedom.

X ·

Transmission

Dawn over an unfinished cathedral. Scaffolds shiver in wind; cranes stand motionless against rose light. On the ground, a mason kneels, tracing chalk lines with gloved fingers, humming an old song. Around him others stir—painters, coders, gardeners, teachers—each carrying the day's first tool. The city beyond still sleeps, unaware that its resurrection has already begun, stone by stone, vow by vow. The sun rises not on walls but on will.

Key 55 · Sovereignty Protocol: The Builder's Covenant and Community Implementation Guide

I.

From Principle to Practice

A rule, no matter how sacred, remains inert until it is lived.

The monasteries of old thrived not because they memorized vows, but because they translated them into rhythm—hours, seasons, work, rest. The Builders of this age must do the same. The covenant is not a creed; it is an operating system that runs on behavior.

Every reader who reaches this point stands at the threshold of embodiment. To believe in renewal is to schedule it. Sovereignty is built not in declarations but in calendars.

The **Builder's Covenant** transforms the Ten Vows of Renewal into tangible systems—governance, finance, ritual, and craft—scaled for communities as small as five or as wide as five hundred. It begins where theory ends: at the table, the workshop, the ledger.

II.

The Covenant Structure

The covenant has **three rings of commitment**: *Personal Discipline, Communal Design,* and *External Integration.* Each ring supports the others like nested orbits.

1. Personal Discipline

Daily, weekly, and seasonal cycles that embody the Ten Vows.

Example template:

Cycle	Practice	Measurable Output
Daily	The Vow of Presence → Morning silence, 15 minutes	Mood and focus log
Weekly	The Vow of Craft → Complete one repair, build, or lesson	Skill documentation
Seasonal	The Vow of Stewardship → Audit of resources shared, waste reduced	Sustainability ledger

By quantifying virtue without commodifying it, Builders anchor ideals in measurable motion.

2. Communal Design

A group of Builders—call it a Circle—operates as a living Rule. Circles have roles, but never ranks:

- **The Keeper:** maintains rhythm, calls gatherings.
- **The Steward:** tracks resources, ensures reciprocity.
- **The Scribe:** records stories, preserves lessons.
- **The Witness:** rotates monthly; ensures transparency.
- **The Novice:** newcomer learning through service.

These titles are functional archetypes, not hierarchies. They prevent concentration of power while keeping accountability visible.

3. External Integration

The Circle interfaces with the wider world through **service projects**—gardens, repair clinics, learning hubs, mutual aid. Every covenant must externalize care. This keeps sovereignty from becoming solipsism. It is the bridge between autonomy and altruism.

III.

Governance of Integrity

Unlike bureaucracies, Builder covenants run on **trust protocols**—low-tech, high-trust agreements verified by transparency.

1. **Open ledgers**: public accounting of funds, time, and commitments.
2. **Consensus minus one**: decisions pass unless one member holds ethical objection, triggering review.
3. **Rotation of roles**: prevents ossified authority; each position expires after one season.
4. **Public apprenticeships**: each member trains another; knowledge hoarding is penalized by loss of status, not punishment but social cooling.

These structures derive from both Benedictine and open-source governance: code reviews meet monastic chapters. Every decision is reversible but recorded. Memory replaces bureaucracy.

IV.

The Builder's Ledger

Where the Rule provides moral compass, the Ledger provides measurable feedback. It is the **instrument panel of sovereignty.**

Each Circle maintains a **Four-Layer Ledger**, aligned to the Sovereign Stack:

1. **Financial Layer** – Transparent record of shared assets and cooperative income streams.
2. **Cognitive Layer** – Collective learning log: skills acquired, texts studied, experiments run.

3. **Social Layer** – Mutual aid hours, conflict resolutions, acts of service.
4. **Cultural Layer** – Rituals, stories, artistic outputs—evidence of meaning production.

The ledger is both audit and narrative. It answers the question: *Are we more whole this season than the last?*

When the answer trends yes, the covenant self-validates. When no, the Circle revises rhythm rather than assigning blame. Adaptation replaces guilt.

V.

Rituals of Continuity

All enduring communities ritualize renewal. The covenant's power lies in repetition, not novelty. Below are **three anchor rituals** adaptable to any geography or faith tradition.

1. **The Lighting of Hands**
2. At each season's start, members stand in a circle, palms up, passing a candle or light source while reciting their chosen vow aloud. The circle closes when light returns to the first hand. Symbol: work completed, cycle intact.
3. **The Ledger Feast**
4. Once per quarter, the Circle hosts an open meal where achievements and errors are read equally. Guests from outside are invited to witness transparency. Food breaks hierarchy; laughter dissolves tension. Humility becomes hospitality.
5. **The Renewal Walk**
6. Annual pilgrimage—urban or rural—carried out in silence for one day. Participants observe the landscapes they sustain and the damage they must heal. At the journey's end, each writes one paragraph of intent for the next year. These paragraphs form the covenant archive.

Ritual here is not superstition; it is mnemonic engineering. Repetition stores virtue in the body.

VI ·

The Currency of Trust

Money in builder civilization reverts to its primal purpose: enabling reciprocity.

Each Circle may create its own **local credit system**—hours, tokens, or direct barter—pegged to real production rather than speculation. The covenant forbids interest accrual beyond maintenance costs. Capital must circulate like blood, not pool like toxin.

For guidance, look to:

- The **BerkShares** experiment (Massachusetts, 2006–present): 10% local discount fostering resilience.
- The **Wörgl Stamp Scrip** (Austria, 1932): demurrage currency that rebuilt a town during depression.

Each example proves that ethical money restores morale before markets. Currency becomes covenantal—its value measured in trust density, not digits.

VII ·

The Discipline of Transparency

Secrecy corrodes every structure it enters. Builders counter it with **radical transparency**, moderated by compassion. All records—financial, procedural, emotional—are shareable unless they betray personal dignity.

Transparency's twin is **forgiveness**. The covenant requires quarterly amnesty: debts of labor, words, or temper are cleared after acknowledgment. Without closure, transparency hardens into shame. The Builder's ethic is clarity without cruelty.

VIII ·

Scaling the Covenant

Replication is the measure of vitality. When one Circle stabilizes, it births another. The model scales like mycelium: decentralized, nutrient-efficient, invisible from above but omnipresent below.

Guidelines for propagation:

- **Split at 150 members** (Dunbar limit for stable cohesion).
- **Maintain inter-circle federations** via seasonal councils.
- **Share resources through open repositories**—templates, rituals, legal documents.
- **Avoid central charters.** The covenant spreads through consent, not command.

Thus the movement evades capture by power or ideology. It remains adaptable as the ecosystems it protects.

IX ·

The Builder's Daily Architecture

Each member structures their day according to a **triple rhythm**—Mind, Matter, Meaning:

Time Block	Mode	Practice
Dawn	Mind	Silence, reading, or reflection (The Vow of Presence)
Midday	Matter	Work in craft or labor (The Vow of Craft)
Dusk	Meaning	Communal meal, study, or song (The Vow of Joy)

This triadic day balances the cognitive, material, and social energies. Neuroscientists identify such balanced routines as buffers against burnout; monastics identified them as salvation. The language differs, the wisdom aligns.

X.

The Covenant's Oath

At initiation, new members recite a condensed oath—a poem and protocol combined:

I stand among Builders.

I will leave no tool rusting, no friend forgotten.

I will keep silence when words wound,

speak when truth saves.

I will trade neither craft for speed nor conscience for gain.

My ledger shall show surplus of mercy.

When called to build, I will build;

when called to rest, I will listen.

May the work endure beyond the worker.

This oath is recited, not enforced. Sovereignty begins with voluntary binding.

XI ·

Continuity Beyond Collapse

The ultimate goal of the covenant is **temporal depth**—projects that survive their creators.

To that end, every Circle maintains a **Legacy Binder**: instructions, contact trees, and philosophies for successors. This is the DNA of civilization compressed into a few pages. When crisis strikes, the Binder revives continuity faster than any bureaucracy could.

Thus the covenant achieves immortality through iteration. Builders die; building continues.

XII ·

Transmission

Evening in a rebuilt town square. The electric grid hums on power drawn from rooftop panels. Children chase shadows between planters carved with the Rule's vows. In a corner workshop, a woman tallies the community ledger as others laugh over shared bread. Above them, faint starlight returns after a long blackout. The clock tower chimes not the hour but the heartbeat of endurance. The covenant has taken root. The world, for the first time in a long time, feels repairable.

Chapter 12

The Children of Ascent

Part IV · The Future

Key 56 · Historical Mirror: The Navajo Continuity of Language and Ritual

I ·

The Song that Survived

When the wind sweeps over the mesas of Dinétah, it carries more than dust. It carries a language old enough to remember when mountains were still molten. The Navajo call it **Diné bizaad**—the People's language—and it endures like desert stone. Empires rose and fell around it, yet its syllables remained the same: rounded, rhythmic, full of verbs rather than nouns. A tongue built not for ownership but for motion.

For centuries, this language and the ceremonies it held formed a civilization without walls. The songs were maps, the prayers were law, and the land itself was scripture. Where others built cities, the Diné built *memory trails*. Every ridge, canyon, and constellation carried instruction—how to live in balance, how to heal, how to walk in *Hózhó*, the state of harmony between body, spirit, and world.

Then came the forgetting.

II ·

The Assault on the Tongue

In the late nineteenth century, the American state sought to standardize souls. The Indian Boarding School system, authorized by the 1887 Dawes Act, aimed to "kill the Indian and save the man." Children were taken from their families and forbidden to speak their mother tongues. Their hair was cut, their clothes burned, their names replaced with English ones.

At Carlisle Industrial School, headmaster Richard Pratt recorded proudly in 1892: "Transfer the savage into a citizen." What he meant was erasure. What followed was silence so heavy it echoed. Elders watched their stories vanish into chalk dust; songs became contraband.

Yet language, like seed, hides resilience in dormancy. Even whispered between sisters at night, even coded in embroidery patterns or rhythm of loom, Diné bizaad survived. Words became underground rivers, flowing unseen until the soil of empire cracked.

III ·

The Code of Return

Irony is one of history's favorite instruments. In 1942, the United States found itself unable to secure radio communications against Japanese cryptographers. The Marines turned to the very language once outlawed. Twenty-nine young Navajo men—farmers, shepherds, students—were recruited to create an unbreakable code based on Diné bizaad.

In the Pacific campaigns, their voices carried commands across chaos. "Turtle" meant tank, "chicken hawk" meant dive bomber. The code was never broken. At Iwo Jima, their transmissions moved faster than machines. What the government had once tried to erase became the cipher that saved it.

The paradox was poetic: language as rebellion turned into language as defense. After the war, those men returned home and were told to keep silent again—classified heroes of a nation that barely recognized them. But they had learned something permanent: survival through sound. The tongue was both weapon and prayer.

IV.

The Geometry of Ceremony

To understand how the Diné maintained coherence under centuries of assault, one must enter their cosmological design. The **Blessingway** (*Hózhójí*) ceremony does not seek to convert or to conquer; it seeks to restore balance. When a person falls ill, the healer sings their world back into alignment. The sand paintings—mandalas of pollen, crushed stone, and sacred earth—depict the emergence of harmony from chaos. After the ritual, the design is erased, returning the materials to the land. Creation, correction, dissolution—three movements of the same melody.

Anthropologist Gladys Reichard, who lived among the Diné in the 1930s, described the experience as "a choreography of cosmos." No sermon, no hierarchy—just pattern. Every brushstroke, every drumbeat reinforces the central theorem: wholeness is not perfection but balance in motion.

The metaphor extends beyond ritual. Community councils operated on consensus, guided by listening rather than decree. Power was diffuse, distributed through kinship and mutual respect. In the Navajo way, governance was an echo of the ceremonial circle: everyone speaks, no one dominates. This is not primitive democracy; it is mature coherence.

V.

The Long Walk and the Return

In 1864, U.S. soldiers under Colonel Kit Carson initiated a scorched-earth campaign, burning crops and slaughtering livestock to force the Navajo into submission. More than 8,000 men, women, and children were marched 300 miles east to the desolate Bosque Redondo reservation. It became known as the **Long Walk**. Hundreds died from exposure and starvation. Yet even in exile, they continued to weave, sing, and teach the young at night. The language persisted in lullabies; the rituals compressed into fragments small enough to hide in memory.

After four years, the government conceded failure. The land at Bosque Redondo could not sustain life. In 1868, the Diné were allowed to return home—the only Native nation to negotiate their way back to ancestral land. They returned walking westward, singing the Blessingway, re-threading broken geography into living myth.

That return became the axis of identity. It taught that sovereignty is the capacity to rebuild alignment after forced distortion. It is not resistance alone but re-harmonization. Every subsequent generation inherited that lesson: harmony can be restored even from ash.

VI ·

Education as Restoration

In the mid-twentieth century, the movement for cultural reclamation began with a single assertion: language is medicine. Activists like Annie Wauneka and teachers at Navajo Community College (founded 1968) reintroduced bilingual curricula. In 1984, the Navajo Nation officially declared Diné bizaad the primary language of government. Today, immersion schools from Window Rock to Tuba City teach math and science in Diné first, English second. Students code-switch between cosmology and chemistry.

Linguists estimate that fluency has stabilized among younger speakers—an anomaly among Indigenous languages globally. Technology, once the colonizer's tool, now becomes ally: apps, podcasts, and VR ceremonies reanimate heritage. The Navajo radio station KTNN broadcasts both powwow music and public policy. The sound of sovereignty is bilingual.

VII ·

The Psychological Continuum

Psychologists studying post-traumatic cultures often focus on survival guilt and inherited fear. The Diné add a third element: **inherited alignment**—the persistence of order-seeking instinct. Generations raised on *Hózhó* internalize the reflex to rebalance. This explains the community's extraordinary rates of mutual aid and low crime despite poverty.

Dr. Teresa LaFromboise's Stanford research (2010) quantified "cultural resilience" among Native youth: identity coherence reduced depressive symptoms by 42%. Ritual continuity functioned as collective psychotherapy. Where trauma fragments the self, ceremony reintegrates it.

The Navajo story proves that sovereignty begins at the level of psyche long before it manifests as politics. Language, ritual, and story act as mental immune systems, defending meaning from erosion. The children of ascent will inherit this principle: repair begins in the grammar of being.

VIII ·

Lessons for the Builders

What the Navajo achieved under impossible conditions mirrors the path ahead for all civilizations approaching fracture. Their continuity was not isolationist; it was integrative. They adopted tools—steel, schools, electricity—without surrendering cosmology. Adaptation without assimilation is the gold standard of sovereignty.

For future societies rebuilding after empire, the Diné example offers a blueprint:

- **Language as Architecture:** Treat words as infrastructure; guard them as cities.
- **Ritual as Technology:** Codify ethics through repetition, not legislation.
- **Harmony as Strategy:** Replace conquest with equilibrium; measure progress by balance restored, not power gained.

In the next deliverable, we will explore this principle's modern counterpart—the Finnish education system—where independence and cooperation coexist by design. But its root is here, in the red canyons of the Southwest, where people once walked home from extinction singing the world back into order.

IX ·

Transmission

Evening settles on Monument Valley. A grandmother hums the Blessingway while her granddaughter records it on a cracked phone. The wind carries their voices toward Shiprock, that basalt monolith the Diné call Tse Bit'a'i—the Rock with Wings. The song loops in digital echo, one line ancient, one newly encoded. A language that survived fire, exile, and empire flows again, unbroken, through circuits and breath alike. Somewhere between the old chant and the new recording, the next civilization listens, learning how to remember.

Key 57 · Modern Parallel: Finnish Educational Independence and the Architecture of Learning Sovereignty

I.

The Quiet Revolution

When Finland rebuilt after World War II, it had no gold reserves, few natural resources, and a population scarred by conflict. The soil was thin, the winters endless, and its people sandwiched between empires that had used their borders as chess squares. Yet within three generations, this small nation transformed into one of the most educated, egalitarian, and innovative societies on Earth. The weapon of their reconstruction was not steel—it was curriculum.

In 1972, Finnish policymakers enacted a series of reforms that would come to define the modern idea of educational sovereignty. They abolished elite tracking, merged vocational and academic streams, and gave teachers—not bureaucrats—control over content. Education was declared not a market but a commons. The result was a system that treated learning as the national immune system. The state could fall; literacy would remain.

By the turn of the millennium, Finland's students ranked among the highest in global assessments without standardized testing, private tutoring, or competition. Behind those statistics was a philosophy: trust breeds excellence, autonomy breeds responsibility.

II ·

Teachers as Architects of the Republic

Every Finnish teacher holds a master's degree and enters the profession as a civic calling, not a fallback career. Admission to education faculties is more competitive than law or medicine. Yet once inside, the system grants near-total autonomy. There is no inspectorate, no external ranking. The trust is radical.

The late Professor Pasi Sahlberg described it as "the quiet revolution." The bureaucracy stepped back so educators could step forward. Teachers design their own syllabi based on national goals but local needs. If one region thrives through forestry, lessons incorporate ecology and trade; if another centers on technology, coding becomes a natural language. The classroom adapts to its landscape, not the reverse.

This decentralization mirrors the Navajo ethos of distributed harmony. Just as the Diné entrusted moral guidance to consensus within clans, Finland entrusts pedagogical design to those who actually teach. Both models assume the same principle: integrity grows from agency, not oversight.

III ·

Learning Without Fear

The Finnish system removed the psychological toxins that cripple most educational structures—fear, shame, and endless comparison. Grades are minimal, tests rare, and recess sacred. The goal is not obedience but curiosity. Psychologists note that stress cortisol levels among Finnish schoolchildren are the lowest recorded globally. The emotional climate sustains the cognitive.

Every element of the system reinforces safety: small class sizes, counseling integrated into routine, meals shared by teachers and students alike.

Education here resembles mentorship within an extended family more than industrial instruction.

The philosophy traces back to postwar trauma. Having seen what centralized control could do to nations, Finland decided that the best defense against tyranny was independent thought cultivated early. The classroom became the republic's conscience factory.

IV.

Equity as Design, Not Charity

Equality in Finland is not rhetorical; it is architectural. Schools are funded uniformly, teachers rotate to avoid hierarchy among districts, and textbooks are shared nationally at cost. There are no elite schools, no private enclaves siphoning talent. The principle is stark: no child's destiny should depend on postal code.

When the global economy urged privatization, Finland resisted. They understood what many empires forget—that talent suppressed by inequality is national entropy. Social mobility is not just moral; it is thermodynamic efficiency. Every human mind left idle is wasted energy.

This ethic extends beyond classrooms. Libraries outnumber police stations. Literacy rates remain above 99%. A taxi driver quoting Rilke is not anomaly but norm. Knowledge is not gated; it circulates like clean air. Civilization, finally, becomes self-lubricating.

V.

The Myth of Enough

Unlike nations that glorify constant growth, Finland embedded sufficiency into its moral economy. Education reflects this restraint. School days are short, homework light, vacations long. The belief:

learning deepens in rest as much as in rigor. Neuroscience later validated this—sleep consolidates memory, play enhances creativity—but Finland practiced it decades before science caught up.

Their unspoken motto could be phrased: "Better fewer, but better." Each subject is taught with depth rather than breadth. A child studies fewer topics, yet each is explored until understanding clicks. The result is not acceleration but absorption. The slower rhythm paradoxically produces faster minds.

This ethos echoes the Navajo *Hózhó*: balance over excess. To live well is not to consume more knowledge but to integrate what one learns into the harmony of life.

VI ·

The Psychological Core: Internal Trust

When asked why Finland excels, teachers often shrug and say, "Because we trust our children." It sounds banal until one measures its effects. Trust increases intrinsic motivation. Studies by the University of Helsinki show that self-directed students sustain engagement 40% longer than those externally monitored. The same pattern appears at societal scale: citizens who feel trusted are more likely to pay taxes voluntarily and to participate in local governance.

Trust converts education from policing into partnership. The child is not a vessel to be filled but a collaborator in their own formation. This transforms the entire power dynamic of learning. Where surveillance breeds rebellion or apathy, trust breeds sovereignty.

VII ·

Global Lessons

In a world obsessed with metrics, Finland's refusal to compete has become its competitive edge. PISA analysts once asked officials why they never published school rankings. The reply: "We don't rank our children." The line became legend, not because it was defiant, but because it was obvious once spoken.

For developing nations and post-collapse regions, the Finnish model offers a template for regeneration that requires no empire, only ethic:

1. **Invest in Teachers** – Education of educators as nation-building priority.
2. **Decentralize Curriculum** – Local autonomy within universal principles.
3. **Democratize Access** – Equal funding, no private distortions.
4. **Embed Rest** – Protect cognitive health through balanced pacing.
5. **Institutionalize Trust** – Design systems that assume goodness before enforcing it.

The results are tangible: youth literacy near universal, suicide rates declining, civic participation among the highest globally. When citizens learn autonomy early, they resist authoritarianism later. Education becomes defense policy.

VIII ·

The Cultural Resonance

Finnish culture encodes humility in its very syntax. The language lacks a word for "please," because politeness is implied. There is little small talk, but deep listening. Silence is not absence; it is respect. These linguistic traits align with the educational temperament: reflection over display, depth over volume.

Art and science coexist fluidly—architect Alvar Aalto designing libraries as cathedrals of light; composer Jean Sibelius turning national trauma into symphony. Even design philosophy (*sisu*) translates to "stoic determination." Every textbook, policy, and meal program channels this ethos of calm persistence.

Through culture, education becomes more than institution—it becomes inheritance. A child raised in such coherence carries the pattern of order into adulthood. The system reproduces integrity generation after generation.

IX.

The Invisible Curriculum

The most radical element of Finland's model is what it doesn't teach: nationalism, guilt, or fear. Instead, it cultivates **meta-learning**—the ability to learn how to learn. Students design projects, fail, reflect, and iterate. Teachers guide rather than grade. This recursive pedagogy mirrors the process of civilization itself: adaptive, self-correcting, humane.

UNESCO analysts once called Finland's education "the quiet software of democracy." Indeed, it runs in the background, stabilizing everything else—economy, health, even foreign policy. When crises hit (recessions, pandemics), the system flexes rather than fractures. Knowledge, evenly distributed, becomes shock absorber.

X.

Transmission

A winter morning in Helsinki. Snow drifts against a school window; inside, a teacher and her students gather around a table scattered with circuits and pinecones. One child sketches how electricity moves through trees; another writes a poem about wind. Outside, the sky brightens to pale gold. No bell rings. The lesson ends when curiosity is satisfied. Across the room, the teacher smiles—not because they finished the syllabus, but because she watched sovereignty take root in a mind.

Key 58 · Psychological Mechanism: Intergenerational Repair and the Biology of Resilience

I ·

The Inheritance Beyond Blood

Every human being is born carrying more than genes. We inherit unfinished emotions, silenced fears, unfulfilled ambitions, and even biochemical imprints of our ancestors' experiences. For decades this sounded poetic; today it is measurable.

Epigenetic research, beginning with Michael Meaney's 2004 studies on maternal care in rats and expanded by Rachel Yehuda's work with Holocaust survivors, shows that trauma alters gene expression. Methylation markers—tiny chemical tags—shift under stress, affecting cortisol regulation, immune function, and anxiety responses. These markers can be transmitted across generations. The body remembers what the mind tries to forget.

But the inheritance is not only damage. Compassion, patience, and courage can also pass through biology and culture. The same neural pathways that encode fear can encode trust. The purpose of intergenerational repair is not to erase memory, but to teach the body that safety has returned.

II ·

The Hidden Weight

Walk into any modern city and you will see people carrying invisible loads—workaholism born from grandparents' hunger, perfectionism from ancestral persecution, or numbness from war. Psychologists call these *adaptive relics*: behaviors that once ensured survival but now obstruct growth.

A grandmother who endured famine teaches her daughter never to waste; the daughter becomes an efficient provider; the granddaughter develops anxiety around scarcity despite abundance. The pattern persists until someone recognizes it as inheritance, not identity.

Family systems theorists such as Murray Bowen described this as *emotional cutoff*: each generation tries to resolve its parents' unfinished story by either overidentifying or rebelling. True sovereignty requires a third way—acknowledgment without entanglement. Healing begins when memory becomes knowledge rather than reflex.

III ·

The Science of Transmission

Neuroscientists distinguish between two primary channels of intergenerational transmission: **biological imprinting** and **social modeling**.

1. **Biological imprinting:** Stress hormones during pregnancy can alter fetal brain development. Studies following the Dutch Hunger Winter (1944–45) found adults born during famine had higher rates of metabolic and anxiety disorders decades later.
2. **Social modeling:** Children mirror not what parents say but what they regulate. If conflict is met with calm resolution, mirror neurons encode safety; if it's met with rage or avoidance, hypervigilance becomes default.

In both cases, what travels between generations is not content but *pattern*. Trauma repeats until someone chooses a different rhythm. Repair is a rhythmic act—the slow re-synchronization of nervous systems across time.

IV.

The Ritual of Recognition

Indigenous cultures have long known what science now rediscovers: acknowledgment heals. Among the Navajo, the *Enemy Way* ceremony cleanses warriors of spiritual residue after battle; in Japanese Shinto practice, *Oharai* purifies communities after disaster; in West African traditions, libations honor ancestors, releasing unfulfilled obligations. Each ritual externalizes invisible burdens, turning inherited tension into communal release.

Modern equivalents need not be religious. Writing family histories, recording elder interviews, or marking anniversaries of migration serve the same function. When stories are voiced, they stop metastasizing in silence. Narrative coherence—organizing events into meaning—correlates with lower amygdala reactivity in trauma survivors. Storytelling is neurochemical therapy.

V.

Repair Through Relationship

Therapy, in its deepest form, is relational apprenticeship. The nervous system calibrates through proximity to regulation. Infants learn calm from caregivers; adults relearn it through empathy. In long-term studies, couples practicing "co-regulation"—steady breathing, synchronized eye contact—lower blood pressure and inflammatory markers. Communities function the same way: coherence spreads through modeled composure.

This principle underlies the builder societies of renewal. Mutual-aid circles, mentorship programs, and intergenerational workshops create feedback loops of regulation. Each act of steady presence rewires a group's collective baseline from survival to creation. Where ancestors built defense, descendants build connection.

VI ·

The Art of Breaking Patterns

To repair inheritance, one must identify the "family myths" that drive repetition. Psychologist James Hollis described these as "invisible loyalties"—unconscious pacts such as *I must suffer to belong* or *I must succeed so their pain meant something*. These beliefs preserve love at the cost of freedom.

The counter-move is not rejection but ritualized rebellion. A descendant who chooses joy without guilt performs psychic alchemy: transforming obligation into gratitude. In that moment, the lineage upgrades. The ancestors' suffering is honored not by mimicry but by transcendence.

Practically, this can be enacted through personal creeds—short declarations reversing ancestral scripts:

"Their fear kept me alive. My courage will keep them remembered."

Such statements are not affirmations; they are treaties with the past.

VII ·

Biological Recalibration

Repair is also somatic. Trauma lodges in the body as hyperarousal or dissociation. Techniques such as EMDR, breathwork, yoga, and polyvagal exercises retrain the autonomic nervous system to differentiate past from present. When the body learns safety, the genes follow suit.

A 2018 study in *Nature Communications* found that mindfulness practice can reduce expression of inflammation-related genes within eight weeks. Cellular coherence mirrors psychological coherence. The frontier of resilience research now measures compassion and meditation as biological interventions. The sacred returns as science.

VIII ·

From Therapy to Culture

When enough individuals complete this repair, culture itself changes texture. The aggressive modern myth—progress through denial—gives way to a subtler narrative: progress through integration. Nations can also inherit trauma: colonial guilt, civil war, slavery, environmental destruction. Collective rituals of apology, truth commissions, and reparations function as societal EMDR—eye movement between denial and memory until emotional balance returns.

Finland's postwar neutrality, Germany's remembrance culture, Rwanda's Gacaca courts—each represents large-scale rebalancing. The same principle applies to any post-collapse rebuilding. Healing the polis begins where healing the person ends: in honest remembrance.

IX ·

The Transmission of Resilience

Just as trauma travels, so does strength. Resilience has its own epigenetic signature. Studies of descendants of Holocaust survivors who developed purposeful worldviews—through activism, art, or education—showed normalized cortisol levels compared to those who remained trapped in avoidance. Meaning metabolizes pain.

Storytelling, education, and craftsmanship create what anthropologists call "resilient cultural capital." These become the new genes of civilization—replicable, teachable, inheritable. When a child witnesses integrity rewarded and kindness sustained, their genome receives a different instruction: trust the world.

The biological inheritance of hope is no less real than that of fear. Both are written in code. The task of our age is to edit wisely.

X.

Transmission

A mother and son sit by a window at dawn. She speaks softly about the famine her own mother endured, not to frighten him but to show him the strength that carried them here. Outside, the first light touches the horizon; he listens, then begins to draw—fields, people, rising sun. She watches his small hand move, the line flowing steady and unbroken. For the first time, the story leaves her body and becomes art. Across generations, the tremor stills. A new inheritance begins.

Key 59 · Mythic Resonance: The Handover of the Flame and the Hero's Return Across Generations

I ·

The Fire That Walks

Every myth begins with fire. Prometheus steals it, Maui snares it from the underworld, the Hopi tend it in hidden caves. The fire is knowledge, courage, consciousness—the animating light within the human story. But the truest fire is not owned; it is passed. The act of transmission, not possession, defines civilization.

The children of ascent inherit a world exhausted by mastery and hungry for meaning. Their task is not to rediscover fire but to remember how to carry it. Where their ancestors sought conquest, they must seek continuity. The mythic challenge of this century is not ascent to heaven but the *handover of flame*—the movement of wisdom across time without distortion.

In every culture, the final test of the hero is return. The dragon is slain, the underworld crossed, but if the elixir is not shared, the journey fails. Joseph Campbell called this the refusal of return: the hero who hoards enlightenment and withers in isolation. The children of ascent must not repeat that mistake. They are both inheritors and deliverers.

II ·

The Pattern of Return

The ancients mapped this archetype long before psychology named it. In the *Epic of Gilgamesh*, the king descends seeking immortality, only to return wiser, not eternal. In Hindu lore, Rama wins victory but finds peace only in reunion. In Buddhist cycles, the Bodhisattva pauses at the threshold of Nirvana to guide others. In each, the hero's greatness lies not in escape but in re-entry.

Return is the hardest movement because it demands humility. To walk back into the ordinary world bearing extraordinary sight is to face incomprehension. Myths preserve this paradox: Moses descending with tablets to a faithless crowd, Odysseus unrecognized in Ithaca, Quetzalcoatl promising to return in a new dawn. All carry the same question—how do you bring the sacred into the everyday without it burning through your hands?

The answer lies in stewardship. Fire must be tended, not displayed. The Builders learned this; now the Children must remember it.

III ·

The Twin Fires

In Navajo cosmology, two fires sustain the people: one external, one internal. The hearth fire warms bodies; the heart fire guides purpose. When one wanes, the other flickers. The rituals of renewal—chants, dances, communal meals—serve to synchronize them. Modern life split the pair: technology as outer flame, meaning as inner ember. The next civilization must reunite them.

The myth speaks plainly: those who guard the hearth of the world must also guard the light within themselves. Every generation that fails to reconcile the two builds machines faster than their souls can steer. The children of ascent will inherit technologies indistinguishable from magic. Their survival depends on moral heat as much as on innovation. Without sacred warmth, the new fire freezes.

IV.

The Council of Ancestors

Every mythic lineage envisions a council where the living and the dead convene. The Greeks imagined it as Olympus; the West Africans as the ancestral grove; the Chinese as the shrine of tablets; the Polynesians as the sea of stars. In each, the message is constant: you are the continuation, not the conclusion.

The Children of Ascent must rebuild this council, not as religion but as remembrance. In their rituals, data archives, and family gatherings, they will create spaces where past and future converse. A recorded voice of an elder played in a classroom, a memorial tree tagged with QR codes linking to life stories—these are the new temples of continuity. The ancestors speak through metadata now, but their tone remains the same: *guard what we learned, transcend what we feared.*

When history becomes dialogue, time ceases to fracture. The flame passes cleanly through generations.

V.

The Myth of the Handoff

Consider the image of the Olympic torch: a flame traveling hand to hand across continents. It is ceremony, yes, but also allegory. The torchbearer does not own the fire; they protect it for the next. The handover lasts seconds, yet the ritual embodies millennia.

In Norse tradition, this idea appears in the *Voluspa*, where the world ends not in silence but in a spark preserved under ash. After Ragnarok, new gods arise from the survivors who remembered warmth. The world is reborn because someone tended embers when all seemed lost.

The modern handover will be no less sacred. It will not occur in temples but in classrooms, workshops, and conversations. When an old craftsman teaches a teenager to mend instead of discard; when a mother passes a family recipe with the story of famine attached; when a scientist mentors an apprentice to choose ethics over fame—the flame changes hands invisibly. That is civilization in motion.

VI ·

The Hero as Teacher

In the next age, heroism will no longer mean conquest. It will mean *instruction*. The hero will not be the one who discovers, but the one who transmits. The teacher, mentor, or artisan who keeps knowledge alive through integrity will replace the warrior as cultural archetype.

Myth has prepared us for this transition. In Hindu philosophy, each epoch is ruled by a different archetype: warrior, merchant, scholar, and sage. The Kali Yuga—the age of disorder—ends when the sage restores equilibrium through teaching. The hero's sword becomes the stylus, the plow, the code. Power dissolves into pedagogy.

The children of ascent will therefore measure greatness by continuity achieved, not monuments built. Their empires will be measured in preserved skill, revived ecosystems, and restored trust. They are both students and stewards in an unbroken lineage of repair.

VII ·

The Mythic Psychology of Legacy

Legacy, at its deepest, is an emotional transaction. The elder seeks assurance that their struggle meant something; the young seek evidence that the world can still be mended. When the handover succeeds, both find peace. Psychologically, this is *generativity*—Erik Erikson's final developmental stage—where care extends beyond the self. Civilizations, too, reach maturity when they invest more in inheritance than in expansion.

In myth, this moment is symbolized by the torch given to the next runner, the ring passed to the rightful heir, the seed planted before death. The gesture unites mortality and immortality: the giver ends, the gift continues. To live this way is to transform fear of death into faith in continuity. The flame absolves the finite.

VIII ·

The Cosmic Perspective

Viewed from space, the lights of Earth resemble constellations scattered on a dark sea. Each city, each lamp, each phone screen is a point of fire—a literal network of Promethean inheritance. Yet beneath the electric glare, another light endures: the moral radiance of human care. Without it, the planetary grid is an empty halo.

Myth reminds us that cosmic fire—starlight, lightning, fusion—is indifferent. Only conscious fire warms. To keep that warmth alive, the children of ascent must rediscover awe, the original renewable energy. Awe humbles intellect, aligns will, and binds communities. It is the emotional equivalent of gravity—the force that keeps meaning in orbit.

When awe returns, arrogance fades. The species becomes teachable again.

IX ·

The Flame and the Circle

In every culture's end-time vision, destruction is cyclical, not final. The Hopi speak of worlds destroyed by flood, fire, and ice, each followed by renewal through chosen survivors. The Mayans encoded cosmic resets in the Long Count calendar. Even physics mirrors this in oscillating universe theories: expansion followed by contraction, then another dawn. The mythic and the scientific converge—the universe itself is a breath.

The children of ascent live within that breath. Their task is not to prevent collapse but to ensure continuity between inhalation and exhalation. If they hold the flame through the dark, the next exhale will light new stars. The circle closes, not with apocalypse, but with respiration.

X ·

Transmission

Night over a rebuilt valley. Wind turbines turn like silent sentinels; solar lamps flicker along a riverbank. On a hill, a group of children gather around a small fire tended by elders. The flames dance across their faces as stories unfold—of droughts and recoveries, of migrations and returns. One child listens, then lifts a torch to light another's. The older hand steadies the younger. Across the valley, thousands of tiny fires answer, each a pulse of continuity. From above, the pattern resembles a constellation coming back to life. The age of ascent has begun again.

Key 60 · Sovereignty Protocol: The Twelve-Year Curriculum of Sovereign Education and Intergenerational Continuity

I ·

From Schooling to Formation

Civilizations fall when education forgets its purpose. School becomes a warehouse of obedience, not awakening. In every empire's twilight—Rome's rote rhetoric schools, Qing China's ossified exams, the late industrial West's standardized testing—the classroom turns from forge to factory.

The Builders understood that renewal required a different blueprint. The Children of Ascent will not inherit schools; they will inherit *learning ecologies*. Education must become apprenticeship in sovereignty: the capacity to think freely, act ethically, and cooperate creatively across generations.

The following **Twelve-Year Curriculum** is not a policy document; it is a living covenant. It can be adapted by homeschools, cooperatives, community centers, or nation-states. Its goal is simple: to raise human beings who do not need supervision to behave wisely.

II ·

Structure of the Curriculum

The design mirrors human development: four phases, three years each, corresponding to body, mind, heart, and legacy. Each year contains one enduring question, one core practice, and one public rite of passage. The system teaches not subjects, but capacities.

Phase	Focus	Years	Primary Mode
I	Embodiment	1–3	Craft and care
II	Understanding	4–6	Inquiry and creation
III	Responsibility	7–9	Mentorship and cooperation
IV	Stewardship	10–12	Leadership and continuity

Each phase spirals back through the same virtues—presence, craft, honesty, stewardship, joy—deepening them like the rings of a tree.

III ·

Phase I — Embodiment (Years 1–3)

Core question: What is real?

Children begin by learning with hands before screens. They garden, cook, build, and play instruments. The body becomes the first classroom; nature, the first teacher. The curriculum pairs every cognitive lesson with a sensory one: measure water to understand fractions, draw the stars to learn geometry, tend an animal to study biology.

Practice: Daily rhythm of work and wonder. Mornings for movement, afternoons for reflection. Attention becomes the foundation of all literacy.

Rite of passage: A "Making Day," where each child completes a handmade object—a chair, a loaf, a song—and gifts it to the community. Creation replaces competition.

IV.

Phase II — Understanding (Years 4–6)

Core question: What is true?

Here the learner encounters logic, language, and history, not as memorization but as mapmaking. They trace how ideas evolve, how empires rise and decay, how evidence becomes knowledge. Instead of standardized tests, each student maintains a *Book of Questions*—a growing record of curiosities answered and mysteries remaining.

Practice: Collaborative projects across disciplines—build a solar oven, translate a myth, write a civic charter for the local garden. Inquiry is communal, not solitary.

Rite of passage: A "Festival of Questions," where learners present one question that changed them and invite peers to explore it publicly. Doubt becomes a sacred act.

V.

Phase III — Responsibility (Years 7–9)

Core question: What is good?

Adolescents enter the civic apprenticeship stage. They learn economics through running cooperatives, ethics through resolving conflicts, politics through deliberation councils. Every student mentors someone younger and reports monthly to a community elder. Governance becomes a lived skill.

Practice: Service-learning rotations—repairing, tutoring, cooking for elders, mediating disputes. Responsibility replaces rebellion by giving agency purpose.

Rite of passage: The *Covenant Walk*—a multi-day trek or project that tests endurance and cooperation. Returning participants share stories around fire, reaffirming their vow to protect life in all forms.

VI ·

Phase IV — Stewardship (Years 10–12)

Core question: What endures?

These final years prepare youth to become transmitters. Each designs a capstone project aimed at continuity—a restored ecosystem, a new invention, an archive of local history, or a program mentoring younger students. The emphasis shifts from accumulation to contribution.

Practice: Independent research coupled with teaching others. Students write their own "Builder's Rule"—ten principles they will live by—and defend it before a council of mentors. The process mirrors ancient initiation: wisdom gained through articulation.

Rite of passage: The *Lighting Ceremony*. Graduates receive a symbolic flame—a candle, lamp, or circuit light—from elders and pass it to the next cohort. It is the visible handover of civilization.

VII ·

The Pedagogy of Trust

The curriculum runs on the same energy that powers Finland's success: trust. Teachers are trained as *custodians of curiosity*, not enforcers. Evaluation is narrative, not numeric. Students are assessed through journals, portfolios, and community testimony.

Neuroscience confirms the efficacy: trust increases dopamine-based motivation and reduces cortisol levels, amplifying creative problem-solving. The brain learns best when it feels safe, seen, and significant. The Children of Ascent will therefore grow up within psychological climates that reward integrity over compliance.

VIII ·

The Community as School

The boundary between classroom and world dissolves. Local farms, clinics, studios, and labs become satellites of learning. Retired artisans teach trades; scientists guide citizen experiments; grandparents tell oral histories. The community becomes both curriculum and textbook.

Economically, this model reduces costs while increasing coherence. Socially, it rethreads generations torn apart by industrial education. The school bell becomes the heartbeat of the town.

IX ·

The Role of Technology

Technology re-enters as servant, not master. Every device must justify itself by deepening human capacity. AI tutors, 3D printers, and global classrooms are used only where they extend empathy or skill, not distraction. Digital literacy is taught alongside digital fasting.

Students learn to code as they learn to compost—each an act of stewardship in different realms. The maxim engraved at every learning center reads:

"Use the tool, never become it."

X ·

The Annual Sovereignty Audit

Every twelve months, each community conducts a *Sovereignty Audit*—a ritual and review combined. Families, educators, and students gather to examine five domains:

1. **Autonomy:** Are learners self-directed?
2. **Integrity:** Are honesty and empathy increasing?
3. **Craft:** Are tangible skills improving?
4. **Culture:** Are rituals alive and meaningful?
5. **Continuity:** Is knowledge being passed effectively?

The audit produces a public narrative report, not a grade. Its purpose is reflection, not ranking. The act of measuring becomes meditation.

XI ·

The Legacy Network

Graduates of the Twelve-Year Curriculum form the *Ascent Network*—a voluntary federation of mentors spanning trades, sciences, and arts. Each contributes one hour monthly to guide someone younger. Over decades, this becomes an intergenerational web of wisdom—an analog neural net stronger than any algorithm.

The Network's creed is engraved in every hub: *"Teach what you love. Share what you've learned. Leave what you build."*

Through this network, humanity reclaims its continuity. Knowledge ceases to be a commodity; it becomes a lineage.

XII ·

Transmission

A circle of young people and elders beneath a night sky. The older ones hold lamps; the younger raise empty hands. One by one, the lamps tilt, transferring flame. Faces glow in the quiet exchange. Beyond them, fields hum with wind turbines, greenhouses, and faint song. The air smells of rain and cedar. Somewhere in the darkness, a bell rings not to end class but to begin the next epoch of learning. The circle closes, bright, unbroken—the Children of Ascent illuminated, carrying the fire forward.

Epilogue

The Return — From Dust to Breath to Dawn

The world ends quietly. Not with the roar of apocalypse but with the whisper of neglect — a power plant unmaintained, a law unenforced, a promise forgotten. Collapse is rarely a spectacle; it is the slow fading of attention.

Yet even as empires dissolve, something stirs beneath the ruins. The pulse of renewal hums through every cracked foundation. Civilizations, like stars, die scattering the elements of their rebirth. And from those fragments, a few who have learned to listen begin again.

You are among them now.

I.

The Return

When the long night finally breaks, it is not banners or armies that mark the return — it is the sound of human hands rebuilding. A hammer against stone. A child reading aloud. A seed breaking open in the thawing soil.

The Ascent begins not with conquest but with comprehension — the moment one realizes that survival without soul is just a slower form of death. What endures is not wealth or rule, but awareness.

The ancients knew this. After the Flood, they built altars, not monuments. After the fires of Rome, monks copied texts by candlelight. After Hiroshima, people planted trees in the ash. Each act said the same thing: that even amid ruin, the human spirit refuses to vanish.

That refusal is the essence of sovereignty.

It is not the crown upon the head but the steadiness within the chest. It is the quiet decision to live by truth, even when systems lie.

You have walked through the architectures of collapse — the fading of empires, the betrayal of markets, the hypnosis of screens. You have seen how power decays, how myths mislead, how meaning fragments. And still, you are here — reader, builder, witness.

The Return is not a coming back to what was. It is a return to *what is real.*

II ·

The Breath

When the first breath of morning enters your lungs, remember that every civilization begins with breath — the invisible covenant between body and world.

In the oldest creation stories, breath is divine technology. In Hebrew, *ruach*: spirit, wind. In Sanskrit, *prana*: the animating force. In Greek, *pneuma*: both air and soul. The act of breathing binds matter to consciousness, chaos to order.

Our ancestors measured life not in years but in breaths. A person's character, they said, was revealed by how they breathed in the face of fear. Shallow breaths signaled panic, deep ones courage.

We forgot this when we industrialized the sky — when the air itself became commodified, filtered, sold, and poisoned. But as the smoke clears, a new discipline emerges: to breathe again as if the planet itself depends on it. Because it does.

The sovereign human does not hold their breath waiting for permission to live. They breathe deliberately, each inhale a declaration: *I am still here.*

This is where ascent truly begins — not in the marketplace or the palace, but in the diaphragm. The breath is the first vote of freedom.

III ·

The Fire

Every civilization runs on fire. It warms, powers, and destroys. The difference lies in how it is tended.

We inherited two fires: the literal one of industry and the metaphorical one of ambition. Both burned too hot, consuming forests and futures alike. The Ascent demands a new mastery — to turn fire into hearth rather than weapon.

This fire burns inward now, purified into will. The Builders learned to forge without frenzy, to labor with grace, to craft beauty not as ornament but as declaration that the human hand still remembers elegance.

You, too, will tend a fire. Perhaps it will be the lamp of knowledge, the flame of courage, or the small steady spark of kindness. Protect it. Pass it. Every age of darkness ends because someone chose not to let their fire die.

There is no empire that can extinguish that.

IV ·

The Circle

On the final evening of the world that was, the Builders gather in a circle. No leaders, no followers — only witnesses. The circle has no top or bottom, no center to collapse. It is the oldest geometry of equality.

They place in the middle the relics of collapse: a broken phone, a burned bill, a torn flag, a jar of soil. Symbols of what was lost — and what will no longer rule them. Then they place beside it the tools of ascent: a book, a seed, a hammer, a candle.

One by one, each person speaks a vow.

"I will not lie to live."

"I will build what I can mend."

"I will teach what I learn."

"I will leave more beauty than I found."

When the vows end, the circle opens — not upward, but outward. Children step through the gap, carrying light into the distance.

The circle never breaks; it expands.

V ·

The Dawn

Dawn arrives without applause. It always does. It does not need to be earned, only seen.

The sun touches the edges of broken towers, and for a moment even the ruins look redeemed. From high ground, the land seems stitched again — rivers of silver, forests reborn, cities quieter and wiser.

There will be new mistakes, new hierarchies, new dangers. But there will also be memory now — memory of fragility, of how thin the line is between progress and pride.

History does not repeat; it rhymes with those who remember. The rhythm of collapse and ascent is the heartbeat of humanity itself.

The question is not whether civilization will endure, but whether consciousness will.

And you, reader, now carry its continuity.

VI ·

The Return Within

Return, finally, to yourself.

Close the book. Feel the pulse in your wrist. That rhythm is older than money, law, or nation. It is the same rhythm that pulsed through the Bronze Age trader, the scribe of Alexandria, the monk of Cluny, the weaver of Kyoto, the coder of the blockchain.

All of them were trying to do one thing: make meaning last.

When you speak truth, you continue their work. When you teach a child, repair a tool, or forgive someone you once condemned, you add another brick to the invisible architecture of continuity.

The empire collapses. The human experiment continues.

This is how the world begins again — not through revolution, but through remembrance.

VII ·

The Covenant Renewed

You began this journey among ruins, reading of shortages and shadows. Now you hold the blueprint of renewal — not as a theory, but as a way of being.

Sovereignty is no longer a word; it is your pulse, your posture, your breath.

The Builders' covenant is simple:

Live as if the world were worth rebuilding.

Teach as if knowledge were sacred.

Love as if time were infinite.

When enough of us live this way, collapse ceases to matter. Because the empire that fails is not the one that controls territory; it is the one that loses meaning.

Meaning is now yours to steward.

VIII ·

The Last Light

As the last page turns, imagine yourself standing at the edge of a quiet field. The air smells of rain. In the distance, a few lights flicker — new homes, new songs, new beginnings. The horizon glows faintly.

Behind you, the old world sleeps in shadow. Ahead, the path ascends.

You take one step forward, then another. You do not rush. You do not look back.

The dawn opens its arms.

And the ascent begins.

Acknowledgments

No book stands alone, and *The Ascent Begins* least of all.

Its roots lie in every conversation that began in darkness and ended with a spark.

To those who endured the long nights of research, revision, and questioning — thank you for believing that ideas can rebuild worlds. To the teachers who taught me that history is not a list of dates but a mirror of choices. To the friends who tested every argument until it bled truth. To the readers who carried these pages in the middle of their own storms.

My gratitude also extends to the countless unnamed Builders — the farmers restoring soil, the artisans reviving crafts, the writers and coders and quiet custodians of culture who prove that civilization is not a structure but a practice.

And to the one who first said, *carry the fire*: this book is the flame you lit.

Notes

All factual references, historical dates, and psychological concepts in this book are grounded in publicly available sources.

Key materials include:

- Joseph Tainter, *The Collapse of Complex Societies* (Cambridge University Press, 1988)
- Jared Diamond, *Collapse* (Viking, 2005)
- Victor Frankl, *Man's Search for Meaning* (Beacon, 1946)
- Mihaly Csikszentmihalyi, *Flow* (Harper & Row, 1990)
- Elinor Ostrom, *Governing the Commons* (Cambridge University Press, 1990)
- Ilya Prigogine, *Order Out of Chaos* (Bantam, 1984)
- Shoshana Zuboff, *The Age of Surveillance Capitalism* (PublicAffairs, 2019)
- David Graeber, *Debt: The First 5,000 Years* (Melville House, 2011)
- Martin Seligman, *Learned Optimism* (Knopf, 1991)
- Daniel Kahneman, *Thinking, Fast and Slow* (Farrar, Straus and Giroux, 2011)
- Yuval Noah Harari, *Sapiens* (Harper, 2015)

Additional case studies draw on data from the IMF, World Bank, UNESCO, FAO, and peer-reviewed archaeology, anthropology, and climate archives. All economic figures cited were current at the time of writing.

Further Reading

For readers seeking to continue the journey:

- Rebecca Solnit — *A Paradise Built in Hell*
- Nassim Nicholas Taleb — *Antifragile*
- Peter Frankopan — *The Silk Roads*
- Lewis Hyde — *The Gift*
- Riane Eisler — *The Chalice and the Blade*
- Wendell Berry — *The Unsettling of America*
- Charles Eisenstein — *The More Beautiful World Our Hearts Know Is Possible*
- David Wengrow & David Graeber — *The Dawn of Everything*
- Ivan Illich — *Tools for Conviviality*
- Maria Montessori — *The Absorbent Mind*

Each work explores a different dimension of sovereignty — moral, economic, ecological, or educational — and together they form a compass for rebuilding culture with conscience.

About the Author

Shanaka Anslem Perera is a writer and strategist focused on resilience, sovereignty, and civilizational renewal.

He has lived through infrastructural breakdowns, currency shocks, and state-level crises across multiple regions, translating hard lessons into practical architectures for ordinary people.

His work merges history, psychology, and cultural design, exploring how individuals and small groups can regenerate coherence when institutions fail. *The Ascent Begins* is his first book.

You can follow his ongoing research, essays, on his X / Twitter profile @shanaka86 or subscribe to the newsletter.

www.ingramcontent.com/pod-product-compliance
Lightning Source LLC
Chambersburg PA
CBHW020512080526
44583CB00013B/578